Themes and Issues
in Christianity

WORLD RELIGIONS: THEMES AND ISSUES

Written for students of comparative religion and the general reader, and drawing on the chapters originally edited by Jean Holm and John Bowker in the *Themes in Religious Studies* series, the volumes in *World Religions: Themes and Issues* explore core themes from the perspective of the particular religious tradition under study.

Other volumes in preparation:

Themes and Issues in Buddhism
Themes and Issues in Hinduism
Themes and Issues in Judaism

Themes and Issues in Christianity

Douglas J. Davies
with Clare Drury

CASSELL

London and Washington

Cassell
Wellington House, 125 Strand, London WC2R 0BB, England
PO Box 605, Herndon, VA 20172, USA

First published 1997

British Library Cataloguing in Publication Data
A catalogue record for this book is available from the British Library.

ISBN 0-304-33848-6 (hardback)
    0-304-33849-4 (paperback)

Library of Congress Cataloging-in-Publication Data
Davies, Douglas James.
    Themes and issues in Christianity / Douglas J. Davies, with Clare
Drury.
        p. cm.
    Includes bibliographical references and index.
    ISBN 0-304-33848-6 (hard).—ISBN 0-304-33849-4 (pbk.)
    1. Christianity. 2. Christianity—Study and teaching. I. Drury,
Clare. II. Title.
    BR121.2.D317 1997
    230–dc21   96-52966
                                                                CIP

Earlier versions of chapters appeared in the following books in the *Themes in
Religious Studies* series, edited by Jean Holm with John Bowker and published 1994
by Pinter Publishers: *Picturing God*; *Myth and History*; *Human Nature and Destiny*;
Sacred Writings; *Sacred Place*; *Worship*; *Rites of Passage*; *Making Moral Decisions*;
Attitudes to Nature; *Women in Religion*.

Biblical quotations are taken from the Revised Standard Version, © copyright 1973
by Division of Christian Education of the National Council of the Churches of
Christ in the United States of America.

Extracts from Dave Richards, 'For I'm building a people of power' and Graham
Kendrick, 'For this purpose' on p. 168 are reproduced by permission of Kingsway's
Thankyou Music.

Typeset by BookEns Ltd, Royston, Herts.
Printed and bound in Great Britain by Biddles Ltd, Guildford and King's Lynn

Contents

Introduction

The Christian religion influences the way of life of many millions of people across the world. Their faith helps guide their actions, supports them in times of hardship, and provides a means of expressing moments of joy. While many born into communities of Christian heritage take their Christian identity entirely for granted some come to appreciate their religion in more personal ways as life goes on and experience deepens. Some others, born entirely outside Christian influence, encounter it anew through missionary or evangelistic activities and undergo some sort of conversion to Christianity. This book focuses on a set of themes as a way of picturing the resources offered to believers by various Christian traditions as a basis for their daily life and for thinking about their eternal destiny.

Methods of study

Several different approaches to the study of religion are integrated in this book to produce a balanced view of Christianity as a religious way of life. The overall approach follows the method of the phenomenology of religions which begins by providing a detailed description of religious practices, beliefs and symbols before trying to identify some distinctive feature underlying the overall religion. So, for example, Gerardus van der Leeuw identified the idea of power as the key feature underpinning a wide diversity of religious phenomena (1967) while John Cumpsty pin-pointed the idea of belonging as basic to religion (1991). The chapters on 'Sacred places', 'Worship' and 'Sacred writings' reflect this phenomenological aspect of religious studies, exemplified in Ninian Smart's *Dimensions of the Sacred* (1996).

The approach of the history of religions stresses more the development of religious ideas over long periods of time, exploring the changes which come about in doctrine under various intellectual, social and religious influences. Good examples are found in Trevor Ling's *A History of Religions East and West* (1968) and Mircea Eliade's *A History of Religious Ideas* (1979). The chapters on 'Human nature and destiny', 'Attitudes to nature', 'Picturing God', 'Attitudes to women', and 'Myth and history' reflect such historical outlooks.

From a different perspective the anthropology of religion describes how religion works in contemporary societies and contributes important concepts for interpreting religious activity. This is especially clear in the chapters on 'Rites of passage' and 'Making moral decisions' where we draw very heavily from the anthropological concepts of ritual and of ethical vitality. Sociologists of religion also try to relate social values to religious ideas showing how, for example, status and identity are expressed through religious organizations. The chapter on women offers a good example of such social pressures.

Theology is, itself, a very important approach to the study of religion which usually bases itself upon certain basic assumptions lying at the heart of a religion. In terms of Christianity, there are several different traditions of theology related to the Orthodox, Catholic and Protestant churches. Theologians may either be very closely linked with the life of these churches or may operate within more secular educational contexts. Even so they often set about discussing topics and developing their arguments within the broad framework of belief in God and in the light of their own religious traditions. This approach is reflected in most of the following chapters which describe the significance of faith for believers rather than trying to argue the case for God's existence.

Religion and faith

One particularly important point which needs to be grasped when trying to understand people's religious life is the way in which the historical tradition of a religion relates to the personal life of the believer. While it is, obviously, quite easy to describe the architecture and history of church buildings or the way rituals are performed, it is more difficult to do justice to the way people feel and think when they are performing rituals in those buildings or when they are in solitude. So, for a more adequate account of a religion, we need to balance the study of its outward, historical, and visible aspects with some account of the inward and personal dynamics of the religious life.

One scholar who emphasized the importance of this complementary balance was Wilfred Cantwell Smith who suggested that the terms 'cumulative tradition' and 'faith' be used instead of the word 'religion' (1962: 194). Cumulative tradition would cover those architectural, symbolic, ritual and theological features which extend over time and provide the framework within which individuals come to a sense of their own personal faith. Smith thought it was important for people to compare like with like when it came to matters of religion. He thought, for example, that confusion emerged when people compared their own faith with the cumulative tradition of others. When they did so it was easy for them to present their own faith as a warm, living and dynamic personal experience and to contrast it with the cold, institutionalized and formal traditions of others. Just as important is Smith's view that 'a symbol in principle never means exactly the same thing to any two persons' (1976: 168).

These cautions remind us of the influence of different contexts on the way people relate to each other and highlights the fact that, when describing religious traditions and religious faith, we necessarily deal in the trends espoused by particular traditions, especially those of the major Orthodox, Roman Catholic and Protestant churches. Taken together the following chapters comprise an introduction to Christian studies, one which balances more abstract doctrinal, biblical and historical theology with the practical life of liturgy and ethics. These chapters first appeared as the entries on Christianity in the series *Themes in Religious Studies* edited by Jean Holm with John Bowker (Pinter Publishers, 1994). Some minor changes to the text have been included in this present book. References within the text refer to full entries in the Bibliography while some further reading on each topic is appended to each chapter. Clare Drury wrote the chapter on 'Attitudes to women' and Douglas Davies wrote all the others and edited the final volume.

FURTHER READING

Cumpsty, J. S. (1991) *Religion As Belonging: A General Theory of Religion*. London: University Press of America.

Eliade, Mircea (1979) *A History of Religious Ideas*. London: Collins.

Leeuw, Gerardus van der (1967; first pub. 1933) *Religion in Essence and Manifestation*. Gloucester, MA: Peter Smith.

Ling, Trevor (1968) *A History of Religion East and West*. London: Macmillan.

Smith, Wilfred Cantwell (1962) *The Meaning and End of Religion*. New York: Macmillan.

Smith, Wilfred Cantwell (1976) 'Objectivity and the humane sciences' in W. G. Oxtoby (ed.), *Religious Diversity*. New York: Harper and Row.

1. Picturing God

For many people the phrase 'picturing God' will trigger the idea of paintings, stained-glass windows, and statues. But the human imagination also has other ways of picturing God through architecture and ritual, and through the lives of men, women, and children. All these help express the sense of God at the heart of Christian faith. In this chapter we think about picturing God both in the literal sense and in other ways which provide people with working ideas of what God is like, and enable them to worship and talk about God as understood by Christianity.

Many pictures

At the most literal level, books and sacred texts give verbal descriptions of God as pictures to the mind's eye, through the verbal descriptions of poetry, sermons or talks. Sometimes these accounts speak in a logical way and try to give a systematic account of what God is like, as in the case of formal systematic theology. But other types of account are more suggestive and poetic, hinting at the nature of God by analogy with human relationships, especially through ideas of love.

Music evokes another realm of sensing what God is like. Not only in hymns and chanting, where words also play a significant part, but also in music on its own, many moods can be formed and a sense of God fostered. The great majority of religious traditions of the world make use of music in worship. And this also applies to Christianity which has, with a few exceptions, taken music as a serious medium for expressing religious faith.

Words and music often benefit from a particular setting and this has certainly been the case in Christianity where cathedrals, churches and chapels regularly serve as the context for worship. Not only can God be 'pictured' through the very architecture of buildings, but the sheer availability of quiet places where people may think, meditate and worship gives opportunity for God to be pictured within the personal experience of individuals.

A final way of picturing God comes through the example of saintly lives as humble and self-sacrificing people give themselves in a life of love for others. This is true not only as Christians look out at other people but also as they gain their own experience of living in a Christian way.

In this chapter we consider all these avenues as ways of picturing God, for each one can enable the imagination to catch a glimpse of what God is like. In practice these media work together to build up a knowledge of God within individuals, drawing as they do from the tradition of their church, from their own experience of worship, and from the facts of daily life and service.

ARE PICTURES VALID?

At the heart of Christianity lies the question which is posed several times in the Jewish Scriptures and which the spirituality of Israel has always taken as its own guide: 'To whom then will you liken God, or what likeness compare with him?' (Isa 40:18). The answer of Jewish Scripture, usually referred to by Christians as the 'Old Testament', is resoundingly clear: there are no comparisons whatsoever that can be made, so that it is wrong even to begin to think of entering God into any set of comparisons. And, to press the logic of this argument further, models, statues, or pictures of God were forbidden.

Some scholars have assumed that this Jewish attitude passed on into Christianity to produce a strong opposition to artistic representation of God which has, in some churches, been a very strong feeling at particular moments in their history. Some other scholars have taken a different line, believing that early Christians used art in a creative way to express their belief in Christ as the saviour of the world, incorporating into their work stories from Old Testament texts along with episodes drawn from classical mythology of that pagan world in which many early Christians lived (Murray, 1981: 13ff.).

Idolatry

The Jewish prophets tended to ridicule the idea of any images of God. To choose special, long-lasting wood, and to cover it in gold, to set it up and worship it was nothing but folly. Isaiah 40 explores this theme and simply points to the heavens as well as to the creation of the earth to show that the one who made all that is beyond comparison, as the Psalmist also makes disparagingly clear:

> Our God is in the heavens;
> he does whatever he pleases.
> Their idols are silver and gold,
> the works of men's hands. (Ps 115:3ff.)

The description of idols presents the ridiculous spectacle of idols that have mouths through which they cannot speak, ears that cannot hear, feet that cannot walk, etc. Idolatry is obviously ruled out of court as dealing with inferior products rather than with the creator of all. In fact, this is the critical point. It is precisely because God is the Creator of all that it is wrong to represent deity in or through any one created thing. A created thing cannot represent the creator, it is by definition a lesser object, an inferior and unworthy focus for worship.

The Ten Commandments, which lie at the heart of the Jewish Law and which have entered so fundamentally into Christian belief, stress the primacy of God with an immediate command not to make any graven image of anything in heaven or earth (Exod 20:1ff.). God is transcendent and beyond any such futile art-work of humanity. God is not to be pictured.

The divine name

Even when God is addressed or referred to in words, the divine name itself must not be taken in vain, as another of the Ten Commandments puts it. The ancient Jews developed the practice of substituting the Hebrew word *Adonai*, or Lord, for the tetragrammaton, or four letters (JHVH), which stood in their Scriptures as the word for the deity. In the Hebrew Scriptures special vowel-points are placed beneath the basic consonants to give the pronunciation of words. Unusually in this case, the vowel pointing for *Adonai* was placed beneath the consonants JHVH, leading to the compound word 'Jehovah', which has come to be common in some Christian use. What this shows is that even in words where, in one sense, God is depicted or identified, respect had to be shown. It is an interesting fact that in Great Britain the letters GOD have never been issued for use on car licence plates, presumably out of some similar respect both for the deity and also for believers who might be offended by such a number plate.

Within the Jewish Scriptures anything to do with God had to be beyond human control. One of the starkest expressions of God's utter reality and transcendence lay in the fact that in the Second Temple at Jerusalem the innermost sacred place of the Holy of Holies was entirely empty. But this strong avoidance of picturing God is a problem for those who have had a deep experience of God and feel the need to express it in some more tangible way.

Divine encounters

There are several incidents in the Hebrew Bible dealing with the early mythical history of Israel, which hint at a physical encounter with God as when Abraham encounters certain visitors (Gen 18:1ff.), when Jacob wrestles with someone until the break of day (Gen 32:30), or when God speaks with Moses, 'face to face, as a man speaks to his friend' (Exod 33:11). But these are all profoundly exceptional moments in the encounter between God and Israel in the formative period of their mutual covenant relationship. For the greater part of Jewish Scriptures encounter with God is expressed in worship (as through the Psalms) or else as inspired utterance by the prophets.

Reflecting God

God is extensively depicted by the prophets in the sense that the divine will, nature, and intention, are all expounded in detail through the prophets and priests of the Jewish religion. The picture that emerges focuses on moral issues rather than on any physical aspect of the divine. God is mirrored in the moral life of Israel. The

Priestly writers and stream of the biblical tradition also depict God through rules for the ritual life of Jews. This led the anthropologist Mary Douglas to propose that the Holiness Codes as represented, for example, in Leviticus, gave laws for social life that tried to make the chosen people a model of the moral nature of God (Deut 14; Lev 11). God was, in a sense, to be mirrored or reflected in the dynamic social and moral life of the Jewish people rather than in any static picture. As we show in greater detail in Chapter 9, even the food laws expressed an ordered world in which animals that conformed to a clear type could be eaten and those that seemed to straddle different groups could not be touched. The dietary laws were 'like signs which at every turn inspired meditation on the oneness, purity, and completeness of God. By rules of avoidance holiness was given a physical expression in every encounter with the animal kingdom and at every meal' (1966: 57). These practical rules for life were contained in Scriptures that were of vital practical consequence for Jews. Given the history of Israel it is no accident that God is approached through the words of Scripture both in the synagogue and in private prayer. The scrolls of the Law were and are treated with respect and honour and they replaced any other representation of God. The symbolic focus of all this lies in the tables on which the Ten Commandments were believed to be written, tables that were, according to tradition, kept in the Ark of the Covenant (Deut 10:1–5).

It is important to recognize that the scriptural religion of Jews emerged and continued in a world of many cultures where gods, heroes, and mythical figures played an important part in the apparatus of worship as did altars, standing stones, wooden posts symbolizing fertility and probably much besides. Episodes such as the disobedient modelling of a golden calf (Exod 32:4) with some sort of worship associated with it illustrate this contextual world of popular religions.

Early Christianity

The birth of Christianity has to be seen against this background of Jewish religion, not least because the Jewish Scriptures became part and parcel of the Christian Scriptures and entered into the way Christians understood God and the world. But – and this is a crucially important point – Christians came to believe that Jesus was divine. The doctrine of the Incarnation is the formal expression of this belief, and it lies central to the creeds of Christianity which were produced in the centuries after the earthly life of Jesus. This doctrine expressed the belief that in Jesus of Nazareth the very nature of God has come to expression in a unique human life. The creeds describe significant aspects of that divine and human existence. By the fourth and fifth centuries they were commonly used in association with baptism and acts of worship. They also included statements of belief about the Holy Spirit, about the Church, and about the salvation of humanity.

These items appear through a threefold pattern of belief. They do not simply assert a belief in God as the one and only deity, they describe God in terms of Father, Son, and Holy Spirit. Before exploring the significance of this threefoldness for picturing God, it is useful to give one of the creeds – the Apostles' Creed – in full because it has played and continues to play an important part in the regular worship of many Christian churches. It will also be a useful way of approaching the ways in which God has been depicted in Christianity.

THE APOSTLES' CREED

> I believe in God the Father Almighty,
> Maker of heaven and earth:
> And in Jesus Christ his only Son our Lord,
> Who was conceived by the Holy Spirit,
> Born of the Virgin Mary,
> Suffered under Pontius Pilate,
> Was crucified, dead, and buried,
> He descended into hell;
> The third day he rose again from the dead,
> He ascended into heaven,
> And is sitting on the right hand of God the Father Almighty;
> From thence he shall come to judge the quick and the dead.
> I believe in the Holy Spirit;
> The holy Catholic Church;
> The Communion of Saints;
> The forgiveness of sins;
> The resurrection of the body;
> And the life everlasting. Amen.

The Incarnation

The doctrine of the Incarnation, therefore, is a formal summary of the way Christians expressed their belief that Jesus was God in human nature. The very word 'incarnation' means 'in the flesh' and it pin-points the radical earthiness and material basis of the Christian faith. It is difficult to exaggerate the importance of this doctrine in Christian thinking and it is particularly important as far as picturing God is concerned. Hand in hand with the growth of belief in Jesus as divine went the writing and interpretation of new Scriptures, of the Christian epistles and gospels, and of other documents that came to form what is called the New Testament. The human life of Jesus was described in the gospel stories, and further, more detailed, interpretations were provided through the epistles and other New Testament documents. Because of the Incarnation, 'picturing God' can now be, directly and simply, picturing Jesus, God in Christ reconciling the world to himself.

THE CRUCIFIXION

Amongst the most frequently represented aspects of Christ's life stands the crucifixion. The crucifix represents the body of Christ on the cross and has been portrayed, both in two-dimensional art and in three-dimensional sculpture, for centuries. The crucifixion was not portrayed in the earliest Christian art and only came into prominence from the sixth century. It is perhaps the most extensively used of all Christian symbols, not only in artistic form but also in ritual behaviour.

In many Christian traditions babies are signed with the sign of the cross at their baptism, and priests often bless their congregations with the sign of the cross. Many of the faithful use the sign of the cross in their public and private devotions. In whatever form it is used it reminds the Christian that the object which caused the death of Christ is the sign of life and hope for the Christian.

THE RESURRECTION

Even though the resurrection of Jesus was, obviously, a matter of belief, some writers spoke of it as a demonstrable fact. Paul outlines his own sense of the Christian tradition and message and expresses his belief in the resurrection in 1 Corinthians (15:3–8).

> For I delivered to you as of first importance what I also received, that Christ died for our sins ... that he was buried, that he was raised on the third day ... that he appeared to Peter, then to the twelve. Then he appeared to more than five hundred brethren at one time ... then to James, then to all the apostles. Last of all ... he appeared also to me.

This factual sense of the resurrection was combined with the historical basis of Jesus' actual life in Palestine to give to all subsequent generations of Christians a firm basis for pictorial representations of Jesus. Because Jesus had been seen by his contemporaries in an ordinary way, he could be represented in paintings, pictures, and other forms of art without any sense of blasphemy or impropriety.

The Holy Trinity

Jesus came to be understood as the Son of God. The language of Son and Father grew and developed in a way that helped to interpret how Jesus could share the nature of his father. The human analogy of father and son was easily applied to the divine nature. Jesus was said to be of the same substance as the Father, and this expressed the idea that Jesus was really divine. But the Christian creeds also added a further 'person' to this group of two. This was the Holy Spirit. That sense of the power and presence of God which had been spoken of in the Old Testament came to prominence amongst early Christians who no longer had the tangible presence of Jesus but who reckoned to share in the life of God through their experience of God, the Holy Spirit. So it was that the Christian Church developed what might initially be seen as a strange teaching, the doctrine of the Holy Trinity. The three persons of this Trinity are the Father, the Son, and the Holy Spirit. Three persons but one God whose very essence is grounded in the relationship between the persons.

This linking of Jesus with his Father and also with the power of God the Spirit had an interesting consequence. Just as Jesus had been portrayed in artistic ways so now the 'Father' and also the Holy

Spirit came to be represented in art. The Jewish idea that God could not and should not be artistically represented was overcome through the doctrine of the Incarnation. Even if in a picture the Father is not actually portrayed he is often symbolically represented by bright light, or surrounded by angels or cherubim, etc. Even so, the very material reality of Jesus as the Son of God made it easier for artists and theologians to think of God the Father in a pictorial way.

One sculptural motif exhibits this well in a fifteenth-century limestone carving from the Netherlands where Christ on the cross is placed immediately in front of a figure of God the Father, and with a dove, symbolic of the Holy Spirit, also as part of the total scene (Christie, 1982: 482). An English example is found on an alabaster of approximately the same period in Nottingham.

Sometimes trinitarian ideas were expressed by utilizing Old Testament images and interpreting them anew in the light of Christian doctrine. A famous icon of the Holy Trinity painted by the renowned Russian Andrei Rublev in the fifteenth century shows three angels sitting at a kind of table and about to share a meal. It is an icon of the Holy Trinity expressed through the story of the three visitors who came to Abraham as messengers of, or as representations of, the Lord in Genesis 18. The three persons of the Trinity are reflected through these three mysterious visitors.

History and life events

The Jewish religion out of which Christianity grew was itself firmly rooted in history: it retained a sense of commitment to the patriarchs, Abraham, Isaac, and Jacob, to Moses who led the captive people out of Egypt, and to many judges, prophets, priests, and martyrs. In Christianity this focus on history becomes even more intense through the belief that God has now, at last, fully shared in human life.

The walls, ceilings, altars, and tombs of Christian churches, and in later years their stained glass windows, not to mention painted icons and statuary, all served as media through which the story or history of salvation could be told. History itself could take shape through art and could come to influence generation after generation of believers.

Great and little traditions in art

Christian churches provide what is probably the most extensive collection of art in the world. The catacombs of Rome with their early pictures of Jesus, magnificent cathedrals with their stained glass, and the millions of ordinary churches in towns, villages, and hamlets from one side of the earth to the other, contain something expressing the nature of God. In many of these there is art based on Bible stories and on the tradition of Christian history.

Sometimes anthropologists and sociologists draw a distinction between what they call great and little traditions. The great tradition of a culture represents its major religion or philosophy as expressed in revered and established texts held and interpreted by trained scholars and priests. The little tradition refers to the local versions and expressions of religion, belief, and thought. The world religions as we now know them have all had complex histories, but one common feature is that they have extended into areas, societies, and cultures, where once they did not belong, but from which they have derived new inspiration and forms of expression.

One interesting side of the little tradition involves the way that many stories from the Bible and wider Christian tradition have been taken up and developed by local believers from many different cultures. They have adapted them to their own cultural idiom at the same time as they have adopted them as basic elements of their faith. This process gives life and power to the stories and allows them to influence new ages and geographical regions. Images of Jesus offer one good example, as he has sometimes been portrayed with the skin colour and bodily features of Africans, Europeans, South Americans, etc.

In this way, the Bible has come to influence the artistic life of thousands of different societies across the world. Because art is visible and more durable than speech and language this one influence upon many varied minds is a profound reminder that Christianity has become a world religion, having taken root in societies that once had their own form of religion but now possess Christianity in a way that makes it seem that they have always been Christian.

Certain works of art become so important that they also help form part of the great tradition. The growth of the media, and especially of books, film, and television, means that pictures and buildings can be seen by millions of people who would not otherwise encounter them. There is a sense in which postcard pictures can take great works of art into places they would never otherwise penetrate. Similarly visitors, tourists, or pilgrims, can buy pictures of religious art and take them back to their own homes. In all these ways the great tradition penetrates the little local traditions of communities and even of individuals' private lives. Some examples featuring pictures of God will illustrate this variety.

God in creation

One of the most famous pictures of God is found in the Sistine Chapel in the Vatican City in Rome. This chapel belonged to the popes and was painted by Michelangelo (1475–1564) in the early years of the sixteenth century. The picture entitled 'The Creation of Man' depicts God as an older man of powerful build reaching out his hand to touch the extended hand of Adam. The human form of God is clear and obvious and shows that in the sixteenth century there was no problem in portraying God, or God the Father in trinitarian language, as a man.

Many reproductions of this fine work have been made and have found a home across the world so that many people who have never been to Rome will be familiar with this portrayal of God. Some might even find it easier to have a reproduction of this picture on their wall than to stand and try to keep their balance while craning their necks backward in the Sistine Chapel trying to concentrate on the original located high in the ceiling amongst other painted panels. But equally many local churches have pictures that can be studied and enjoyed even though they are not regarded as world class works of art. Similar themes and links can often be found between artistic motifs. In Uppsala in Sweden there is, for example, an interesting mural painted high in the north transept of the Lutheran Cathedral which echoes Michelangelo's 'Creation of Man' in the Sistine Chapel. The Swedish painting is much later, coming from the 1890s. In it, God is shown as standing as a man, once more as older rather than as younger; he has slightly long hair and a white flowing robe. On the ground before him and asleep on his right side lies Adam. From Adam's left side, from a rib, Eve is emerging as the first created woman. She is depicted as actually coming from Adam, with only the top half of her body yet visible. God stands leaning slightly forward and with his left hand he holds the hand of Eve, leading her into the world. God's right hand is raised in the form of a blessing.

Through the medium of creative art, in both pictures and music, the biblical stories were given a much wider exposure than could have been achieved through the printed page alone. One good example of a work that took a biblical passage into thousands of homes is Holman Hunt's famous 'The Light of the World', painted in 1854. Hunt (1827–1910) was a founder of the Pre-Raphaelite group of painters in the mid-nineteenth century, and he travelled extensively in Palestine getting detail for his many pictures on biblical themes. His 'Light of the World' shows Jesus as a tall man dressed in a long robe or cloak standing outside a closed door and knocking on it. In his hand he holds a lantern. This painting expresses the idea of Jesus himself being the light of the world (John 8:12) but combines with it this text from the book of Revelation (3:20): 'Behold I stand at the door and knock; if anyone hears my voice and opens the door, I will come in to him and eat with him, and he with me.'

Other texts from the book of Revelation have become widely known through being set to music by Handel in his oratorio *The Messiah*. One of the best known pieces of religious music in the Western world, the 'Hallelujah Chorus' (along with 'Worthy is the Lamb that was slain', Rev 5:12), comes from this source.

Both the art of painting and the creativity of musical settings of Scripture provide magnificent complements to religious architecture. Sight and sound combine with the physical place of worship to furnish layers of rich symbolism for the faithful in their worship.

From catacombs to cathedrals

Christian worship has not, however, always been conducted in the splendour of large buildings. The subterranean catacombs surrounding Rome, where the dead were often placed for burial, also became the tombs of many early Christians for about the first four hundred years of the Christian era. Early Christians also met in these hidden places, especially during times of persecution, for worship, to celebrate the Eucharist, and to remember the dead.

It was here in the catacombs that the first Christian art was developed. Pagan art had long been associated with funerary monuments and had used figures such as Orpheus and Helios from mythology and classical authors to express beliefs in immortality. By the third and fourth centuries Christians were also using such figures, adapting them under the control of the image of Christ and his resurrection.

Funerary art, painted both on wall panels and also on special coffins or sarcophagi, was a particularly appropriate art form to carry the Christian message concerning resurrection and life after death. The grave, after all, had been the place of Christ's victory over death, and that was a key element in Christian thought.

The Jewish Scriptures, which Christians had also made their own, gave to artists of the new faith a wealth of stories which could be used in sculpture to illustrate Christian themes. So, for example, Jonah's delivery from his 'death' in the great fish that had swallowed him, or Noah's delivery from the flood through his ark, are both used on tombs of the third and fourth century. As Mary Murray (1981: 98), a specialist in Christian art, has shown, Rome is very much a centre for Noah portrayed in his ark, now carrying a Christian significance; these Noah sculptures start from about the year 200 CE. It is thought that the overall meaning is that the Christian, represented by Noah, has been through the water of death and rebirth in baptism, and this is a basis for life after death. It is also true that this particular biblical picture echoed some pagan mythology of Perseus.

But Christ is also an important figure, sometimes depicted through classical mythology as Orpheus or Helios, but also in more direct biblical expressions. A typical and important representation is of Christ as a young man carrying a sheep over his shoulders. This idiom of the good shepherd also has its forerunner in art of classical antiquity where the shepherd figure was widely used, but in Christian contexts it takes an additional significance directly from the gospels (John 10:11; Luke 15:4) where, in literary form, Jesus is strongly depicted as the good shepherd who loves, seeks out, and lays down his life for his 'sheep'. Once more, the human reality of a historical Jesus gives the artist a strong foundation for realistic picturing of the divine Son involved in earthly activities.

From the fourth century, art becomes increasingly more plentiful and devoted to wider themes than death and baptism. Broader aspects of the life and ministry of Jesus are drawn upon. One ivory plaque from northern Italy from approximately 400 CE shows the resurrection and ascension of Jesus. After speaking to the women who come to visit his tomb, he is seen walking up on a cloud into heaven. Christ has a halo painted around his head, a feature that occurs very frequently in pictures of Jesus from now on, representing his holy status. Sometimes a cross is designed into the halo to represent the form of his death and victory over sin.

The hand of God

In this, and other, resurrection and ascension pictures the right hand of God can be seen from the wrist down emerging from the cloud and taking Jesus by the right hand to receive him into heaven (Christie *et al.*, 1982: 60). Other pieces of art of many sorts use the hand of God to represent God or God the Father in relation to other activities. So, for example, some pictures of the transfiguration of Christ have the hand of God extended towards the figure of the glorified Jesus, representing in pictorial form the words of God on that occasion, 'This is my beloved Son with whom I am well pleased, listen to him' (Matt 17:5). Some scenes of the crucifixion also have the hand of God poised above the cross.

At the baptism of Christ it is usual to have the Holy Spirit represented in the form of a dove placed above the head of Christ as he stands in the water of the river Jordan to be baptized by John, but sometimes there is an additional symbol, with the hand of God emerging from a cloud just above the dove, as represented for example in an illustration of an Armenian gospel book of the sixth century (Beckwith, 1970: plate 118).

This clear symbolism of God through the divine hand also occurs in some Christian art portraying Old Testament stories, as when the hand of God is shown in a mosaic of the sacrifice of Isaac in the church of S. Vitale, Ravenna, or in the hand of God delivering the tables of the Law to Moses, from an illustration from a tenth-century Bible (Beckwith, 1970: plates 91, 172).

Icons

At their simplest, icons are paintings made on wooden panels and having religious themes. They are characteristic objects within the

Eastern Orthodox Churches and have a significant part to play in the history of picturing God.

Icons picture the holy in a special way. The logic behind their construction and use is grounded in the assumption we have already discussed for religious art in general, namely, that the Incarnation of Christ gives a positive significance to the material world. Because God in Christ shared in human nature and in the material dimension of the world that dimension is acknowledged as worthy. Then, in addition to this, it is believed that the divine essence or the divine aspect of holy persons can be encountered or experienced through their material representation. So a picture of Christ is not simply a likeness presented in paint, it is a means of experiencing and sharing in the divine attributes of the one portrayed.

In this sense icons provide a medium of contact, a channel to gain access, a kind of window or door into the divine world. They are not an end in and of themselves, and that is why they cannot rightly be regarded as a source of idolatry. Rather, like the sacraments in wider Christian thought icons have an outward and visible form, but through them it is possible to encounter an underlying spiritual grace.

This idea of communicating spiritual realities to the believer becomes very evident in the architecture of many Eastern Orthodox churches. As well as having icons around a church the Orthodox have developed a large partition called an iconostasis which separates the altar from the rest of the church building. As its name suggests the iconostasis is a picture stand and on it are painted or hung many large, often life-sized, icons of saints, angels and other holy persons. These structures were greatly developed in the twelfth century to reach from floor to ceiling instead of being low walls, as they were originally.

One important feature of many Orthodox churches is the central place given to large-scale pictures of Christ placed at the dominant point in the building, often in its dome. This frequently takes the form of Christ as Pantokrator, the one who creates and rules over all. In theological terms, Christ stands absolutely central in these paintings, and for all practical purposes serves as the one divine referent: he stands as God and for God.

The area of the altar behind the screen is often interpreted as representing heaven while the area where the people stand, in front of the iconostasis, represents this life on earth. During the liturgy the priests pass through doors in the iconostasis from the altar to the people, from 'heaven' to 'earth'. In its own way this ritual passage pictures God in terms of a divine heavenly dwelling place which, through worship, the believer may share. The priests serve as mediators between the two realms, and in the work of the Liturgy they bring the faithful to participate in the heavenly kingdom of God. The icons of the angels and of saints help mark out the heavenly territory, encourage the faithful in their lives and worship, and help convey to them spiritual strength and power.

In the Western churches, it became usual for the long nave, where the people gathered, to be separated by a choir from the sanctuary where the altar was located. Often this separation was marked by a screen which divided the church into two major sectors. Although there was no formal theological association of these areas with earth and heaven, as in the case of Orthodoxy, in practice the 'altar end' came to be viewed as especially sacred while the nave might even be used for popular local activities of a much more secular type. This distinction between holy and ordinary activities itself classifies God in the minds of worshippers, and can give the impression that God is distant, removed from ordinary life events. It may well be that the immense size of some cathedrals, especially in the light of the size of ordinary houses in the tenth to thirteenth centuries when many of them were built, gave the impression that God was transcendent over human activities.

Objecting to pictures of God

Some modern Christians find great cathedrals a problem as far as faith is concerned. They think that immense buildings, along with their apparent wealth and richness of art and architecture, detract from both the simple teaching of Jesus, and the importance of sincere groups of believers. Slightly similar concerns were also mentioned early in this chapter when referring to idolatry as the process of making objects to represent God and then offering worship to those objects. In other words, idolatry pays to immediate objects the due that rightly goes only to the ultimate being of God. Christianity, as Judaism, has always disowned that sort of practice.

But it is very easy to misunderstand the behaviour of other people, especially when it comes to matters of religion and worship. We have already seen that Eastern Orthodox believers use icons as part of their worship of God, but they would adamantly deny that they treated icons like idols or that they practise idolatry. They would say that the icon is a medium or vehicle through which the power and grace of God come to the faithful. Some Protestant Christians would not be persuaded by this and would prefer to see icons eliminated, so that a more internalized form of piety might come to the fore. This kind of objection to the dominant force of outward objects used in worship has not only been made from Protestant quarters: one of the most important debates in the history of Eastern Orthodox religion concerned icons, with those who would have had them destroyed understanding themselves to be keeping the purity of the faith.

ICONOCLASM

From early in the eighth century a debate raged in the Eastern Church over the use of icons. The Emperor Leo III sought the destruction of icons in 726 for a wide variety of reasons, including the argument that such material representation of holy things hindered the conversion of Jews and Muslims. Theological arguments also focused on whether icons did justice to the human nature of Christ or over-accentuated the divine nature. This Iconoclastic Controversy, as it is called, involved some monks losing their lives for the cause of icons as a true form of spirituality, a position that was established by 842 CE, after which icons became a natural part of Orthodox worship.

ANTHROPOMORPHISM AND PROJECTION

Despite the vehemence of debates about icons and idolatry, the arguments involved are relatively simple. But there is another area that is much more complicated and perhaps even more important. It concerns anthropomorphism.

21

'Anthropomorphism' comes from the Greek and means that something is given the shape or form of man. This can apply to obvious things such as physical objects but it also has another sort of application as when a dog, cat, or some other animal is said to behave like a human being. We read into the animal's behaviour some of those features which are characteristic of human beings. But it is not only animals that can be viewed as though they are human beings. Supernatural entities can also be regarded as though they are human. One very direct and obvious case concerns ancestors, for in some societies the dead are believed to pass to the after-life where they become ancestors and as such continue to play an active part in the affairs of their living descendants. An ancestor may curse or bless the living depending on their behaviour. The issue that has to be raised is whether the entire enterprise of 'picturing God' is a massive case of anthropomorphism − of projecting human ideas and ideals, and calling them 'God'. Thus in the history of Western thought on religion, some scholars have approached the whole of religion on the assumption that God does not exist and that everything said about God is really the outcome of human imagination.

A PHILOSOPHICAL VIEW

One of the best and historically most significant examples of this approach comes from the German philosopher Ludwig Feuerbach (1804–72). In his book *The Essence of Christianity* (1841) the idea of God as a transcendent and self-existing deity is denied. Philosophy and theology, he thought, were really about humanity and not about God. What human beings say about God are not really statements concerning a deity at all, they were statements about the human condition arising from human thought. This is why it is often said that Feuerbach wanted to replace theology, as a study of God, by a philosophical anthropology which dealt with human nature.

A PSYCHOLOGICAL VIEW

From the quite different direction of psychology, though with an equally direct atheistic commitment, Sigmund Freud argued that ideas of God were the outcome of human thought and, in particular, expressed a kind of wish-fulfilment. For Freud, the pictures of God which traditional Christianity possessed were only an illusion. Men and women want to believe that there really is a 'heavenly father' because they desire a strong father figure but know that their human fathers are inadequate. Life experience shows that earthly fathers are not always dependable, and in the end they die.

But, according to Freud, the human mind was not content to accept these harsh facts of life. Instead, it constructed this image of a heavenly father to help make life bearable. Freud used the word 'projection' to describe this process through which the idea of God came into existence. For Freud, religion was an illusion, and in his suitably entitled book *The Future of an Illusion* (1913), he spelled out this theory of how human beings had created the idea of God, an idea that has no future if men and women are ever fully to understand themselves and come to a mature insight into the nature of existence.

Feuerbach had also used this idea of projection in his theory of religion: 'Man projects his being into objectivity and makes himself an object to this projected image of himself' (1957: 29). Feuerbach thought that the process of human self-understanding was very complex and took a long time, and he thought that religion played a vitally important part in it. Since there is no actual God, as far as Feuerbach is concerned, religion is really about human beings. What people say about God they are really saying about themselves. It is this that makes it possible for Feuerbach to believe that 'religion is man's earliest and most indirect form of self-knowledge' (1957: 14).

A SOCIOLOGICAL VIEW

From Feuerbach's philosophical perspective, it is to be expected that in each society the idea of God, gods, or spirits will be directly related to its values, organization, and culture. This, obviously, makes the issue open to sociological and anthropological analysis. One attempt was made by Guy Swanson (1960) who tried to relate the way different societies are organized to the way their gods are organized.

One classic text on the relationship between gods and society was written by the French sociologist Emile Durkheim. In his *Elementary Forms of the Religious Life* (1913), he argued that what people believe to be an experience of God is really the experience of being together in a group ritual. The idea of God was 'really' a picture of society even though ordinary people were unaware of this real meaning. This kind of argument is often called a reductionist argument in that it reduces the point at issue to some underlying process which is known only to the expert.

Another expert, the sociologist Max Weber, also saw the importance of anthropomorphism in his *Sociology of Religion*, first published in German in 1922. Having focused attention on the process of drawing analogies between things which lie behind mythology and magic he argued that analogy also underlay the personification of gods, just as it does certain kinds of magic (1965: 10). Gods were regarded much as human beings were regarded, and the dynamics of human life were visible anew in the world of the gods as humanity perceived it, or reckoned it to be.

The social basis of religious ideas was very extensively pursued in the twentieth century in what is called the sociology of knowledge. Peter Berger and Thomas Luckmann's book *The Social Construction of Reality* (1967) gave a sociological explanation of how societies come to have a sense of meaning in life and in the organization of culture. Berger took this further in *The Social Reality of Religion* (1969), where he showed how religious ideas are born out of ordinary social life. This was such a reductionist form of argument that he wrote a follow-up study called *A Rumour of Angels* (1971) to offset its hard-line approach and to suggest that there were certain 'signals of transcendence' to be found in play, hope, damnation, humour and the sense of good order in the world. He thought that these showed that people are not totally conditioned by their social existence.

Even so the strictly sociological view of religion generally makes out that religious ideas are the outcome of society and are, therefore, human in origin. Pictures of God are, necessarily, human constructions and projections of the human imagination.

THEOLOGICAL VIEWS

One theological view that disagrees with this interpretation and tries to argue with it comes from John Bowker (1973, 1978). On the assumption that God exists and creates a universe in which we find ourselves, Bowker suggests that certain 'cues of meaning' are picked up by humanity and enter into ideas of God. Religious ideas are not simply the product of the human imagination but of the human imagination in relation to encounters with God. People may decide to develop and use the experience of encounter or they may decide to ignore it, but the importance of the possibility of God influencing us must not be overlooked.

The great art of the world treats physical things such as landscapes in very different ways with, for example, some Impressionists giving a sense of a scene through thousands of small dots of paint, while more traditional painters draw detailed representations of what is there to see. In each case there is an actual scene before their eyes, but their picture of it comes out in many different ways because of the difference in perspective, creativity, and fashion.

This process of feedback between external source and human appreciation is evident in many aspects of daily life. In the gospels of the New Testament, for example, the disciples try to understand and form a 'picture' of Jesus and often get it blurred through misunderstanding, as when they try to prevent Jesus being crowded by children but he calls them to him and says that the Kingdom of God belongs to children (Luke 18:16). In the end, therefore, the 'picturing of God' is always a tentative and provisional activity, open to being corrected: no one has ever *seen* God (1 John 4:11), and therefore any imaginative representation of God must always be suggestive, pointing towards the only possible encounter with God in prayer and worship – above all in liturgy.

God as Christ in priests

One feature of the rise of the priesthood as a special order of leaders was the medieval doctrine that through ordination the priest was given a special character or power by means of which he could perform sacramental rituals. His key task was to celebrate the Eucharist or the Mass. In one sense the priest represented Christ. He was Christ at the altar. So in a symbolic sense it is true to say that the ritual of the Mass was a means of picturing Christ.

The Mass or Eucharist is a remarkable rite which can be understood in several different ways. At one level it is a form of memorial which simply enables people to remember the past. As such it is a kind of practical history. For many in the Protestant traditions of Christianity this memorial element predominates; it often goes hand in hand with a very simple form of ritual in what members of those churches often call the Lord's Supper or Holy Communion.

By contrast, in the Orthodox traditions of Greece and Russia, the Church on earth comes to share in the eternal Kingdom of God through the worship of the Eucharist. In the Roman Catholic Church the doctrine of transubstantiation (which became popular in the twelfth and thirteenth centuries) asserted that through the prayer of consecration the body and blood of Christ came to replace the inner substance of the bread and wine. This brought the real presence of Christ into the Mass as a focus for devotion and worship, as we shall see in Chapter 6, and also as the basis for a constant re-presenting and sacrificial offering to God.

These rites can often be complex, involving the priest and other clergy and assistants wearing special clothes or vestments which carry a heavy weight of symbolism. One interpretation sometimes given for the eucharistic vestments is that they blot out the personal identity of the ordained individual to emphasize the role and nature of the priest. This is all the more significant when the priest is believed to represent Christ, for not only is the Mass a kind of representation of the Last Supper, but it also represents the sacrificial death of Christ with the priest being a symbol of Christ. As such this ritual offers a way of portraying and depicting Christ through a ritual act rather than through art.

Whether at its simple or most elaborate level this ritual of taking bread, blessing, breaking, sharing and eating it with others links the present with the past. The historical Jesus and the original Passover meal become intimately bound up with the present moment of faith. The past mixes with the present. Just as believers are taken in heart and mind back to events recorded in the Bible, so they feel the effects of those events in their life today. For many believers their experience of God focused in Jesus and active in their personal faith is nurtured and fostered through the Holy Communion.

Changing times and changing images

These images of Jesus cover a wide spectrum of belief. As both artistic and verbal images, they move from a picture of Jesus as the mighty conqueror mirroring the Old Testament idea of God as the warrior, through the image of the dying saviour sacrificed for sin, to the gentle carer concerned for those he loves.

Christian doctrine is intimately associated with these images of Jesus because they are deeply influenced by the theological meaning that a tradition wants to express. This makes Christian art in the widest sense a useful key to the belief of Christian groups at different times and places. This includes the images of God and of Jesus Christ which theologians construct in their writing.

One very explicit example of this can be found at the end of Albert Schweitzer's *The Mystery of the Kingdom of God* (1914), which was itself part of a longer study of the Holy Communion in Christianity. His work was very influential at the beginning of the twentieth century, not least because he sought to explore the life of Jesus in a historical and critical way. He wrote a very telling postscript saying that the aim of his book was 'to depict the figure of Jesus in its overwhelming heroic greatness and to impress it upon the modern age and upon modern theology' (1914: 274). Schweitzer thought that the modern world-view had taken the heroic aspect away from the picture of Jesus, and because of this had 'humanized and humbled him'. Referring to two philosophers of religion of his day, he went on to say what he thought about the verbal pictures of Jesus they had painted in their work:

> Renan has stripped off his halo and reduced him to a sentimental figure, coward spirits like Schopenhauer have dared to appeal to him for their enervating philosophy, and our generation has modernised him, with the notion that it could comprehend his character and development psychologically. We must go back to the point where we can feel again the heroic in Jesus. Before that mysterious Person, who, in the form of his time, knew that he was creating upon the foundation of his life and death a moral world which bears his name, we must be forced to lay our faces in the dust, without daring even to wish to understand his nature. Only then can the heroic in our Christianity and in our world-view be again revived. (1914: 274)

As we shall see later, Schweitzer was committed to this heroic aspect of Jesus and to a degree reflected it in his own life. In the mid-twentieth century the picture of Jesus as deeply socially involved helped fire a series of theological views focused on political and social theology aimed at justice for oppressed people. This made him more of a revolutionary than a hero, but the general trend was similar. For others it is the humility of Jesus, or Jesus as the key to the mystery of the universe, or as a miracle worker, which stands to the fore.

So it is that sometimes these pictures are images for the mind to dwell on in an intellectual and poetic kind of way. But they may also be more three-dimensional and tactile, for it is equally possible for a tradition to stress that we 'see' God at work today through the lives and service of faithful followers of Jesus. The following section is devoted to this idea because it plays an important part in the total picture of Christian living.

God depicted in people

Christians sometimes stress the fact that the true faith has more to do with people than with buildings. They emphasize the idea of the faithful gathered together as the body of Christ more than they do the building where they gather. Following the biblical point that where two or three are gathered together in his name, there Christ is in their midst (Matt 18:20), such Christians see themselves as the dynamic expression of God's activity. Where the Christian community is active, there God can be 'seen'. This is an ethical expression of God's nature and though it may seem far removed from artistic pictures of God or Christ, yet, in its own way, it can be a powerful expression of the divine nature.

A charity such as the contemporary Mission to Lepers provides an obvious link between what Jesus did in his earthly life and what Christians should do today. Similarly movements like Christian Aid, and many other charities, provide a kind of moral sketch of the divine nature through human activity.

CHRIST-LIKE LIVES

And as with groups of people so, too, with individuals. In most generations church historians can point to particular individuals who have been regarded by others as examples of a Christ-like life. The martyrs, or 'witnesses', as the word means in Greek, of the early Church were typical examples of lives in which the divine power was expressed. And such martyrdom continues today, especially in South America, as Christian leaders advocate justice and freedom in the face of hostile political regimes.

Many others live less dramatically but also furnish examples to their generation of what Christian life should be. We have already talked about Albert Schweitzer as a New Testament scholar. He was also a fine musician as an organist, conductor, and historian of J. S. Bach. While at the peak of his influence in Europe he decided to train as a doctor to serve as a medical missionary in Africa and went to Lambarene in French Equatorial Africa (as it then was) in 1913.

When the influential Dutch phenomenologist of religion Gerardus van der Leeuw wrote his classic study in 1933, he included Schweitzer in the category of 'The Exemplar'. An anecdote explains why Schweitzer was included in this category of those whose faith is seen through the example of the life lived. An ordinary workman who attended one of Schweitzer's organ recitals given to raise money for Africa was asked why he had come to the concert. He said he had come to hear the one who had done something while everybody else talked (1967: 664).

THE GENDER OF GOD IN HUMANS

Another twentieth-century example of a life that expresses the life of Jesus through service to others is that of Mother Teresa of Calcutta. Throughout the 1980s and 1990s she has gained wide public recognition for her work and that of the sisters of her religious order who serve the destitute not only in India but in many parts of the world.

Mother Teresa is, obviously, a woman. Although this point may sound absurd it raises a most interesting question for religious studies in relation to picturing God. There is a great tradition in Christianity of nuns living lives of service to others, and there is no practical problem interpreting this as Christ-like behaviour.

It is all the more interesting, then, when the question of gender emerges in relation to the priesthood. The Eastern Orthodox,

Roman Catholic, and some Anglican churches have argued against the ordination of women on the assumption that because priests are today's representatives of Christ and are, in a symbolic sense, a kind of Christ when they celebrate the Eucharist they must be male to fully represent Jesus who was male.

This is a good example of how Christ is pictured in different genders. It also raises another key yet subtle point which needs to be spelled out with care.

CHRIST IN HELPER OR HELPED

In the case of Schweitzer, Mother Teresa, and many hundreds of saintly people of both genders, the picture of Christ comes through them as individual servants of God. Christ is seen in the helper. This has a firm biblical basis in the idea that whoever listens to or rejects Christ's disciple listens to or rejects Christ (Luke 10:16).

But it is equally possible to focus on Christ in the person who is helped. In the gospels this emerges in a discussion about who is the greatest in the Kingdom of God. Jesus tells his disciples that whoever receives a child in his name receives Jesus (Matt 18:6). This insight has been taken up in a radical way by one of the most influential of all twentieth-century theological explorations, that of Liberation Theology. Gustavo Gutiérrez wrote *A Theology of Liberation* in Spanish in 1971. At its heart is the practical concern to love through living by becoming a neighbour to those suffering injustice. Here theology, ethics, and spirituality lie close together and are combined on the assumption that God is best seen today in the lives of other needy individuals:

> God is revealed in history, and it is likewise in history that men encounter his Word made flesh. Christ is not a private individual ... We find the Lord in our encounters with men, especially the poor, marginalized, and exploited ones. An act of love towards them is an act of love towards God. (1974: 201)

Source of Christ's image

Yet another angle on picturing Christ in other people comes from the

Russian Orthodox Archbishop Anthony Bloom. Speaking of the 1960s, he reflected on how popular it was to 'look for God in one's neighbour', and noted that the third- and fourth-century desert fathers used similar language. But he went on to make the very important theological point: 'In order to see the features of Christ in our neighbour's face, which is sometimes very difficult to read, we have to have in us the vision of Christ so as to be able to project it on to them' (1971: 112). For Bloom the source of Christ's image first lies within the Christian, within the helper. It is there because of God's grace which enables the life of faith to learn about Christ through the Scriptures, the tradition of the Church and worship. In Christian living this internal sense of Christ is then 'projected', as he puts it, on to those who are served and helped. It is interesting to see him use the idea of projection in this way. It takes into account the fallenness of people, which makes the image of God difficult to read or to perceive, something the Orthodox speak of as the 'coats of skin' which cover humanity after the Fall (Yannaras, 1991: 87), but it also shows the importance of the process of being made new in the image of God which is an important feature of Orthodox theology and belief.

THE MARKS OF CHRIST IN THE BELIEVER

St Paul speaks of bearing in his body the marks of Jesus (Gal 6:17). Whatever he meant by that, some Christian saints have spoken of receiving in their bodies the marks of the passion and crucifixion of Christ. These marks, or stigmata as they are called, were quite uncommon until the thirteenth century, a period when devotion to the sufferings of Christ became common. More than three hundred cases are referred to by the Catholic Church, notably St Francis of Assisi who is said to have been the first to have been granted these signs of Christ's suffering. These marks are dramatic 'pictures' of Christ within the life of a faithful devotee.

In terms of picturing God we have traversed a great distance from the ethical reflecting of God in the Old Testament, through the belief in God's self-manifestation in Christ expressed in the New Testament, to the representing of Christ in the sacred buildings and ritual of the medieval period, and to the modern world where God is reflected in the moral behaviour of believers and even in marks on the actual bodies of a select few individuals. These varied depictions of God serve as a most appropriate background for moving on to discuss the relationship between historical and mythical aspects of Christian thought and life.

Further reading

Baggley, J. (1987) *Doors of Perception*. London: Mowbray.
Colvin, H. (1991) *Architecture and the Afterlife*. London: Yale University Press.
Stevenson, J. (1978) *The Catacombs*. London: Thames and Hudson.

2. Myth and history

In the Christian tradition, an understanding of the nature of God as intimately connected with a belief in divine action discernible within human events has made history, as the interpretation of events befalling peoples, a crucial field of study. But, because history shares with myth ideas about significant events, and how they bear on life, it is important to consider them together. Both also reflect a characteristic search for meaning which is typically human, and which takes many forms from science to poetry. By such means the world is made less strange, and a degree of order and certainty is brought to what otherwise might be seen as chaotic and dangerous. Both myth and history are of fundamental importance to Christianity, providing two axes between which the meaning of this faith emerges. Just as science has recently come to give an account of the natural world, so history has, for many nations, provided an account of their social world. Myth too has a similar explanatory power, especially in preliterate cultures, where it has provided an account of how things came to be and why certain values of life are important.

Texts and history

It is very likely that, for millennia, the stories lying at the heart of myths gave people a picture of reality and allowed them to interpret the complexity of life. Myths told of the origin of the world, of men and women in their dealings with supernatural beings and powers, of the source of good and evil, and of the institutions of society. Sometimes they also spoke of the future and of life after death. Myths show how imaginative people can be as they reflect upon existence. Before the invention of writing myths exist as part of an oral tradition and often exhibit a considerable variation of content and presentation; once written texts come to exist, myths can easily turn into a more formal statement of belief (Goody, 1986).

As we will see in Chapter 4, Christianity has, from its outset, been a religion possessing sacred texts. Initially they were those of Judaism but in quick succession there emerged letters written by the early Christian leaders to various new congregations of believers, followed by the gospels, which presented outlines of the life and teaching of Jesus. Other documents, like the Acts of the Apostles, gave an account of the life of early Christians and of their experience of God and of Jesus.

The Scriptures deriving from Judaism contain some material, such as the creation stories (Gen 1 – 4), which probably existed as myths prior to being written down and gaining the status of sacred Scripture. As time went on some of the letters and documents of the early Christian Church were counted along with the older Jewish Scriptures as part of what is now accepted as the Christian Bible. Many of these documents, such as the Gospel of John and the Letter to the Hebrews, are not simple descriptions but are clear theological interpretations of the life of Jesus and of Christian communities. The Acts of the Apostles also has its definite theological concerns, which influence the way the activities of the Apostles and others are recounted.

So it is that within one single book, the Bible, we find side by side material that many theologians would define as either more mythical or more historical. But, for a variety of reasons, many believers look at the Bible as a whole rather than as a collection of different material. They see it as a book inspired by God and telling the truth about God and humanity. Many such readers find it difficult to distinguish between the different kinds of literature within the Bible and, because the word 'myth' has come to assume the meaning of something that is false or untrue, such believers reject the view that the Bible has 'myths' within it at all.

CHANGING VIEWS

The Bible has existed for a long time. This rather obvious fact must not be ignored in trying to understand myth and history in Christianity because, as times change, so knowledge about the nature of myth and the nature of history has increased. Both myth and history have become topics of academic study, undergoing considerable analysis, and becoming more identifiable as forms of human understanding. This can influence the practice of Christian religion if believers become aware of the part myths play in their sense of their own history. Once people know that history involves the interpretation of events, they can quickly appreciate the importance of an individual historian's outlook on the way the past is presented. In other words, history is not just about dates, happenings, and 'facts' of the past, but is very much concerned with how they are interpreted.

This makes it quite obvious that, for example, Marxist, feminist, or evolutionist historians are likely to interpret the past differently. Similarly, Catholic and Protestant historians are likely to give different emphasis to periods such as the Reformation. Ideology and theology are radically important influences on the way history is written.

CHRISTIANITY AS HISTORY

As far as Christianity is concerned there is one factor which makes this picture doubly interesting and complicated. It is that Christians believe God to have been active in or through historical events, and in this sense Christianity is often said to be a 'historical religion'. The very fact that by what we now call the sixth century of the Christian Era the history of the world came to be divided into two major periods, representing time before Christ (BC) and then time after Christ (AD; Latin *Anno Domini*, meaning in the year of Our Lord), demonstrates this sense of divine activity.

This does not simply mean that Christianity has a past, though in a very simple sense this is obviously true, but that past events have had more to them than simply meets the eye. But this is where a major theoretical problem arises, because it is only to the eye of faith that certain events can be seen as the result of God's activity, and not all historians are Christian believers. As will be seen later, some theologians even speak of what they call 'salvation-history'. This is best understood by beginning with Jesus of Nazareth.

There is little doubt that there was a man called Jesus who came from Nazareth, and who was a wandering Jewish religious teacher who ended up being put to death by crucifixion. But Christianity grew and derived its very significance from the belief that this man was also divine. This belief assumed that divine activity took place amidst actual mundane events. This belief implies that history cannot simply involve the interpretation of human behaviour, but has to be read as possessing an additional dimension, one of divine influence and significance.

This raises the critical issue of whether this sort of description of the past constitutes history or a kind of myth. Does the belief that God became man in Jesus, who then died to redeem people from their sins before being resurrected and returning to heaven, constitute a myth rather than history? Christians deal with this question in different and sometimes opposing ways because of the variety of stances adopted over ideas of faith, over the way God operates, and also over the way myth and history are defined. Much depends upon basic premises and whether someone starts from a particular doctrinal belief or from a more philosophical perspective. This chapter links the concerns of religious studies with a broad theological position, and in line with that we begin by considering human creativity as a force behind humanity's myth-making and history-writing tendencies.

Creativity and the image of God

From the Christian belief that humanity is made in God's image, this drive for meaning can be interpreted as a human reflection of divine creativity. Made in the image of God, men and women possess this creative dimension to their lives, which they bring to bear on events in the world around them. This creativity begins in childhood as the young learn about the world in which they find themselves growing up.

Reason, imagination, and emotion all lie at the heart of this human creativity and are fostered by the many cultures of humanity through science, myth, and history. But myth and history, like science, also exist as part of the knowledge and tradition held by certain groups, movements, and societies. This total social base influences myth and history and needs to be considered in its own right.

The words 'science', 'religion', and 'history' all point to the fact that Western society has divided information into distinct categories which are taught as separate bodies of knowledge. Although there are advantages in doing this, there is also the danger of thinking about the world and human existence in a fragmented way, and of assuming that other cultures, or people of former ages, also classified life in a similar way when they often did not do so.

This is a very important point for interpreting Christianity, because over its two thousand years' existence Christianity has become established in many different cultures with their own attitudes to the world of nature and to the realm of faith. For this reason it is important to understand something about the culture of a people when talking about myth and history. This is where the academic discipline of social anthropology is useful within religious studies because it concerns itself with the pattern of human cultures and social life.

Traditional, modern and postmodern societies

Although it involves an over-simplification, societies may be divided into three types according to their approach to knowledge. These are traditional, modern and postmodern societies. It is probably best to think of these terms as describing trends or broad attitudes rather than as describing an entire society. Indeed, many question the very idea of a 'postmodern' trend, and there is considerable debate over the whole issue of defining 'modernity' and 'postmodernity' (Harvey, 1989; B. S. Turner, 1990). But the issues are so important that they are worth sketching even though accepted definitions do not exist. With this caution in mind we outline some distinctive features of these different social attitudes to knowledge, time, and life's significance to give a framework for understanding myth and history.

TRADITIONAL SOCIETIES

A traditional society is one where knowledge is handed down from generation to generation as a precious commodity. In the history of mankind this has included very many tribal groups of hunters and gatherers, of pastoralists, and agriculturally based peoples who often were preliterate. Knowledge in the form of songs, stories of the past, and religious beliefs, along with basic practical knowledge of nature and of crafts, was passed from parent to child over many generations. Great respect was shown to such traditional wisdom, and care was taken to instruct particular people capable of perpetuating it. Many of the so-called primitive peoples studied by anthropologists over the last hundred years have been of this type. In Europe, too, many rural communities have operated in this way until fairly recently.

MODERN SOCIETY

Over the last hundred years many deeply significant changes have come about in what is called the developed world of industrial and modern agricultural societies. Urbanization and the great development of industry involved science and engineering to a great extent. A key feature was discovery.

Discovery involves new things. New ideas came from science and new techniques from engineering. Old ideas and ancient traditions were no longer prized simply because they were old. Old things were abandoned as new discoveries offered possibilities of development that quite transformed human life. Perhaps electricity and the steam engine were two fundamentally important discoveries, but many drugs and medical techniques also changed the pattern of human life.

Modern society emerged as the desire for discovery replaced respect for traditional knowledge. Modernity itself shifted respect to newly discovered ideas and to principles that now held sway over life. The theory of evolution was one such principle of modernity and was applied to aspects of social life just as to animal life. In its own way Marxism also offered a modern theory of social existence. As we shall see, modern society, especially since the middle of the nineteenth century, has had a considerable impact upon religious life and in particular upon religious belief.

POSTMODERN SOCIETY

It is only since perhaps the 1970s that the idea of postmodernity has been discussed by intellectuals. In simplest terms postmodernity refers to life that has no simple theory to unite people in their motives for living and for interpreting the world. A deep awareness of the way social customs influence people leads the postmodernist into a sense of the fragmented nature of each individual. There is no overarching focus to guide thought in any collective way. Meaning becomes a shattered concept, and each thinker has to make do with the fragments that lie to hand. Language itself becomes the very tool to tear to bits theories of life that have guided many.

The three forms and Christianity

These three forms of social outlook have dramatically different consequences for religious belief and especially for the Christian faith. It is important to spell out some of these even though the terms traditionalism, modernism, and postmodernism involve a simplification of social situations.

People in traditionalist societies speak in the plural and say 'we have always believed' that such and such is true. They accept a belief because it has been handed down to them. They learn the stories of old times and pass them on to their children because they are important in maintaining their identity as a tribe, group, or nation. Old things are good and must be preserved through their customs.

Modernist societies speak in the singular and say 'I believe' that such and such is true, as do many others because this theory has been discovered to have great power in explaining the world. Individuals are important as they commit themselves to a theory of life whether it is Christianity, Marxism, liberalism, evolutionism or whatever.

Postmodernists doubt the existence of a definite individual, deny the truthfulness of any one theory of existence to which individuals might commit themselves, and certainly deny the worth of simple acceptance of schemes of life interpretation passed down from the ancient past.

As far as the Bible and religious teachings are concerned, traditionalists accept the past because the source of religious inspiration was located in the life of Christ, his apostles, the written Scriptures, and the early decisions of the Church.

Modernists qualify traditional teaching in the light of discoveries about evolution and the development of the Bible. They develop theories about the sources and forces lying behind Scriptures and doctrines, and seek to interpret these for their own day.

Postmodernists deny the wisdom of seeking interpretations of texts to find out what their original meaning might have been. They deny the right of great institutions to pronounce on truth or on theories of truth which others should accept. Instead the post-modernist prefers to play with ideas which are seen as flitting aspects of questions rather than arrive at concrete answers to problems. Postmodernists toy with the surface of things, while the modernists reckon to seek the depth beneath the surface, and traditionalists assert the ancient wisdom in the depth and in the transmission of its truth to future generations.

TRADITIONAL CHURCHES, MODERNITY AND POSTMODERNITY

In the light of what has already been said, one issue becomes dramatically obvious. It is that most mainstream Christian churches have strong traditional dimensions to them even when they exist in largely modern, and increasingly postmodern, societies. As tradi-tional bodies, they perpetuate beliefs and values from the past and seek to hand them on to future generations. Many aspects of church life foster this attitude, including the existence of bishops, celibate priests, and many forms of ritual which have an authority of their own. So, too, when it comes to doctrine, the very idea of discovery seems to contradict that of divine revelation.

But, at the same time as they emphasize their obligation to the past, churches often strongly assert the need to be part and parcel of modern society and to speak in ways that are relevant to the present day. In saying this they may not fully appreciate the contradiction that exists between tradition and modernity, between perpetuating the past and discovering new things, as far as basic attitudes are concerned.

Cultures and Christianity: types and time

Sometimes this paradox is not obvious because Christianity has long ago penetrated societies that are traditional. In many such cases, as in Catholic South America, a Christian-influenced mythology has replaced, or merged in a significant way with, pre-existing myths, just as Christian ideology has come into close relations with the thought-forms of modern societies.

Two interesting features are to be found in the traditionalist perspective on life experience and events that take place in society. First, traditionalists see some period in the past as a golden age, or as a period when the supernatural world was very close to the world of humanity. Often God was nearer then than now. In many tribal religions this is a major area in which myth operates to describe the original time of creation when gods, humanity, animals, plants, and the rest of nature had distinctive relations to each other. Invariably this scene of idyllic relations is brought rudely to an end by some sort of wickedness on the part of human beings. The creation myths in the early chapters of Genesis are typical of this depiction of a primal time when God walked in the garden in the cool of the day and spoke to Adam and Eve, and when there was a serpent that tempted the unfortunate pair (Gen 1 – 4). In a slightly similar way the Acts of the Apostles speaks of the nearness of God through the Holy Spirit, expressed through the flames of fire that danced on the Apostles' heads on the day of Pentecost when the Christian movement was propelled into a new intensity of life (Acts 2). Secondly, ordinary life in the present world operates according to a cyclical programme. This repetitive scheme of things was often associated with the cycle of the year grounded in the economic life of a society. In agricultural societies there were times for seed-sowing and harvest, just as in pastoralist and nomadic societies there were times for moving flocks to different pastures.

The paradox of Christianity in this kind of society is that in theological terms, it cannot simply accept time as a constantly repetitive cycle of events because of the Christian belief that God started with creation and is now working towards a future goal which will overthrow the present ordinariness of life. This was part of a problem that Augustine devoted himself to in the fourth century in his book *The City of God* (XII, 13–15). In developing his own philosophy of history he argued that God had actually created time which passed in a flowing way rather than as a repetitive cycle.

This is symbolized to a certain extent in those ritual moments when the doctrinal–mythical domain penetrates the cyclical and repetitive life of everyday existence. These moments can be viewed as 'outside' time, expressing a kind of 'ritual time' when the normal routine of life is put aside to enter into ritual activity where mythical material is rehearsed. These moments can be backward- or forward-looking, as in Mass or Eucharist. During the service people are reminded of the events of the passion of Christ and of the Last Supper and, in some sense, come to share in those past events through the ritual events of today. But the Eucharist also looks forward to the coming kingdom of God.

Early Christian traditions developed an annual calendar to govern worship, prayer and theological thinking. It focused on events in the life of Christ from his birth to his resurrection and the sending of the Holy Spirit. But this calendar was directly related to pre-existing Jewish festivals such as Passover. The particularly important factor in this Jewish background is that key festivals, such as Passover, were held to acknowledge divine acts in the history of Israel. Even though their timing was linked to phases of the moon, as Easter still is in Christian churches, this was not because of any power of nature but because of a way of timing events. Over the centuries many other days were incorporated into what is now called the Liturgical Calendar, and these celebrated the lives of various saints or theologically important events.

Such ritual knowledge is a fundamentally important aspect of human experience, and it probably exerts a great influence on how people think about their religion. It is likely that people come to a sense of their religion as being true because of experiences they have in life, often in connection with worship, prayer or other religious activity. We explore this dimension shortly in connection with the Eucharist.

MODERNISTS

Using the term in a general cultural sense, Modernists see the radical importance of their own day as a period of discovery and advance. This key-note of discovery typifies the modern world-view and offers an opposite picture to that of tradition. Tradition hands things on, discovery finds new things. But the 'things' that are found tend to be theories, broad-scale ways of interpreting reality. So, for example, both evolutionism and Freudianism were nineteenth-century discoveries of 'theories' which explained many aspects of life.

The word 'Modernist' also has a specifically theological meaning, used to describe a group of Catholic scholars of the late nineteenth and early twentieth century, including A. Loisy (1857–1940), G. Tyrrell (1861–1909), and the Anglican F. B. Jevons (1858–1936), who is mentioned elsewhere in this chapter. All these saw deep significance in the symbolic meaning of doctrine rather than in its literal truth.

In the mid and late nineteenth century other Western Christian thinkers also developed the idea of 'salvation-history' (a translation of the German *Heilsgeschichte*) to interpret the way God deals with humanity. In many respects salvation-history resembles evolutionism and Freudianism as a theory explaining human destiny. Like Marxism it suggests that history is not simply a series of random events but involves the outworking of underlying principles.

Some Christians combined grand theories with basic Christian doctrine so that their explanations of the meaning of life could make its appeal at both levels. So, for example, both F. B. Jevons and his close contemporary, Teilhard de Chardin, combined evolutionary thinking with a belief in a progressive revelation of Christian truth, as discussed more fully in Chapter 3.

The general scheme that salvation-history followed argued that it was God's initial action which created the world, after which divine activity was focused on mankind through the people of Israel, their prophets and spiritual leaders, until, in a new way, God entered human life through the person of Jesus of Nazareth. His life, death and resurrection herald a new and distinctive phase within the history of salvation and lead on to a future Kingdom of God in which the divine purpose is fulfilled.

Many religious movements, such as the Jehovah's Witnesses and Seventh-Day Adventists, have become narrowly interested in *dispensations*, or particular phases of divine activity during which God is believed to be engaged in particular tasks working towards the salvation of people. Very often such groups use biblical texts, especially from books such as Daniel and Revelation, to provide blueprints for the pattern of history which they believe God has revealed to them.

Theologians of more mainstream traditions have also set about interpreting God's work in connection with humanity through various time series, as with Karl Barth and Paul Tillich. Barth stressed the nature of faith in perceiving the events of Jesus' life as a work of God, events which ordinary historians would read in a secular way. Tillich showed how time can be divided into categories depending upon its quality or significance. *Chronos* refers to 'clock-time' or the constant passing of equally significant moments, while *kairos* refers to periods of deep significance for Christian people (1953, vol. 3: 395). This distinction between *chronos* and *kairos* shows how important the perception of events is in interpreting historical events.

Another fundamentally important contribution comes in Oscar Cullmann's book *Christ and Time* (1962). This was first published in 1946, and is an important analysis of Christian ideas of time and history. For Cullmann the coming of Christ provides the central focus, which he calls 'the middle' of time, for a Christian understanding of history – a history which he calls redemptive history. Basic to this perspective is the fact that Christianity inherited the idea of 'linear' time from Judaism. Time has a beginning in the creation of the world and presses on in a linear way towards a goal set by God. The coming of Christ is the profoundest of all events, punching its way into the midst of time and providing a profound significance for all other periods both before and after it. Both preaching and, as we see below, the Eucharist are moments when the significance of Christ's intervention into time becomes apparent and deeply significant for many Christians.

POSTMODERNITY

Postmodernists announce the death and end of history. They believe there is no validity in grand theories of history grounded in underlying principles or laws. Inevitably, postmodernists assume that there can be no overriding theories of existence, including religious theories. This means that it is impossible to interpret the past in ways that imply an inherent reason for events and occurrences. Individualism and personal idiosyncrasy are the best that can be anticipated and even the idea of an individual is radically questioned.

The idea of an eternal truth can have no place in a postmodern outlook whether that truth is experienced through a cyclical view of nature or in a sense of linear time working towards a goal. This makes postmodernity an uncomfortable context for Christianity with its commitment to aspects of historical tradition and to a divinely influenced future.

Churches and forms of knowledge

We have already said that Christian churches exist in a paradoxical situation as far as these three approaches to knowledge are concerned. In what follows we see some of the ways in which Christianity has responded to this problem.

BIRTH OF TRADITION

Christianity's Jewish background held the view that God acted in particular events set within history. The message of the prophets about a coming reign of God set a stamp on the idea that times would change and that there was a purposeful flow to history.

Christianity emerged within this pattern of thought and was specifically rooted in a group of disciples of the historical person Jesus of Nazareth. Early generations of Christians believed that Jesus had overcome death through the resurrection, and many seemed to hope that quite soon a supernatural event would take place with the risen Christ's Second Coming to inaugurate the Kingdom of God (1 Cor 7:29–31). As time went on the Second Coming did not take place, but believers did not simply give up their faith, they went on to develop it in complex ways. Of central importance was the increasing commitment to the belief that Jesus was both human and divine.

In this doctrine of the Incarnation (already discussed in Chapter 1 as a key element in the Apostles' Creed) the belief is expressed that God participated in real human life, and human nature, through the individual Jesus of Nazareth. This was believed to have taken place in a quite literal sense. Someone whose very nature was divine in a way that no other human had ever been divine had walked the streets of Jerusalem. God had in a quite new sense 'entered' history and changed the way time was viewed. Central to this scheme was

45

the ancient history of the Jews which was part and parcel of early Christian self-reflection. The Christian Bible came rapidly into existence as sacred Scriptures over the early centuries of Christianity. It was divided into Old Testament and New Testament, the clearest example of a cutting up of time into periods of differing significance. In the first God dealt with the Jews through prophets, priests and kings, and in the second with all mankind through a 'Son'.

CHURCH AND BIBLE

Throughout the subsequent history of Christianity this sense of a historic foundation for belief has been significant in two major ways; one focuses on the Church, and the other on the Bible. In the Catholic and Orthodox traditions great stress is placed on the belief that the Church continues the ministry of Jesus. The Roman Catholic Church sees itself as having the successor of St Peter as its head and regards the Pope as a guardian of true doctrine. Great emphasis is placed on the line of succession, or apostolic succession as it is called, from Peter the apostle to the present Pope. Bishops are also a central feature of this line of authority and they ordain priests as part of the total ministry of the Church. God is believed to guide the decisions of this Church, not least in the way it understands and interprets the Bible. The early Church Fathers are also relied upon as sources of theological material so that the past remains an important centre of gravity of belief.

In a very similar way the Greek Orthodox Church sees itself as a guardian of tradition and places heavy emphasis on the ritual of the Holy Communion, or the Liturgy, as it is called. In many ways Orthodox tradition consists in maintaining the faith through maintaining the Liturgy and the bishops and priests. The Protestant churches stemming from the Reformation, including the Anglican and Lutheran churches, stress very much the importance of the Bible as an authoritative basis for faith precisely because it deals with periods when God is believed to have communicated with humanity through prophets, the historical Jesus and the apostles. These accounts of early Christians are as important to Catholic as to Protestant strands of Christianity and demonstrate the importance of history to Christian theology and religion.

Ritual activity also gives believers an experience of the historical aspects of religion. The Christian Eucharist is a very fine example of this, working as it does to link the present day with the earliest days of Christian history. It takes the Last Supper, held between Christ and his disciples, as the model for today's Eucharist. The Eucharist is a kind of memorial. Christian traditions differ in the interpretation they give to this memorial in quite subtle ways. In Catholic tradition a link is made between the Last Supper, Christ's death on the cross, interpreted as a sacrifice, and the present-day rite of the Mass. This emphasis on what is called the eucharistic sacrifice is associated with another doctrine, that of the 'real presence' of Christ in the bread and wine used in the ritual. In this way there is a kind of 'collapsing' of time into one moment of devotion and worship. Historical events of the past are integrated with a theological interpretation of those events and with the individual's own inner experience of God in the present day.

There is yet another dimension to this spiritual tradition of Catholic thought which is related to the Eucharist. For not only do believers share in what happened in the past, they also share in what, in a sense, also happens now 'in heaven'. The sacrificial offering of Christ in his death has an eternal significance to it, and each Mass enters into that eternal mystery of Christ's sacrificial death. Past, present and eternity are related through the Mass.

In more Protestant traditions time and worship are viewed quite differently in theological terms. The historical death of Christ is strongly emphasized by saying that he died once in a completed sacrifice which does not have that eternal dimension to it in which later worshippers may share. Protestant Eucharists stress a memorial, a looking back in thanks for the forgiveness of sins, rather than a looking into an eternally present sacrifice. There are many theological arguments involved in this difference, including a radically different doctrine of the priesthood and ministry.

Churches make history

Despite these variations in doctrine one vitally important point emerges from the variously named Christian ritual of the Eucharist,

Mass, or Lord's Supper. It is that a present-day rite is believed to be integrally linked with deeply significant past events. In a very significant way Churches sustain and develop a sense of history, so that Christian ritual not only grows out of past events but also generates history.

This raises a theoretically interesting question. Does the idea of tradition arise in the past and then get passed on to today's generations, or does the present-day life of churches generate the interest and energy which gives life to past events? In terms of common sense the answer is obvious. Tradition starts in the past and comes on to the future. But from another perspective it is perfectly possible to say that it is the present-day activity of religious groups which gives the past any significance at all. In practical terms there is an interplay between these two perspectives.

For Christianity, as a living religion, this is a very important point. Christian tradition is not, for example, like the 'tradition' of ancient Egyptian religion. It is possible to study ancient Egyptian religion and many other 'dead' traditions which no longer have active groups of believers. But those traditions do not have the power and significance found in religions which still have adherents. It is contemporary Christians who make Christian tradition live. There are many institutions which help sustain the past and which place a tremendous emphasis upon it, so much so that the centre of gravity of the religion seems to lie in history rather than in the present. Some people might see the Pope and the hierarchy of the Roman Catholic Church in this way possessing a weight of tradition coming from earlier centuries.

Other Christians see God at work today in such a way that the centre of gravity of Christianity lies in their own group in the here and now. This is especially important in newly emerging religious groups as in the case of many sects. They will, almost always, see the Bible as important in recording the times of Jesus but they tend to jump over the intervening centuries as periods of reduced Christian commitment until they come to the present day when God's power through the Holy Spirit restores the fullness of faith to humanity.

In these ways Christian Churches 'make history'. They draw significance from historical events at the same time as they give significance to them. And as with the Eucharist so with other rites. Baptism, for example, and the washing of feet, are used in Catholic traditions and also in other groups such as the Seventh-Day

Adventist Church. Biblical accounts of these rites feed into present use and often validate what is done today.

It is in this sense that dynamic religious groups are likely to stand in firm opposition to the postmodern idea that history is dead. To speak of the death of history may sound odd but, as already mentioned, some contemporary scholars argue that history has come to an end in the sense that postmodern people can no longer believe that history is influenced by laws, trends or processes (Fukuyama, 1992). The collapse of Communist regimes in many European countries in the 1990s offers one example of this, but can also be argued as demonstrating a rebirth of history (Glenny, 1990). Another objection to the idea of the death of history comes from Christian religious practice.

From what has already been said it is obvious that active Christian groups and congregations do see themselves as an expression of God's activity in the world. In this sense the idea of the 'kingdom of God' stands in sharp contradiction to a postmodern world view. This opposition is not simply philosophical, but is grounded in the practical life-experience of believers who think of themselves as part of a long series of divinely influenced events. Their commitment can be very widely or narrowly conceived. Some churches see their own history as the truest and surest expression of God's activities, and to be certain of salvation people should be members of that particular group. Here the Catholic Church has traditionally argued that individuals need to receive the sacraments of that Church before they attain salvation, while many Protestant groups have argued that the individual needs a personal experience of God's forgiveness. Some other Christian churches think more in terms of a broad movement of God's activity in the development of many Christian churches. But for all these groups history is not dead but dynamic and alive.

Facts of history and myth

The importance of faith in interpreting history as a divine process cannot be overemphasized because what may appear to one person

49

as a divine history to another can seem to be a simple mythological account of events. Faith is a key factor in discussing the relationship between history and myth, a discussion that must now be considered from several different angles.

Two well-known phrases summarize the difference between history and myth. The one is '1066 and all that', and the other is 'once upon a time'. The first reminds us that history is grounded in past events, in dates when things happened. But history is about more than simple dates; it concerns the significance and interpretation of events and periods in the life of human societies. The second signals the fact that the account that follows the introductory phrase is a story and does not refer to events that have actually taken place.

In one sense 'facts' are very rare in the realm of human behaviour. They seldom come 'pure'. Each culture deeply influences the way its members look at things. This is true of simple objects and is even more significant when it comes to ideas, values and beliefs. This is exactly the case with history and with myth. It is often said that it is the victors who write the history of a society, and recent times have witnessed the writing and rewriting of history in the decline of the Communist world of the USSR.

So, though for many people history means a list of dates which are seen as basic facts about events that once took place, in practice history involves complex debates about the relative significance of different interpretations of events. In the Bible this is the case as scholars argue over the way different authors present the story of the life of Jesus. Do they do it as historical fact or more as a story that reflects a mythical concern over issues of God, and truth, of life and death? A good biblical example of the shaping of historical accounts concerns the event when Jesus made a whip and drove out the traders from the temple at Jerusalem. In the gospels of Matthew (21:12), Mark (11:15), and Luke (19:45) this takes place towards the end of Jesus' earthly ministry, as events move to the climax of his passion and death, while in John's gospel it is placed very early on, at the outset of the public life of Jesus (2:14ff.). For a variety of reasons it is likely that, historically speaking, the event that lies behind these accounts took place once and towards the end rather than at the beginning of Jesus' ministry. But the theological significance John wishes to develop, that Jesus is more significant than the Temple in the life of believers, makes him bring the event forward in the account.

This kind of emphasis is not far removed from stories that are told to make a point without the events contained in the story ever having taken place. In fact many people think of myth as interesting stories about persons and places which exist in imagination but not in real life. This is so much the case that the word 'myth' has come to have the popular meaning of something that is untrue, of being 'just stories'. This is why the question of defining myths is particularly important and must be approached with care because misunderstanding is very easy.

LITERAL, POETIC AND MYTHICAL WAYS OF THINKING

'Truth' is the most important theological issue at stake in the relationship between myth and history, but it is not easy to define truth, as another biblical and well-known example will show.

As discussed more fully in Chapter 10, the early chapters of the book of Genesis focus on the creation of the world and of the human race. Some Christians see these chapters as myths. They do not for a minute think that there was an actual garden in which a real-life Adam and Eve walked in the cool of the day and heard God speaking to them. Even so they think that the stories do present truth because they speak of God's responsibility for creation and of human responsibility towards God. The truth of the story does not lie in whether the events actually occurred, but in the ideas expressed through the events of the story.

But there are other Christians who do believe that there was a real garden possessing the real first parents of mankind. For these believers the truth of the story lies in the events actually having taken place. The first kind of interpretation accepts that some biblical material is mythical in form and resembles the myths of many other cultures, while the second line of interpretation says that the biblical material must be accepted in a literal rather than in any allegorical or metaphorical way. This is a fundamentally important point for Christianity and must be spelled out in more detail because it adds a further dimension to the question of truth, and truth is a key concept in the Christian religion.

TRUTH AND MYTHICAL THOUGHT

The literally minded Christian believes that God has inspired the Bible in a way that makes the printed book authoritative as a source of religious truth. All human attempts at interpretation must be secondary to the Bible itself. But almost all modern scholars accept that the Bible must be approached through other forms of interpretation before its significance becomes apparent. This assumes that reason and scholarship and a knowledge of the development of ideas and social life play a tremendously significant part in understanding the Bible. The problem is that literal-minded Christians often accuse others of not accepting the plain meaning of the Bible, just as the more liberal thinkers see the literalists as naive fundamentalists. In other words, the very word 'myth' has come to be a kind of shorthand term expressing quite different attitudes towards knowledge, literature and faith.

In terms of religious studies, scholars like Mircea Eliade have paid particular attention to what they call mythopoeic thought (1960). This refers to the human ability to create and use mythical stories as a way of expressing particular ideas about life. For Eliade, mythical forms of thinking are associated with the idea of the sacred, which reflects a constant capacity of human consciousness rather than a phase in the evolution of consciousness. From the work of historians and anthropologists of religion the importance of myth in the kind of traditional societies often studied by social anthropologists is well established. What is less easy is to grasp the significance of myth-like aspects of stories, accounts of events, and of more clearly historical occurrences.

Especially since the nineteenth century, science has come to play an increasingly important part in influencing the idea of truthfulness and certain knowledge in the population of modern societies. The experimental method is specially important in this process, so that the phrases 'prove it', or 'can it be proved?', throw light on how some people at least think about particular ideas.

Sigmund Freud's psychoanalysis is one example of an interlinking of what appears to be both scientific and mythical ideas. He reckoned to have discovered the existence of the unconscious mind with its power to influence ordinary life. Taking the Oedipus myth as the model for what happened in humanity's earliest history, he argued that early men grouped together to kill their father to gain access to the forbidden women. Overcome by guilt, they initiated the incest taboo in human culture. The great majority of psychologists do not accept that there is any truth in Freud's interpretation, yet it has profoundly influenced Western society (Rieff, 1966; Badcock, 1980).

Freud interpreted Christianity as an extension of Judaism and as an outworking of the Oedipus complex. The death of Christ becomes another kind of killing of the primal father, with the Holy Communion as a meal related to the reduction of the sons' guilt after murder. In *Totem and Taboo* Freud spelled this out with history being a process of human encounter with guilt. In *The Future of an Illusion*, already mentioned in Chapter 1, Freud depicted religion as an illusion preventing individuals from encountering the harsh realities of existence. Knowing that parents ultimately fail, people put their trust in a heavenly father, thus failing to mature and stand alone. This theory of history and culture is fundamentally mythical and has influenced many, despite its complete lack of any scientific base.

ANTHROPOLOGY AND MYTH

Some social anthropologists have been among the most influential group in the study of myth because, unlike Freud, they have lived among peoples who used myth in a normal and regular way as part of their ritual life and as a way of explaining aspects of their own social custom.

The French anthropologist Claude Lévi-Strauss argued that myths were a way of trying to overcome problems posed in a society through a series of binary oppositions. These were statements giving opposite views of a cultural problem through stories which explored various options for its resolution. Lévi-Strauss tended to avoid using biblical material but the English anthropologist Edmund Leach specifically took up myths from the Old Testament to study by this method of 'structuralism' (1969). The Old Testament scholar John Rogerson has analysed this work, along with many others, and presented a reliable analysis of many approaches to myth in the Old Testament (1974).

DOCTRINE AND MYTH

One key issue in this often hostile debate lies in the fact that Christianity asserts as doctrinal fact things which are regularly regarded as myths when found in non-Christian religions. Obvious examples lie in the creation stories, the Virgin Birth of Christ, the miracles associated with the life of Jesus, as well as the idea of the Incarnation itself.

There is probably no doctrine more central to Christianity than the belief expressed in this doctrine of the Incarnation. As we saw in Chapter 1, the creeds of the Christian churches have this teaching at their heart, as does all Christian worship. At one level it is an incredible statement and begs to be interpreted along with other human myths about the gods coming to visit humanity. But the Christian faithful, along with the great majority of Christian leaders, are adamant in their view that God actually became human in Jesus at one point in time. A story which has the marks of myth about it is said to be true in the sense that the events it describes actually took place within human experience. In other words, it is said to belong to history and not to mythology.

Many of the writings of the popular theologian C. S. Lewis flow around this idea that the wonder of Christianity lies in the fact that what seems almost totally impossible actually happened: a mythical scheme of things actually occurred in the real life of mankind and not simply in the imaginative and myth-making or mythopoeic capacity of humanity. This belief in Christ, expressed as the doctrine of the Incarnation, came to assume an increasingly important place in the history of Western culture, notably from the establishment of the Holy Roman Empire by Constantine in the fourth century. It became focused in the Mass or Eucharist, and from that ritual base exerted a strong influence on church architecture, music and art. With the subsequent establishment of theology as a major subject in European universities from the Middle Ages, Christian doctrine became established as a statement of fact about reality.

Power and truth

This is a particularly important point that is often ignored in theological studies. It concerns power in society. Each society explains its significance in terms of some theory of origin or principle of life and these religious, political, and ideological explanations become normative and authoritative for its members. Christianity has been one such explanatory principle, and Christian ideas or doctrines, such as that of the Incarnation, came to be unquestioned and even unquestionable. Although the rise of modern thought from the Enlightenment, and especially since the nineteenth century, has altered this state of affairs, it still remains true that Christian doctrine is often treated differently from the doctrines of other world religions and from the 'myths' of preliterate societies. For complex social, historical and philosophical reasons centred on cultural ideals of status, influence and power, it is difficult to equate a professor of theology with a local myth-teller and wise-person of a preliterate society, yet for many practical purposes they serve a similar purpose.

In this sense European history itself gave an authority to Christian doctrine which allowed it to function as a factual and empirical truth. For, as we have just argued, there is a sense in which the accepted truthfulness of an idea or belief is associated with the assent given to it by those who hold and control power in a society. This was the case, for example, in the USSR until the 1990s with the Marxist interpretation of history as a struggle between social classes in an evolutionary development of society. With the decline of the Soviet Union the history of Russia and aligned countries is being rewritten and Christian groups are free once more to express their own theory of history in relation to the kingdom of God.

The history of many countries in other parts of the world was also deeply influenced by Christian ideas of history as a result of European colonization and missionary work; this was especially true, for example, in South America and South Africa. The South African theory of apartheid involved a Christian doctrine of racial groups and of the duty and prerogative of white people in relation to black races. This, too, has undergone serious change as other Christians have argued against the Dutch Reformed background to white South Africans' religious views of history.

Story and truth

As times change the status of belief alters. In Christianity, for example, the centrality of the Mass led to an entire theology explaining its nature. In the thirteenth century this was explained by the doctrine of transubstantiation. For many Catholics this was a vitally important doctrine which helped feed their faith and form the ritual of the Mass. For many Protestants it is simply not accepted as a true explanation of how Christ is present for the faithful at the Eucharist. To non-Catholics, and especially to non-Christians, this transubstantiation doctrine can easily be viewed as a myth explaining how divine power comes to inhabit material objects.

Following on from the life and death of Jesus, his earthly representatives, the official priests whose ordination makes them stand in a historical succession to St Peter as Christ's prime apostle, perform the ceremony and say the prayer of consecration through which God miraculously transforms the inner nature of the bread and wine so that the very body and blood of Christ can be eaten and drunk by believers today.

Is this a myth or is it a doctrine? Is it a myth that functions as a doctrine, or a doctrine that functions as a myth? Or are the words doctrine and myth largely interchangeable and only avoided because of the cultural status of Christian religion compared with preliterate religions or religions long dead?

Myth and spiritual development

Christian doctrine has to battle with this relationship between history and fact, myth and doctrine, just as many individual Christians, past and present, have to do for themselves. This is particularly important in an individual's religious and intellectual development in relation to a maturing idea of God.

To think of God as a pleasant and generous old man living amongst the clouds is obviously an immature and vastly childish image. Yet, to speculate without any real factual evidence, many Christians probably do think of heaven as a place and of God as an identifiable 'person'. The work of theologians such as Paul Tillich, who have spoken of God in a less literal and more existential way as 'the ground of being', has not been particularly welcomed by people at large.

This was made very obvious in the 1960s when the then Bishop of Woolwich, John Robinson, wrote several books, including the famous *Honest to God* in which he simply reflected the existential theology of Tillich and denied the simple images of a supernatural heaven, etc., much to the dismay of many ordinary Christians (Towler, 1984). Many felt that he was taking away the truthfulness of the faith they had held throughout their life.

Since the 1970s a similar concern has been expressed by the Cambridge theologian Don Cupitt, whose many books basically argued that all religious ideas were constructed by human imagination and influenced by social contexts, so that Christian doctrine was not basically different from preliterate mythology. For Cupitt, along with a significant minority of Christians, this view must be accepted as part of a maturing of thought and faith, while for many others it involves an abandonment of the Christian claim to exclusiveness through an actual divine revelation.

Part of the issue of history and myth concerns the way individuals evaluate their religion, because the distinction between history and myth is, at one popular level, simply the distinction between fact and fancy. For some, it would be impossible to believe and live as Christians if they felt that there never was an actual historical pair called Adam and Eve. For others, it is perfectly possible to continue in faith even if, for example, Jesus had not actually been raised from the dead but that a memory of him had somehow inspired his disciples with hope for the future and love amongst themselves.

Many Christians who give serious thought to doctrine find these issues of tremendous importance as their life proceeds. Many people are brought up as Christians, or are converted to Christianity as children or teenagers, and tend to have a relatively simple view of God, Jesus and the Bible. For them the factual and historical nature of Christian religion is vitally important because it has formed part of the belief which is intrinsic to their sense of identity. As time goes on, and especially if they engage in academic study of religion, some of these perspectives no longer hold. They come to see parallels between stories of supernatural persons and miraculous events in other religions, and wonder whether Christianity works in the same way? There is no easy answer to this question, because a simple rationalistic perspective gives a clear negative answer even to the existence of God, let alone to more particular religious ideas. One problem lies in the fact that the idea of history has been accorded high intellectual status, while that of myth has been given a low status because of its association with 'primitive' peoples. This was especially true in the nineteenth century but it also continued into the first half of the twentieth century.

MYTH AND EXPLANATION

Comparative study of religion and culture has shown that myths have been extremely widespread in the history of human civilization. They take the form of stories which spell out basic truths or values held dear by a particular society. These often touch on general features of human nature, including love, hate, parenthood, sexuality, obedience and disobedience, fate, bravery, generosity and meanness. They sometimes give an account of how things came into existence for the first time. This varies from the geographical realm of how a particular mountain or river came to be, to the social realm of particular human relationships of kinship, marriage and incest. Myths also often deal with the question of how humans relate to their dead ancestors or to the realm of the spirits, or gods. A very short definition of myth might sum up these points in this way: *myths are stories enshrining cultural values*.

BIBLICAL MYTH AND DE-MYTHOLOGIZING

Scholars have discussed the idea of myth in relation to the Bible from the later part of the eighteenth century until today. Originally the greatest weight was placed on the Old Testament (Rogerson, 1974), but the New Testament has also received considerable attention (Bultmann, 1960), not least in connection with the doctrine of the Incarnation which has been derived from it (Hick, 1977).

The German New Testament scholar and theologian Rudolph Bultmann broached this question in 1941 with his study of *The New Testament and Mythology*. He provoked one of the most famous recent debates in theology with his argument that the New Testament emerged from a world where mythological forms of thought and expression were commonplace. We, in the modern Western world, educated by science, philosophy, and not least by a growing awareness of history, no longer found the mythological perspective persuasive. On the contrary, myth spoke more of error and immature thought than of educated insight. Accordingly, he proposed a scheme of *demythologizing* which sought to translate the meaning of biblical myths into a message which could be understood by contemporary believers. Mythology must be translated into existentialist philosophical terms appropriate to the modern world. Bultmann was worried that modern people would pay no attention to the Bible because of its obviously mythical and therefore (according to popular thought) untrue content; they would throw out the baby with the bath-water.

In a characteristically Lutheran way Bultmann saw the crux of Christian belief lying in the decision that each person had to make within their own lives in relation to God's grace. They should not be hindered in doing this by outmoded biblical images, expressions and stories. He retained as central the doctrine of Justification by Faith as the key-note doctrine which made Christian faith authentic. In fact Bultmann saw his own task as resembling that of Luther:

> De-mythologizing is a task parallel to that performed by Paul and Luther in their doctrine of justification by faith alone ... De-mythologizing is the radical application of the doctrine of justification to the sphere of knowledge and thought. Like the doctrine of justification, de-mythologization destroys every longing for security. (1960: 84)

The last sentence is particularly important because Bultmann's prime concern is with the life of faith and not with an attempt at destroying faith by rationalizing it away. He defines faith as 'the abandonment of man's own security and the readiness to find security only in the unseen beyond, in God', and argues that 'faith itself demands to be freed from any world-view produced by man's thought, whether mythological or scientific. For all human world-views objectivize the world and ignore or eliminate the significance of encounters in our personal existence' (1960: 40, 83).

History as myth?

But history was also central to Bultmann's discussion. This became very apparent, for example, in a discussion on myths and demythologizing between him and the German philosopher and psychiatrist Karl Jaspers, especially in their small but significant book *Myth and Christianity* (1958), subtitled 'An Inquiry into the

Possibility of Religion without Myth'. Bultmann wants to keep a stress on the historical revelation of God to humankind in Jesus despite a strong avoidance of the language of miracle, but Jaspers criticizes him for retaining the idea of God speaking to humanity at particular historical moments, for to claim that God does such things is to speak in a mythical way; that, at least, is what Jaspers thinks.

Jaspers was not opposed to mythological thought. On the contrary he resembled another influential figure, the psychologist Carl Jung, and considered myth to be a basic element of religious reflection upon life. For Jaspers, myths composed 'a language of images, ideas, figures, and events ... which point to the supernatural. When translated into mere ideas their actual meanings are lost.' More than this, he saw that myths are important not as, 'objects of historical study, but as presences, as legitimate modes of existential insight' (Bultmann and Jaspers, 1958: 85).

Jaspers included the idea of a divine revelation in history as also belonging to the mythical world of understanding. This is an important and crucial point, for it is the issue which divides thinkers. On the one hand, there are those who see Christianity as a fundamentally historical religion because at one place and at one time God was revealed through the actual man Jesus; on the other hand, there are those who see that belief itself as a mythical statement about reality. It is, after all, a matter of faith as to whether the historical Jesus was anything other than a Jewish teacher who won disciples and influenced the subsequent history of the world.

In practical terms this division is likely to continue for as long as some Christian theologians identify myth as a category of thought alien to theology and to the human nature of Christians. These will continue to stress the literal truth of Christian doctrine focused on the wonder of the Incarnation. For others, and here the study of religions exerts a strong influence, myths are categorized as a perfectly normal mode of thought in the lives of people of all levels of society and in every culture. Religious life for such people may well include a commitment to accept the mythical formulation of belief, knowing full well that it is not a literal statement of truth but a way of formulating their inner experience. For some contemporary Christians, especially some who have been born into a more traditional and literalist form of religion, this outlook can be a freeing possibility, enabling them to develop in their experience of God.

Myth and history continue to exist as directly related categories.

Where history is prized as the medium of religious revelation myth will be ignored or devalued. Those who see history as a radically problematic medium for gaining religious certainty will value myth highly.

But other important consequences follow these trends, not least the significance given to non-Christian religions. A spirit of exclusivity rules if history is deemed the canvas on which God is revealed through events in the life of Israel, through Jesus of Nazareth, through early church councils and their creeds and doctrines, and then either through the great tradition of Thomas Aquinas and ongoing Catholic tradition, or else through the Reformation of Martin Luther and others. Catholics argue that their history gives more of the total revealed truth than the history of the Protestants. The Protestants see the Reformation as a major turning point in religious knowledge and freedom. The Eastern Orthodox see their constantly ongoing liturgical tradition as continuing the Christian truth through history and not losing out as the other two Christian streams have done. Smaller Christian groups then add their own version of historical revelation to show how their doctrine is closer to God's truth than the doctrine of the other churches.

But through all this there is the doctrinal certainty that God is revealed in Christian history in a way that is not the case for non-Christian religions. Their gods, scriptures and worship are seen to be strongly mythical and to lack the stamp of religious truth, which is none other than a direct contact from God in history. Any idea that the supernatural world may have interacted with this world through actual personages such as the incarnation or avatar of Vishnu in Hinduism tends to be quickly relegated to the realm of myth and thereby to a lower order of knowledge.

In other words, Christianity's sense of being a historical religion is part of its own identity as a superior form of religious knowledge when compared with 'mythological' religions. This is why many theologians would deny that Christian doctrine was mythological in any real way.

NARRATIVE, MYTH, AND THEOLOGY

The constant importance of myth and history within Christian theological thinking can be seen in Narrative Theology. This theological approach emerged in the second half of the twentieth century as a way of allowing groups of ordinary Christians to develop their own theological understanding of their life and local circumstances. It has been an important aspect of Christian thought in disadvantaged social groups in South America and South Africa.

Instead of approaching the Bible through a detailed analysis of the text they see it as an extensive set of stories about God's dealings with many earlier believers. Because no great scholarly skill in knowing many languages and how to interpret the Bible is required, ordinary believers can practise this kind of theology. They are encouraged to see their own life circumstances as another story of God's relationship with people. The idea of a narrative lies behind this approach, which is why it is often called Narrative Theology or the Theology of Story. As people see their own local history as a narrative of events, often focused on elements of injustice, they find it easy to see the Bible as one large set of narratives concerning God's people and their search for justice and salvation (Stroup, 1981).

This approach shows the clear importance of history as the framework within which Christians see themselves as related to God. But it also involves a kind of myth-making activity, a sort of mythologizing of events which otherwise might be seen as economic, political, or ordinary social history. While this approach resembles the nineteenth-century idea of salvation-history it adds to past events a strong emphasis upon today's deliverance. This complex interlinking of history and myth can now be taken further, in the next chapter, as we see how Christian theology sets about explaining human nature and destiny.

Further reading

Bultmann, R. and Jaspers, K. (1958) *Myth and Christianity*. New York: Noonday Press.

Kirk, G. S. (1970) *Myth: Its Meaning and Functions in Ancient and Other Cultures*. Cambridge: Cambridge University Press.

Munz, P. (1973) *When the Golden Bough Breaks*. London: Routledge & Kegan Paul.

3. Human nature and destiny

For Christians, human nature and destiny are to be understood through the doctrines of creation and salvation. Traditionally speaking, God creates and sustains the world and humanity. Human beings, both through their own God-given freedom and through the actions of others, experience evil. They are saved from the consequences of sin by Jesus Christ who is believed to be both human and divine, and who conquers sin and death through his own death and resurrection. God is committed to humanity and to a future kingdom of moral righteousness, and believers are called to work for this goal through the Church which already symbolizes God's work.

This world-view is drawn from the Bible, which itself clearly poses and sets out to deal with the great issues of human nature and destiny. 'What is man that Thou art mindful of him?' asks Psalm 8, which is a good place to begin exploring the Christian view of life's meaning, reminding us, as it does, that Christianity owes much to Jewish Scriptures as a basis for later Christian thought. This psalm begins with the glory of God expressed in the grandeur of the heavens, with moon and stars all speaking of God through their very existence. It is in the light of this wonder and magnificence that the question of human significance is raised. What can human life, in all its apparent smallness, mean when set against the immensity of the heavens? The Psalmist answers that humanity is made by God and placed in dominion over the 'work of God's hands' in the form of the animals of earth, sea and sky. Humanity itself is part and parcel of the wonder of the creation, but a part given special responsibility for the earth, as we see in greater detail in Chapter 9 of this book.

So it is that the doctrine of creation answers human self-reflection. But if the Psalmist, centuries before Christ, could be moved to question human significance in the light of the dome of heaven, how much more demanding this question becomes after the modern scientific revolution in understanding the immensity of space and of the universe. Can people, not to mention plants and animals, have any significance when we think of our earth as the smallest of small flecks in an unimaginably immense universe? For most ordinary individuals, untrained in astronomy, physics or mathematics, the size of the universe simply does not make sense – it is too big to understand, we have no way of comparing it with anything. And even when scientists say that it is statistically very probable that there are other civilizations out there in the universe, we find it hard to understand or accept. Because such descriptions of the cosmos give to human nature and destiny a dimension that many individuals do find impossible to understand, significance is lost within the vastness of it all and the key issue of the relevance of persons is brought into sharp focus, and, as far as faith is concerned, becomes vitally important for Christian theology.

Persons at the heart of everything

Many things in life depend upon our perspective, not least the significance of the universe where these factors of size and personal significance offer two potentially different outlooks. We have already said that if size is the basis of judgement, then men and women count for infinitesimally little on the scale of the universe. But, if we ask about significance, we can say that human beings are the most important part of the universe since it is humans who are doing the thinking about space and time and are raising these very critical issues.

This raises a curious fact that is often overlooked, namely that it is these large-brained human animals' own reflections upon the size of the universe that make them feel insignificant. It is as though the very genius of thought turns against itself when size is the key consideration. If love, or human relationship, or scientific discovery, or poetry, or any other creative product of human life is taken as the basis for judgement, then human beings come to assume immense importance when compared with millions of light years of dust-strewn space.

Christian belief has firmly embraced this issue of perspective, and has appreciated the issue of the immensity of the heavens against the smallness of human stature. The outcome of its reflection on the problem has resulted in a commitment to the doctrine of creation. A doctrine which allows for both the immensity of the universe, in terms of size, and the immensity of human beings in terms of self-conscious life. Human nature involves life in an immensity of space. It involves the drive to try to understand the physical universe, and it also involves the rise of worship of the God who could create both the great size of space and the worth of human personality.

This worth of human beings was central to the world-view of European Christianity for many centuries, with the Bible-fed belief that the earth, as humankind's home planet, was the centre of the universe. It has often been fashionable to criticize this view and say that humanity had an inflated image of itself and, like a spoiled child, wanted to be at the centre of everything. More realistically, we should appreciate that the biblical myths of creation, as spelled out in Genesis, inevitably fed the view of human priority, and nothing in human experience contradicted it.

INTERPRETING EXISTENCE

It is more than likely that these creation stories were read by many generations of Christians as factual accounts of human origins. It made very good practical sense to think of human nature as created by God and, following human disobedience and the entry of sin into the world, as redeemed by God through Jesus. The picture painted by Paul in his Letter to the Romans draws close parallels between the first Adam who sinned and Jesus, as the second Adam, who redeemed humankind. This world-view accorded with human experience of wickedness and of forgiveness, as well as answering the obvious question of life's significance. The traditional Christian interpretation of existence possessed an explanation for moral evil within itself. It is perfectly understandable that the Genesis creation stories should have been read in a literal way as explanations of life. Other parts of the Bible, especially the New Testament, played a further part in explaining what happens after this life. The accounts of the resurrection of Jesus and beliefs about life in heaven after death complemented the Christian theory of life, especially when read in an equally literal way. Human nature and destiny could be adequately explained through the Bible.

INTERPRETING THE WORLD

While Copernicus and Darwin stand out as two scientists who helped alter this world-view, many theologians of the nineteenth and twentieth centuries went further in changing the way we understand the biblical accounts of creation and life. Copernicus (1473–1543) was a canon of Frauenberg Cathedral in Prussia who had studied astronomy and mathematics in Poland and Italy. He came to realize that the sun was the centre of the solar system, a view that contradicted the age-long theory that the sun went around the earth. This finding laid the foundation for other discoveries about the universe which, in a philosophical sense, can be said to have shifted humankind from the centre of the universe. This astronomical outlook has come to be very influential in the birth of the 'size and distance' perspective on human life.

More dramatically still, Charles Darwin (1809–82) altered the way people understand themselves within the world. From his work on evolution it became increasingly obvious that humans had an animal ancestry. While the Bible spoke of all living things coming from the dust of the earth and, in that sense, having a common identity, evolution spoke of a more direct form of descent. From the later nineteenth century and throughout the twentieth century the animal nature of humans has assumed an increasingly important place in human self-knowledge and self-discovery.

For some people these two perspectives – Copernicus on cosmic size and Darwin on animal ancestry – have been highly influential in forming an overall perspective on human nature which differs from the biblical picture of humankind as a special creation. Instead of God creating a universe as a home for human beings, there emerges a picture of an unexplained universe in which the human species simply happens to have evolved and finds itself engaged in self-reflection.

INTERPRETING THE BIBLE

Just when Darwin was fostering the idea of evolution, some biblical scholars and theologians were studying the Bible and producing a new more liberal view of it than traditionally had been held by Christians. As already discussed in Chapter 2, the issue of myth and history was central to this new form of biblical criticism, and stressed the various sources or documents from which the Bible was derived rather than the idea of divine revelation and authority lying behind the scriptures.

Hermann Hupfeld (1796–1866), for example, wrote in 1853 a important study on the sources underlying the book of Genesis. Still better known are Julius Wellhausen (1844–1918), who was concerned with the way Jewish institutions and ideas had developed through history, and Hermann Gunkel (1862–1932), whose work in the history of religions led him to talk about the ways in which the Israelites adopted and transformed beliefs that originated in other religions. These, along with other forms of biblical study, deeply influenced the way the Bible is interpreted and understood. This applies as much to the creation stories in Genesis as to any other part of the Bible. For some Christians, this involves major problems, especially when questions of biblical criticism are placed alongside scientific accounts of creation and both are seen as attacks upon traditional Christian explanations of the origin of human life.

Creation or evolution?

'Creation or evolution?' – this stark opposition is often presented as the choice Christians have to make when they decide on the meaning of life. But the apparent simplicity of this three-word phrase hides a series of complicated issues that need elaborating.

The first issue involves the word 'creation'. It is surprising how often people, even moderately well-educated individuals, assume that orthodox Christians believe that God actually created the universe in six days. There is no doubt that some Christians do believe in a six-day creation, especially those who would be happy to call themselves fundamentalists and who believe that the literal meaning of biblical passages is the proper way to understand them. But there are many problems involved in this view of the Bible, including the fact that there are two creation accounts in the first two chapters of Genesis each approaching the idea of God's creation of humankind in rather different ways.

The first account (Gen 1:1 – 2:3) gives an orderly and sequential account of what God did on each 'day' of creation, including the fact that the sun and moon were created on the fourth day, leading up to the creation of male and female on the sixth day. In the second creation story, the male human being is created on the very first day when 'the Lord God made the earth and heavens' (Gen 2:4). The man is taken and placed in the garden of Eden and, only after all the other plants and animals are made does Eve, the first woman, get to be made from one of Adam's ribs (Gen 2:21). The differences between these two accounts of creation are stark, showing how inappropriate it is to try to harmonize them into a single scheme. It becomes doubly difficult to try to harmonize them with certain geological theories about different rock strata as some people have occasionally tried to do.

The most obvious way to understand these passages is to see them as myths of origin which deal with different themes and which seek to establish some basic values. Both make it obvious that God is responsible for the universe and that humanity's existence is not accidental or arbitrary. They also emphasize the divine command that humanity should obey God and act responsibly in the world. But the first account works out these ideas in an orderly progression of events, while the second puts the male–female relationship at the centre of the story.

Many Christians would be happy to see these stories as contributing to their knowledge of God, and of human life lived in obedience to God, without taking them in a literal way. Instead of reading the accounts as some sort of history or science, they take them as theological statements about the human condition. The stories are seen as answering the 'why?' of creation rather than the 'how?' of creation. They remind us that another aspect of the 'creation or evolution' distinction lies in the fact that, since the nineteenth century, certain ideas have actually changed their meaning or have arisen for the first time. The theory of evolution, for example, has changed the way many people understand human, animal and plant life. Similarly, the very idea of history and the way people tell stories and build up religious and other texts has been transformed over the last hundred years. This means that modern interpreters have to choose between many different categories of literature when trying to understand a text that has come down from much earlier times, when these categories were not explicitly understood. This is a difficult point to make clear but it means, for example, that at a time when science did not exist as we know it today, it would be natural to accept a mythological explanation of something because no other explanation existed. Given the modern choice between science and myth, and many other categories of classification, more sophisticated descriptions are possible.

CREATION THROUGH EVOLUTION

For many modern Christians, the choice between creation and evolution is unnecessary once the Genesis stories are accepted as dealing with religious truths about God and humanity while scientific theories attempt to explain how the universe has come to be the way it is. For them, creation is achieved through evolution. But this perspective has its own problems, because, if Christians hold to it, they do so believing that God intended to create humanity. An evolutionist who is speaking only in scientific terms can make no such statement of belief and can only assume that what emerges through evolution does so accidentally.

Some scientists have even spoken in more recent years about what they call the 'anthropic principle', the idea that the universe is not random and works in such a way as to produce humankind. This view would certainly not be acceptable to the majority of scientists, but it shows that scientific interpretations can also vary. In a broad sense, many modern Christians have accepted the evolutionary and scientific view of the way the universe works, and some have found their own theological thinking stimulated by it. It is worth considering several trends associated with such scientific perspectives, because they deeply influence Christian ideas on human nature and destiny.

THE CHALLENGE OF EVOLUTION

It is hard for late twentieth-century people to grasp the impact made by evolutionary thought on their nineteenth-century forebears. So many new ideas have emerged in the twentieth century that we have become familiar with novelty and quickly take for granted something that was quite unknown only decades earlier. This is especially true in the two areas of science and technology which have radically influenced human life in both great and small ways. For example, the discovery of DNA, as the chemical basis of human chromosomes containing the basic biological information on the make-up of individuals, took place in the late 1950s, by the mid-1960s the topic was on the school syllabus and by the 1970s it formed part of popular knowledge about life processes.

When Darwin published his discoveries on evolution in *The Origin of Species* (1859) and *The Descent of Man* (1871), he was presenting material that dramatically altered the way human life and identity were understood by his contemporaries. It had been customary to think of the origin of humanity in terms of a special divine creation with the biblical stories of Adam and Eve under-pinning the world view of the general public as well as the thinking of most church leaders. To have this established assumption challenged was a major problem because it raised the issue of authority. What was the basis of truth about life? What was human nature? What source of information and method of study should be followed to know the truth about humanity?

For many centuries theologians had debated with philosophers about the nature of life, but always it was one person's opinion against another. And more than that, there was the weight of tradition and social influence that came from the churches to back up ideas drawn from the Bible, and from earlier church authorities. Complex webs of influence linked churches, schools, colleges, powerful families, moral rules and the secular law makers.

With Darwin, and other important thinkers of the mid and late nineteenth century, science began to emerge in a quite new way as a source of authority about life and the world. This was also the period when industry and engineering were making Western nations uniquely powerful and wealthy, and making Britain's the greatest Empire in the world. Science was able to demonstrate its discoveries and not simply to argue them as earlier critical philosophers had done. The Bible and theology were set against scientific theory, the laboratory, and the age of new engineering. It is no wonder that some church leaders quite simply set themselves against this new knowledge and argued that it was godless. But it is even more important to appreciate that some Christian thinkers saw these discoveries as valuable insights into the way God worked in the world. Rather than turn their backs on evolution, they eagerly explored it and sought to apply it in Christian reflection on the world and on human life. For them, at the beginning of the twentieth century, the question of human nature and destiny had to be approached in quite different ways than had been appropriate in preceding eras. Many churches of the late twentieth century are still coming to terms with this fact, and the challenge is still dramatically insistent.

Some evolutionist Christians

The following individuals are a few among many who have taken up the challenge of evolutionary ideas and used them in developing their own theological perspective on human nature. Though each went in a different direction they stand as useful examples precisely because of their varied emphases in taking up the challenge to interpret the world anew. Jevons was concerned with social life, morality and the individual, Whitehead with a philosophy of the universe, and Teilhard with the spiritual life and with Christ.

JEVONS (1858–1936)

The Englishman F. B. Jevons spent his whole life as a university teacher in the University of Durham. Beginning with Latin and Greek, and with a deep interest in philosophy, he rapidly came to see the importance of evolutionary ideas in the development of religion and human personality (1896, 1906). The new discipline of anthropology, with evolutionary theory at its heart, provided Jevons with a key for understanding the emergence, through various stages of primitive and world religions, of the kind of human personality capable of love, service and self-sacrifice. Such a personality was, he believed, also able to understand God in increasingly clear ways. This sense of revelation, coming through the natural religion of humanity, was very important to Jevons because he did not want to make any distinction between natural religion and revealed religion.

On a more religiously conservative front, another Englishman, L. S. Thornton, also took modern science seriously, relating it to the tradition of Christian theology, and especially to the theology of the church and of society. Like Jevons, Thornton's work has been largely forgotten, but it offers a good example of a serious Christian thinker seeking to relate theology to science in order to understand more of human nature within the overall activity of God (1950).

Unlike Thornton, who was an Anglo-Catholic priest and scholar, Jevons was an Anglican liberal in theological terms; he argued that experience in relation to social life and ethics was vitally important (D. J. Davies, 1991). He was more concerned with what a person felt than with some abstract notion of what a person ought to think. In the evolution of religion Jevons believed there was also a development in what people felt of God, an intuitive foundation for their lives and for their theology.

WHITEHEAD (1861–1947)

Alfred North Whitehead was a mathematician and philosopher who became committed to an evolutionary view of the universe and humanity (1926). Because he spoke so much of the process underlying the universe and its development he, and other theologians such as Charles Hartshorne (1967), Schubert Ogden (1979) and Norman Pittinger (1967), were called Process Theologians. One of their concerns was to see the universe as full of a potential which is in the process of being worked out in an open and dynamic way and in close relationship with God. This dynamic aspect of God's being reflects their belief that these processes of change all take place 'in-God'. God is not far removed and untouched by events in the universe but is, in some sense, involved in all of them. For Process Theology, because the main focus of Christian 'tradition' lies in the present rather than somewhere deep in the past, Christians have to be aware of the present activity of God in and through the evolutionary processes of life which influence humanity's destiny. Love and the love of God are key ethical and theological features here and touch the way people live and interpret their lives.

TEILHARD DE CHARDIN (1881–1955)

The French Jesuit Teilhard de Chardin spent much of his earlier life in China working as a physical anthropologist on human evolution and, later, in America for an anthropological research foundation. The Roman Catholic Church in France was suspicious of some of his researches because he sought to interpret theology through the idea of evolution. He saw humanity as caught up in both a material and a spiritual realm, despite the fact that few are aware of it. The universe is forever stirred by divine activity as God leads it and humanity on to the future goal of love. Christ as the risen Son of God is the 'Omega Point', the centre of this creating power. Teilhard even thought that this theological belief ought to be given some part to play within a fuller scientific understanding of evolution. Christ was the focus of love, giving meaning to the universe as it developed and progress into the future and into God. In other words, science should not be separated from religion, with one explaining the 'how?' and the other the 'why?' of the universe. According to Teilhard, a unity exists between God's purpose and energy within creation and Christ's power of love within salvation. This sense of unity is part of his deeply mystical and poetic sense of the presence of Christ with the universe and within his own consciousness so basic to Teilhard as a priest and as a scientist (Teilhard de Chardin, 1965). Teilhard's perspective originates in and through faith, and not through traditional methods of science, so there is no way in which it could be taught as a standard scientific approach. In fact, it raises the question of faith, which needs to be considered in its own right at this point because, as far as the Christian tradition is concerned, faith lies at the heart of human nature and destiny.

Belief and faith in human nature

Belief is complex. From a practical point of view it involves an intricate combination of reason and emotion, set within the life context of each individual. The element of reason concerns thought and logical reflection, and can be developed through study and training. Emotion, by contrast, involves a complicated bundle of processes involving the human capacity for insight, along with moods and feelings that surround our experiences in life. Belief involves all three elements of reason, emotion and autobiography.

Belief is central to the Christian view of human nature. Men, women and children are persons capable of belief and of a knowledge of God. For Christianity, belief represents a fuller and more intensely human life than a life lived in disbelief. This is because belief involves the rational acceptance that the universe is created by God and is therefore an intelligible place in which to exist.

But it also involves the sense of trust in God as redeemer. Disbelief or unbelief is regarded as a negative feature. Faith and unbelief need to be considered together because human nature and destiny cannot be understood by Christians apart from faith and the nature of God; indeed, in many respects the Christian idea of human nature is determined by the Christian doctrine of God.

GOD AS CREATOR

In Christian thought, God is uncreated, and is the source of all things while human nature is part of a world lying within a cosmos that is entirely God's responsibility. Whichever particular theory is held about how God created the world, the fundamental Christian belief remains that God is the creator and, as such, sustains the creation. In many respects the first creation myth in Genesis can be misleading when the idea that God 'rested on the seventh day' is taken literally especially for those, already mentioned, who want to talk of the creator as constantly involved in the developing creation, and who see the changes and developments which are still occurring as part of the creative activity of God.

HUMANITY AND THE IMAGE OF GOD

Because, as we described in Chapter 1, men and women are said to be made in the image of God they, too, have a responsible part to play in the ordering of creation. This idea of being made in the image of God has been taken from chapter 1 of Genesis and interpreted in different ways within the Christian tradition. In part, it embraces the rule and dominion given to humanity by God (Gen 1:28), but it has also been seen to lie in human reason, in the moral sense and in creativity. In more literal interpretations of Christianity it has even been understood as a physical resemblance, a view which comes to full expression in the Mormon doctrine that God actually possesses a body which is the model of the body of human beings.

One major feature of the image of God that has tended to differentiate Catholic from Protestant theology is the question of how much the image was influenced by the Fall. Here there are several strands of argument to contend with because of the issue of a historical Fall of Adam. In much early theology the idea of a historical Adam and Eve was largely accepted in a natural way and, until the nineteenth century, both Catholic and Protestant theologians were agreed on this point. Where they disagreed was on what happened at the Fall. One particular point of contention was whether the image of God, whatever it was, had been completely erased or merely, in some way, flawed and impaired. In the light of modern science and technology, the interpretation which emphasizes the creative aspect of human reason has a important part to play alongside the moral aspect of life. Now, more than ever before in human history, human beings can directly engage in manipulating aspects of the world through genetic engineering. The moral dimension of human nature, however, does not seem to evolve to produce saints at the same speed that reason produces new discoveries. It is to this moral realm that we now turn.

Sin and evil

While the creation stories of Genesis do talk of God as creator and of the world as a perfect place, they quickly pass on to speak of evil as a radical flaw running through the otherwise perfect creation. This flaw embraces the two aspects of temptation coming to human beings from beyond themselves, and of evil emerging from other individuals.

THE DEVIL

The external source of evil is symbolized in Genesis by the serpent as an independent agent throwing a question mark over what God has said (Gen 3:1). In other biblical passages this personalized focus of evil appears as Satan (Job 2:1ff.) or the devil. By the time of the New Testament this picture of the devil, as an enemy of God and source of problems for humanity, is widespread. At the outset of his ministry, Jesus is said to have been tempted by the devil in the wilderness (Matt 4:1ff.). Similarly, in their turn, Christians are exhorted to resist their adversary, the devil (James 4:7), who prowls around as a lion seeking his prey (1 Pet 5:8). In the Apocalypse this evil figure reappears as the ancient serpent, the devil, and Satan, the deceiver of the whole world (Rev 12:9). However portrayed, the figure of the devil expresses the belief in a real power of evil that is set against good. J. B. Russell's study *The Devil* (1977) traces the many ways in which believers and professional theologians have described or tried to interpret this awareness of evil.

POSSESSION

At times in the history of Christianity the sense of the objective existence of the devil has been very strong, as in the fifteenth-century Inquisition with its belief that witches actually did enter into pacts with the devil and needed to be punished for this for the good of their eternal souls. A belief in the devil, along with a belief in evil spirits, has also played a part in the practical faith and spirituality of some modern trends of contemporary Christianity. The Charismatic Movement, for example, which emerged and grew dramatically from the 1960s in the USA, in Britain and in many other developed countries was, in part, associated with a belief both in the devil and in evil spirits. This belief could take the dramatic form of serious possession by the devil, requiring exorcism.

It is interesting to see this attitude emerge in the later twentieth century which is often considered to be a more secular age. Still, with the growth of popular cinema and video, a spate of films on objective, evil forces was brought into the everyday world of ordinary people. In the 1970s, for example, the Church of England became increasingly aware of popular beliefs in evil spirits, and encouraged each diocese to appoint a priest with special responsibility for this area. In practical terms this sort of 'ministry of deliverance', as it was often called, embraced a wide variety of behaviour, including experience of ghosts or frightening presences as well as the fear of some who had engaged in seances or games seeking to contact spirits.

Within some Charismatic churches the idea of possession could take a rather different form, with the belief that particular Christians could come under the influence of various sorts of 'spirits', such as the spirit of rebelliousness or apathy. This shows how wide the idea of spirits and spirit influence can be within Christian churches, varying from a full sense of devil possession, requiring formal exorcism, to a state that is more of a personal disposition (or even clinical illness) interpreted almost metaphorically as 'possession' or evil influence.

In their own way these ideas also raise the issue of human nature and show how Christians can differ in interpreting human life. For, just as some believe in the objective existence of evil spirits and the devil, there are many others – and certainly they would be in the majority among professional Christian leaders – who hold no such belief.

The language used about evil is very important for the way believers understand and interpret their lives. Many Christians do not accept the objective 'existence' of the devil or of evil spirits, yet still talk of evil, as in the example provided by Paul Tillich (1886–1965) in his twentieth-century existentialist theology. He chooses to speak of the 'demonic-tragic structures of individual and group life', and not of the devil or of evil spirits. Tillich sees this demonic element embracing 'disruption, conflict, self-destruction, meaninglessness, and despair in all realms of life' (Tillich, 1953: 55). This focus makes individuals more responsible for their lives, and does not shift blame to the devil, or even to God, by saying that God may tempt them to do something. In practical terms this is important because failure to take responsibility for our own temptations and sense of sin makes it more difficult to face up to problems and take decisions for ourselves. In the New Testament, the Letter of James gives clear voice to this very issue: 'each person is tempted when he is lured and enticed by his own desire' (James 1:14).

SPIRIT-POSSESSION: ANTHROPOLOGY AND CHRISTIANITY

Any serious discussion of spirits and spirit-possession in Christianity cannot be separated from the kinds of issues studied by social anthropologists who, formally, work on the basis of practical disbelief in the gods and powers acknowledged in different human societies. This approach enables anthropology to focus on the social forces at work in people's lives and on the cultural expression of human beliefs.

Despite human diversity it is interesting to see some distinctive patterns emerge through anthropological research. So, for example, beliefs in spirits can be taken as expressions of evil and of negative life experiences and pressure, as Ioan Lewis argued for possession cults in some Islamic groups in Africa. Among some Somali wives, spirit possession was a way of allowing them to exert pressure on their husbands to pay attention to them and to their needs (Lewis, 1986: 94). In an interesting study of women in South Wales, the medical anthropologist Vieda Skultans (1974) showed how women were the regular clients of male mediums through whose trance state and contact with the spirit world benefit was brought to the women. She interpreted this situation as one where women gained some consolation from contact with the sensitive male medium in contrast to the lack of personal concern shown them by their husbands. In this case, there is no full-scale possession by spirits but there is a belief in spirit involvement with the life of human beings. What is particularly significant is that, in this context, human life is understood against the complex and mysterious backcloth of spirits, mediums and trance states. In other words, human nature cannot be understood in and of itself but only with the help of some additional forces of a spiritual and personal nature.

Many other examples of possession could be given to show that, from the perspective of social anthropology, possession is not a random event but befalls particular individuals in particular social situations. This helps demonstrate how much social life affects human nature and brings us to the important theological point that a major dimension of human nature is social.

Human nature is social

One of the most fundamental Christian beliefs about human nature is that individuals belong together as a community of people. One of the Genesis myths makes this dramatically clear when God says 'It is not good for man to be alone' (Gen 2:18), and goes on to create a partner to establish humanity as male and female. Much of the rest of Genesis is taken up with an account of the kinship groups, clans and finally a nation which God establishes as part of a covenant relationship. The Jewish religion and culture born from this divine endeavour was community-minded to its core, as the Ten Commandments make crystal clear by spelling out each person's social obligations.

The emergence of Christianity continued this theme, with the covenant relationship between God and Israel opened up to all humankind as driven home by the Acts of the Apostles in the conviction that people from 'every nation under heaven', whether Jews or Gentiles, were open to the salvation provided by Jesus Christ (Acts 2:5; 10:1ff.). Just as the congregation of faithful Jews meeting in the synagogue expressed the community nature of Hebrew religion, so the emergence of the company of believers meeting as a church expressed the Christian commitment to life as a social fact. Paul helped to forge early Christian ideas to a great extent, and the idea of Christians as the body of Christ firmly reinforces this corporate image of human life as social life. When Paul says 'You are the body of Christ and individually members of it' (1 Cor 12:27), he is not simply talking about being a member of a group; he is taking the idea of a human society further by linking it with Christ. This is one reason why the Church is sometimes called a supernatural society or a spiritual society. This is especially true for those Christians who interpret the world and Christian life in a sacramental way, seeing material things as symbolic of divine truth. For example, the Christian socialist thinker F. D. Maurice (1805–72) pinpointed the family and the nation as two 'spiritual orders' which indicated the nature of human nature as intended by God. In his influential book *The Kingdom of Christ* (1837), he argued that the Church took up and transformed these basic institutions to ensure that they did not turn in 'on themselves and become negative and destructive features of life.

SERVICE AND FULFILMENT

Profound ethical consequences flow from this social view of the world and life. Service to God involves a service to our neighbour and to society at large. Human nature comes into its own when it gives itself to others. The idea of self-sacrifice as an ethical principle of Christian living comes to be seen as intrinsic to human success and fulfilment because the individual is turned from self-concern and self-obsession to a concern for others. This has become an integral part of Christian spirituality as a basis for ethics, and often surfaces in prayer and worship, as in the well-known 'Prayer of St Francis' asking God to grant that 'we may not seek so much to be consoled, as to console; to be understood, as to understand; to be loved, as to love; for in giving we receive, in pardoning we are pardoned'.

Service is about the relationships we have with others and, more specifically, about the quality of those relationships. It is tied to the Christian idea that service to God is both a kind of slavery and a kind of freedom. This underlies the history of Christian churches in their charitable work through hospitals, schools and places of refuge for the needy. Though dramatically evident in European society in earlier centuries, before modern states took over these welfare duties for their citizens, the ideal of care remains a key Christian concern in the modern world, especially in developing countries. This concern for people is not without a reason, and it too plays an important part in the Christian idea of human nature–human worth.

Human worth in human nature

In terms of Christian understanding, all human beings have an intrinsic worth for three reasons: God creates them; God in Christ loves and redeems them; and, being made in God's image, they are persons in their own right. One of the central tasks of Christianity is to teach people that they have a worth because God sees them in a positive way and calls them into a sense of their own significance.

CREATION AND MYSTERY

The processes of creation give to human beings a sense that the universe is not a random and meaningless background to their own meaningless lives. This is not to say that atheists are, necessarily, despondent people. It is possible for someone who does not acknowledge a creator to be fascinated and absorbed by life and by the nature of the universe. That same fascination has an important place in Christian thought, too, because religious belief does not immediately make everything obvious and clear as far as the universe is concerned.

Though from some simple, and perhaps fundamentalist, perspectives religious belief may clarify all intricacies of the universe, for many other Christians the universe and life itself possess a tremendous mystery and wonder. The essence of human nature involves this sense of mystery about reality. The fact that a Christian may believe that God is involved with this creation and is active within it can add to the mystery, precisely because there is a personal element, a sense of expectation, surrounding the meaning of life. It is in this sense that belief in the universe as made for humanity possesses an integrity rather than a selfish self-centredness.

GOD IN CHRIST LOVES AND REDEEMS

The central message of Christianity is that the God revealed in creation as an outgoing source of life, is also revealed in salvation as an outgoing source of love. The universe reveals God's creativity, and Jesus reveals the divine love. The belief that God engages with sin and evil through the life and work of Jesus is taken by Christians to show the personal nature of God. Evil and sin are moral ideas and relate to the experience of persons, so it is that, in and through a person described theologically as the Son of God, God encounters these things – a point that is so important that we return to it below when considering the Incarnation.

One important question in Christian theology concerns 'theodicy', or the problem of evil. In essence, it asks how a good and almighty God can allow dreadful suffering in a world for which he is responsible. Christianity responds to these great problem by talking of God being involved in the suffering of the world through Jesus. In a formal sense the question is side-stepped and not answered, but for many, the example of Jesus' suffering along with a sense of God's presence with them in their suffering furnish a practical way of coping with their own problems of evil.

GOD'S IMAGE AND PERSONAL WORTH

Despite the Fall, however it is interpreted and understood, men and woman still have the capacity to be creative and loving people, even though they may sometimes choose to be destructive and hateful, human life is precious because of this capability. In strictly biological terms, it is true that any particular individual could turn out to be astonishingly gifted, so that every child should be cherished because of that fact. But in terms of Christian morality and ethics, all human life is precious because it expresses the divine creativity and is the object of divine love. It is this conviction that lies behind the argument that some Christians expound over abortion, and all Christians share in concern for the deprived, oppressed and poor. As children of God, all are valuable. It is an idea inherent in the teaching of Jesus, when he says that things done to others can be understood as things done to him (Matt 25:35). This identification of Jesus with other people brings us to the doctrine of the Incarnation, which is the key issue for a Christian understanding of human nature and destiny.

THE INCARNATION AND HUMAN LIFE

Several important councils of early church leaders, especially the Councils of Nicaea in 325 and Chalcedon in 451, established the doctrine that Jesus of Nazareth was both fully human and fully divine. This was no easy conclusion to arrive at, and the way to it was strewn with many variant attempts at defining and explaining just who and what Jesus was. All this is perfectly understandable given the Jewish background of strong monotheism alongside beliefs in a coming Messiah and in intermediary figures between God and humanity (Casey, 1991).

The Council of Chalcedon, for example, argued forcefully that Jesus should be viewed as being one person having two natures both a human nature and a divine nature. This commitment to the belief that Jesus was both human and divine came to typify mainstream Christian orthodoxy even though it has sometimes proved difficult, if not impossible, to spell out in any real detail the 'chemistry or biology' of how this was possible. More than anything else, the deity and humanity of Jesus express a belief in his uniqueness and in his competence to be the saviour of the world.

Perhaps one of the most interesting aspects of these debates about Jesus Christ – christological debates as they are called – is that they do two things at once. They talk about God and they also talk about humanity. This means that the question of human nature is at the very heart of christological debates, not simply the nature of Jesus, but the nature of all people. To talk about Christology is also to talk about what is called 'theological anthropology', i.e., the doctrine of human life and nature. This becomes particularly apparent through one of the major theological concerns of the Councils that produced the creeds: the belief that though Jesus was fully human he was sinless. Such a contrast between this one man and all other human beings highlights the place of sin within ordinary human nature, and defines the relationship between Jesus as the saviour and the rest of humanity in need of salvation. Here human nature is defined by contrast with the nature of God which is sinless. And yet, at the same time, it outlines the human vocation to be sinless, and therefore the process of salvation.

SIN IN HUMAN NATURE

We have already seen the centrality of sin to the Christian doctrine of human nature; it is one point on which most Christian traditions are largely in agreement with the very heart of the Christian message announcing Jesus as the saviour of sinners. Sin itself has to do with the way individuals understand and treat both themselves and others, and most especially how they relate to God.

Basic aspects of sin in the Christian tradition involve human disobedience to God, grounded in human self-love. Pride is thought to be so deep-seated that the self is placed before God and before other people. Humility is the opposite of this, and puts both God and others before the self; but humility cannot emerge and develop of its own accord because of the flawed quality of human nature. This flawed nature of things is related to the idea of the image of God, the *Imago Dei*, in which humanity is said to have been created (Gen 1:27), already alluded to in this chapter. In all of its meanings the *Imago Dei* has been a very important issue in the history of Christian theology, lying as it does at the heart of differing doctrines of salvation. It is also important because the idea of creation underlying it is rather literal in its reading of the Bible and assumes that humans were initially made perfect and existed in a state of original righteousness. This involved a closeness of relationship to God prior to a fall into sin through disobedience. Theologians have discussed various consequences of this Fall on the image of God in humankind. For some, the image was totally destroyed through the Fall; for others, it remained, but only in a distorted and mutilated form. For the early Fathers, for medieval theologians like Thomas Aquinas, and for Reformation theologians, the idea of the Fall as being a historic event is an important implicit assumption. After the period when God and humanity were closely related, there came a time when sin caused a separation and distance between them.

The Incarnation, then, becomes doubly important – not only as the means for God to share in human nature, through Jesus of Nazareth, and to save mankind, but also as another momentous event in humanity's history when the Fall is reversed and the image of God is visible once more. Jesus is seen as the 'Second Adam' who achieves where Adam failed: 'For as by one man's disobedience many were made sinners, so by one man's obedience many will be made righteous' (Rom 5:19). Death is seen as the outcome of the Fall and of the sin of Adam. The spoiled image of God is overtaken by death. But resurrection and eternal life come through the obedience of Jesus as the second Adam, who is the very image of God because he is himself divine. The following quotation shows how part of the New Testament sees the idea of the image of Adam as a negative and sorry thing, but the image of Jesus as its saving correction: 'Just as we have borne the image of the man of dust, we shall also bear the image of the man of heaven' (1 Cor 15:49). In Jesus, the image of God is restored to humanity and, through the work of the Holy Spirit, individuals can come to share in its restoration: 'And we all ... beholding the glory of the Lord are being changed into his likeness from one degree of glory to another' (2 Cor 3:18).

Processes of salvation

Although they all agree that this depends upon the grace of God, churches differ in how they think grace works. The Catholic traditions stress the sacraments; from baptism through to the last rites, the grace of God is passed to people through the sacraments of the Church administered by priests. Protestants emphasize the inner working of the Spirit in relation to the teaching and the preaching of the Bible and the conversion of the individual, while the Greek Orthodox traditions emphasize the resurrection power of Christ to bring all people to share in God's life and nature.

One significant doctrinal issue, focused on the fifth-century historical debate between Augustine, Bishop of Hippo, and Pelagius, a British monk, argued the case on sin and salvation asking whether human beings can, themselves, aid the process of salvation. Augustine said that humans could do nothing to advance their own cause as far as salvation was concerned; God does it all by grace. Pelagius argued that God had given people the capability to do good if only they would do so. While the foundation of the argument is found in the New Testament (Rom 5; James 2:17, 18) it also resurfaced in the Reformation when Luther echoed both Paul and Augustine in seeing God as the sole source and means of salvation.

So it is that human nature and destiny lie within the scheme of sin and salvation. But to many modern thinkers the framework of a historical Fall is unacceptable, especially if the Genesis accounts are regarded as mythical material. This is where another approach to the human predicament is useful and needs careful exploration.

HUMAN EXISTENCE AND SALVATION

Just because Adam and Eve may be regarded as figures in a myth does not mean that the Fall ceases to be theologically important. The human experiences of alienation from others and from God, of being inwardly divided and emotionally torn, of being lost and a stranger in life, all speak of that flaw which lies at the heart of fallenness. So too does an awareness of guilt and shame over one's life and actions. The moral sense surrounding us in society, and especially in Christian teaching, and even within our own conscience, brings us to a knowledge that we are divided beings. As Paul expressed it, 'I can will what is right but I cannot do it' (Rom 7:18).

This led Paul, and after him both Augustine and Luther, to dwell on and to develop the doctrine of predestination, the idea that we are all so lost and dead in sin that God alone can bring life to us. The pathetic moral weakness of human nature in its fallen state, irrespective of whether we believe in a historic Fall or simply see the Fall as a way of describing the way we are now, depends on divine help. Unless God specifically wills our salvation, we would be ultimately and certainly lost. Luther spoke of people as being 'curved in on themselves'. This deep awareness of one's plight lies at the heart of the sense of gratitude to God for taking us in hand and drawing us out of ourselves and into Christ.

Here the doctrine of predestination is important, expressing the strong belief that we are so helpless that even our will is corrupt and cannot bring about the good we might believe we ought to do. Although many look upon predestination as a negative and unfortunate doctrine, one causing some Christians to be rather over-sure of their own salvation and overly eager to see others as damned, it is more properly viewed as a means of gratitude to God for saving helpless people. This can be seen theologically in the doctrine of double-predestination developed by John Calvin (1509–64), whereby God was believed to predestine some people to salvation and others to damnation. Karl Barth's twentieth-century theological position changed this quite dramatically, as he focused predestination within the person of Jesus. Jesus is the one predestined to death and also to life.

HUMAN DESTINY AND JESUS CHRIST

Jesus is the measure of humanity and the ground of its destiny. This centrality of Jesus, as both God and Man, is crucial for under-standing the Christian view of human nature and destiny. In some ways this is a strange emphasis, since humans are defining themselves in terms of what they are not. The one who is taken to be the model human being is everything that ordinary human beings are not, in that traditional theology strongly argues that Jesus was like us in every respect except that he did not sin. In practical terms this is difficult to sustain, because it is not only his sinlessness that differentiates Jesus from others but also the fact that he is believed to be both God and Man. The divinity of Jesus Christ means that he is worshipped, and, despite the fact that doctrinally it is heretical to separate his divinity from his humanity within his total identity, it is the divinity which tends to be accentuated in worship.

Human destiny lies in being transformed into the likeness of Jesus in some moral sense, in a process that will be completed after death in the new order of heaven. Indeed the place of heaven and an after-life is quite crucial in the Christian doctrine of salvation, or soteriology as it is called, but here there is a possibility of a major difference of interpretation within Christianity depending upon whether one believes in an after-life or not.

HEAVEN AND EARTH

It has been traditional in Christianity to see human life as one phase of a total existence which will be perfected in heaven. One view sees heaven as the answer to the problem of why people suffer on earth: there they will obtain the reward for earthly suffering. An additional Catholic view presses the thought of an after-life in another direction through the idea of purgatory as a process through which God's grace operates on individuals to prepare them for the holiness of the divine presence.

More recently some Christians have tended either to ignore the heavenly dimension or else to reject it when considering human nature and destiny. Though it is something of an over-generalization, we might say that movements like Liberation, Black, and Feminist Theologies have tended to emphasize the vital importance of social justice in this world as the goal of Christian endeavour. This shows how varied ideas of human destiny can be since, for many Christians, the hope of heaven is real. While they normally regard it as a 'place' where they worship God, they may also think in terms of heaven as a place to meet their dead relatives and friends – all as part of the process of their own coming to fulfilment as persons.

DEATH, DESTINY AND SALVATION

Even if life after death plays a very small part in the faith of some Christians, death remains a central issue for Christian faith itself because the death of Jesus is an absolutely crucial part of Christianity because of the belief that his death on the cross was the key sacrifice for sin. Various interpretations explain this sacrifice in different ways. 'Substitutionary atonement' identifies Jesus as taking the place of guilty humans, dying in their place, and being the fulfilment of the animal sacrifices for sin in the Old Testament. Some of the early Church Fathers regarded Jesus as a ransom paid to Satan, because Satan had gained authority over humanity after the Fall. Martin Luther in the Reformation and the twentieth-century Swede Gustav Aulén saw the crucifixion as some sort of encounter between Christ and the devil. The following quotation is from the end of Aulén's small but important book *Christus Victor* (1970) and expresses in a personal way the dynamic importance of the death of Christ for many believers.

> The Atonement is, above all, a movement of God to man, not in the first place a movement of man to God ... God, the Infinite, accepts the lowliness of the Incarnation ... We hear again the old realistic message of the conflict of God with the dark, hostile forces of evil, and His victory over them by the Divine self-sacrifice. (1931: 176)

In the 'exemplarist' view of the atonement, Peter Abelard (1079–1142) saw the death of Jesus as the supreme example of the love of God, which triggered or stimulated a human response of repentance and responding love. At around the same time, Anselm (1033–1109) interpreted atonement in a more legal or juridical theory, which made sense in the feudal society of his day. According to Anselm human sin was a disgrace against the dignity of God. The price that was paid through the death of Jesus was paid not to Satan, but to God as a satisfaction for his outraged honour.

Types of salvation

The idea of salvation can also be usefully explored in religious studies from the perspective of sociology. Early this century Max Weber discussed the idea of salvation at some length in his *Sociology of Religion*. Working on the assumption that 'every need for salvation is an expression of some distress', he characterized religion as one aspect of life that helped reduce the distressed condition (1965: 107). So, for example, he speaks of disprivileged groups as primarily needing a release from suffering: 'they do not always experience the need for salvation in a religious form' (1965: 108). What some rich people want, by contrast, is a sense of legitimacy – to feel that the good things they have are theirs by right. Intellectuals, in their turn, seek a sense of meaning for the world. When Christianity is the official religion of a country, its theory of divine grace administered through the Church can easily serve to provide just such a validation for the life lived by people in positions of power and responsibility. Salvation has also been interpreted sociologically as a means of attaining a higher level of identity or a kind or super-plus of meaning in life (D. J. Davies, 1984).

In a very similar style to Max Weber, the English sociologist B. R. Wilson discussed salvation in religious sects and his classification of sects is an interesting way of approaching human nature and destiny as far as religious people are concerned. Despite the fact that mainstream churches give an interpretation of life for millions of members of society, an important aspect of human nature in itself, there are many others who reject the dominant cultural interpretation and follow an alternative explanation of things. While Wilson's scheme or typology is, obviously, useful for describing sectarian groups it also depicts some of the characteristics found in mainstream religions. Wilson's basic argument is that each distinctive sect first describes evil and then proposes a remedy for it.

Conversionist groups say evil lies in the individual heart which needs to be converted through the Holy Spirit. *Revolutionists* say that the organization of society is itself corrupt and can be changed only through a supernatural revolution brought about by God. *Reformists* also see evil in social structures, but think that they can bring about change through human endeavour. *Utopians* try to avoid the evil of society by setting up their own ideal social world apart from everyone else. Something similar is done by *Introversionists*, who try to live within holy groups of their own, surrounded by the wider evil society. *Manipulationists* try to pinpoint evil and cultivate a way of manipulating it so as to overcome it; secret knowledge or practices, known only to members, are the basis for manipulating those negative and destructive tendencies. Finally, *Thaumaturgical* sects, a name from the Greek verb for wonder-working, specialize in dramatic acts such as healing or snake-handling to focus on evil and to show that its members have the means of overcoming it (Wilson, 1970: 37ff.).

MOOD, HUMAN NATURE AND SALVATION

One of Weber's many insights is that some groups cultivate a 'religious mood' as an instrument of salvation (1965: 151). This is an important point for religious studies, since human nature is capable of being trained in many different ways. Weber emphasizes the way different cultures and religious groups express their ideas and doctrines, and relate them to the active life of people. The way ideas are worked out in actions is related to the kind of mood which each group develops over time. A similar point was made by sociologist Robert Towler who associated what he called 'cognitive styles' with particular patterns of belief as when pinpointing assurance as the cognitive style of the conversionist form of religion (1984: 66).

One aspect of human nature that is deeply involved in theories of human destiny is that of music. As discussed in Chapter 6, music is important for religious studies because human beings not only have the capacity to speak and to enjoy the power of words, but also to sing and to be inspired by the power of music. This must not be taken for granted. In practice, most Christian traditions use music in worship. Though the Greek Orthodox forbid musical instruments in worship they sing or chant the largest part of the Liturgy, and do so with great power. Catholic and Protestant traditions have been even more significant as sources of musical creativity in Europe, and, through missionary work and emigration, also in many other parts of the world.

Doctrinal ideas about God, humanity, life, and death have all been expressed poetically in hymns, and song. Such singing in worship has helped millions to grasp the hope of divine help and to pursue the eternal dimension of life. Sometimes music on its own inspires people to transcend the ordinary levels of daily existence, yet sacred music exists in many forms, from the military style of Salvation Army bands to the mystical chanting of monks. Though, in popular thought, even the angels are said to play harps in heaven, in practical terms music has the effect of uniting people together as a group and of giving a sense of unity to individuals within themselves. This brings us to the question of what makes up a human being.

Human nature: soul and/or body

Two broad kinds of explanation of human nature are found in Christianity. Perhaps the one that has been, and continues to be, dominant divides human beings into body and soul, or into body, soul and spirit, as in 1 Thessalonians 5:23. This internal division has a long pre-Christian history and was widespread in ancient Greek thought. In Plato, for example, the soul is a prisoner within the body set free only by death. Much of this has had an influence on

Christianity. The other tradition, with its roots in Jewish thought, sees people more as a single physical entity. Though in a rather metaphorical way the body may be said to possess the breath of life, human nature remains a physical thing that ceases existence at death. The idea of the resurrection of the body relates to this view, and sees any future life after death as dependent upon a new creation and a definite act of God, rather than upon some immortal soul passing on its way from earth to heaven.

Much modern Christian thinking prefers this unified approach to the individual, and uses it to talk of salvation as wholeness of the entire person rather than as the salvation of the soul. The ethical issue of abortion is, for example, one practical area where this question of what constitutes human nature becomes deeply significant for people. To believe that the soul comes to the growing embryo at some specific point of development, defines human nature in quite different terms from that which emphasizes the ongoing development of the body and its personality through relationships with other people, involving no single moment which stamps the human animal as a human being.

Human nature: society and individual

One final and radically important aspect of defining human nature from a Christian perspective concerns society. From its Jewish background, Christianity took the idea of a community of people existing in a covenant relationship with God and, to this, added the belief that, in Jesus Christ, God had participated in human life and opened the boundaries of the covenant to include all people. The Church was to be seen as a kind of symbol of this total human group linked to God.

One feature of what is called 'theological anthropology', or the doctrine of human nature, is that Christianity sees individuals as members of a group, whether a covenant community, a family, or the Church. While individuals are important, their prime place is within a community. The New Testament idea of a community existing as the 'body of Christ', with everyone linked in to others through the varied gifts, duties and responsibilities of each, is basic to the Christian view of human nature and destiny (Rom 12:4). In theological terms, the social nature of human life is sometimes seen as a reflection of the Holy Trinity as a group of 'persons' interacting with each other. This 'social' model of the Trinity is one way of seeing humanity made in the image of God, with a capacity for relationship with others and, even more than that, a necessity of relationship with others. Following this line of thought, human nature is essentially social, and human destiny lies in developing relationships with other humans and with God.

FAITH, LOVE AND HOPE

It is as the collective body of Christ that Christians live by faith in God and seek to express the love of God to others through their own ethical living. While faith and love express two aspects of life that are intrinsic to Christian values, hope furnishes the third 'theological virtue' characterizing the Christian understanding of human nature (1 Cor 13:13). Hope is grounded in the will and purpose of God for humanity. Together faith, hope and love are opposed to unbelief, despair and egoism, in the total life of Christians.

Destiny's goal

We began this chapter by focusing on creation. We said that Christian wonder at the world's complexity, and at the very fact of its existence, came to centre on the doctrine of creation. In an interesting way this stress on God's act of making the universe draws attention away from God's more immediate nature. This is a rather subtle but important point. The doctrine of creation looks at an empirical and factual world of things; it asks Christians to see God through and behind the creation so that this doctrine comes to be one of the working perspectives of daily Christian life.

We have also seen that the greater part of the Christian tradition asserts that human existence does not end with death. Human destiny is said to come to its true goal in a relationship with God after death. And it is here that a shift of focus takes place, moving away from the doctrine of creation to the nature of God in a more direct way. Instead of revelation through the medium of creation there is a direct knowledge of God. Human destiny shifts from the creation to the creator.

Further reading

Buber, M. (1958) *I and Thou*. Edinburgh: T. & T. Clark.

Cupitt, D. (1979) *The Nature of Man*. London: Sheldon Press.

Dillistone, F. W. (1981) *Religious Experience and Christian Faith*. London: SCM Press.

Tillich, P. (1953) *Systematic Theology*. London: Nisbet.

4. Sacred writings

Christianity, along with other great world religions, especially Islam and Sikhism, has a book – in this case the Bible – close to the centre of its life. As we have seen in Chapter 2, it even shares a large part of these Scriptures with Judaism, for what Christians call the Old Testament the ancient Hebrews and modern Jews have long held as their own Scriptures. To share Scriptures in this way means, amongst other things, that there is a focus for both agreement and disagreement between Christians and Jews, and to an extent with Muslims when it comes to reflect on human nature and destiny as well as on the nature of God.

The Bible has been translated from its original texts into many other languages, and this involves trying to grasp what the original authors meant in their own day, and then seeking to communicate those ideas for other societies. This involves the difficult task of 'cultural translation' running alongside the obvious task of interpreting words, of getting the right degree of fit between the original message and the message for today. Through its missionary ventures Christianity has extensively given itself to this task because of its commitment to translate the Bible into the languages of as many people in the world as it possibly can. The belief that both church leaders and ordinary church members should be able to read the Bible in their own language has motivated both Bible translation and educational programmes teaching people to read in many parts of the world. They believed that knowledge of God could be gained from reading the Bible both publicly in church and also in private worship. The Society for Promoting Christian Knowledge (SPCK), for example, was founded in 1698 to build schools for educational purposes in England and Wales and to distribute Bibles throughout the world.

The issue of interpretation, or hermeneutics, has never been more important than at present because twentieth-century scholars have become more aware than ever of the social and personal factors influencing authors and readers of texts. Also of great importance is the context in which sacred Scriptures serve their purpose, the setting where they come into their own and are perceived as sacred. A Bible on a bookshop shelf may have the title Holy Bible written on it but be viewed as just another book; but once it is placed in a church and read, or used as part of an individual's private devotions, then it comes to be something far more significant. One decision Christian leaders have to take involves balancing accuracy of translating the Bible from its original languages against making it easily understood in the language of the reader. This is especially important for people who are normally unfamiliar with books or whose level of education in reading and literature is low. Even in Britain, for example, some religious organizations use films, videos, slides, and comic-strip papers, to convey the message and stories of the Bible.

Scriptures in context

Christian worship is so closely linked with sacred Scriptures that it is almost impossible to think of any formal Christian service taking place without some use of the Bible. This centrality of the Bible is due to the fact that Christianity stresses its past through the belief that God's self-revelation has occurred within history at particular times and places through religious leaders such as prophets, but most especially through Jesus of Nazareth. The Bible is the central deposit of witness to this divine revelation.

Because Christianity grew out of the Jewish religion of the time of Jesus its first sacred writings were those of Judaism. Not only would most of the first Christians, as Jews, have been familiar with having the sacred Scriptures of their Jewish tradition regularly read in the synagogue, but they would also have been accustomed to those Scriptures being studied and debated, especially by the rabbis. As time went on Christians drew a distinction between the writings of the Jewish religion prior to the life of Jesus and those writings which Christian communities produced for their own purpose. As we said when looking at the birth of the Christian tradition in Chapter 2, the former were not abandoned but came to be called the Old Testament in contrast to the New Testament writings produced by the new Christian leaders. So it is that the Bible known to modern Christians is made up of pre-Christian Jewish material seen as a foundation for the new Christian writings. Getting the actual separate books together into an authorized and accepted collection was neither a simple nor a rapid task. The authoritative list, or Canon of Scripture as it is called, did not take place for the Jewish Scriptures until about the end of the first century of the Christian era. It took nearly four hundred years after the birth of Christ before the emerging Christian Church produced its own definite list including both Old Testament and New Testament sections. This collection came to be called the Bible, from the Greek word *biblia*, meaning books. Subsequent generations of Christians saw the Bible as a special book that was, in some way, inspired by God, and containing truths vital for instruction in living the Christian life, with both Old and New Testaments having their part to play in drawing the picture of divine activity and purpose.

At the heart of Jewish Scriptures for Jews lay the idea of the Torah or divine Law believed to have been given by God through Moses and focused in the Pentateuch or five books of Genesis, Exodus, Leviticus, Numbers, Deuteronomy, which were the first books of the Jewish sacred Scriptures. At the time of Jesus this group of 'Torah' Scriptures – the Law – along with those of 'the Prophets', were clearly identified as sacred Scripture while some other 'Writings' were deemed less authoritative; these included all the other books presently in the Old Testament as used by most Christians, plus Ecclesiasticus, Tobit, and Maccabees, which were later excluded by Jews.

One of the interesting facts of early Christianity is that it relatively quickly produced written documents of its own. Paul, a convert to Christianity from Judaism, who was a highly educated and literate person, saw himself as having been charged by the risen Christ to take the gospel message to the non-Jewish world. This he did by a series of missionary journeys, by preaching and debating not only with fellow Jews but also with Gentiles, the name Jews gave to non-Jews. He later wrote to these new Christian congregations he had helped create and in his letters spelled out his beliefs concerning the significance of Jesus of Nazareth viewed as God's chosen and anointed One or Messiah (or Christ – *christos* in Greek). Christ fulfilled God's promises to the Jews and, through his death and resurrection, also opened up the divine plan of redemption for the Gentile world. The message of Christianity focused on a divine plan of salvation motivated by God's love for mankind, executed through the man Jesus who was believed to be God's Son in some special way, and experienced through the power of the divine Spirit within the company of believers. The very use of the terms Old and New Testament reflects the idea that God has established a relationship of salvation with mankind, since the word 'testament' comes from the Latin word for 'covenant'.

A New Testament sketch

The New Testament is made up of letters, of four gospels, of the account of the Acts of the Apostles and, finally, of the Apocalypse. Of these 27 New Testament documents some 21 are letters. Their authorship varies and the actual author of some of them is disputed or unknown even when an epistle stands under the name of a particular apostle. As to their content, it also varies from clear affirmations of faith and expressions of doctrine to pastoral encouragement and moral instruction. The following selections drawn from each basic type of New Testament document illustrate this variety of early Christianity's self-understanding.

LETTERS

Christians at Corinth

The First Letter to the Corinthians presents a sweep of Christian understanding. Based on the belief that Paul was 'called by the will of God to be an apostle of Christ Jesus' (1:1), whose cross is the power of God for salvation (1:17), it is grounded in the message of 'Jesus Christ and him crucified' (2:2). His hearers are no mere audience but are God's temple where God's Spirit dwells (3:16). But Paul has heard that in this community of the saved there are members living immorally, including an incestuous relationship (5:1). He calls them all to moral living and gives advice about marriage. There is some suggestion in the text that Paul thinks that the period of the Christian Church's existence will be short given the fact that Christ may return to judge and change the way the world is run; given the shortness of the duration of things even those who are married might live as if they were unmarried (9:29). Even so he is concerned that they should know that Christians have a great deal of freedom from a multiplicity of religious regulations because of Christ but they should not use their freedom for selfish ends. So too in connection with idols and non-Christian religions, a Christian may eat food that has been offered to idols because it is of no importance to the believer, but if non-believers see some problem in it then the believer should desist from eating because of the other person's conscience (10:28). This kind of ethical approach to life reflects Paul's view of the universe as an ordered scheme of things from God, through Christ, to men and then to women (11:3–16). The life of the Christian group must also express this sense of order, which is why dissensions and divisions are wrong and why worship should be an orderly affair and not a time of chaos. This is especially true when they meet to break bread together. He emphasizes his status as an apostle in touch with Christ when he tells them that what he received from the Lord he gave to them, that 'the Lord Jesus on the night when he was betrayed took bread, and when he had given thanks, he broke it, and said "This is my body which is broken for you. Do this in remembrance of me"' (11:23). This element of tradition is important for Paul because it links the historical life of Jesus with the present day life of the Christian community: 'You are the body of Christ and individually members of it' (12:27).

Some of the Christians at Corinth possess religious experiences which are publicly significant because they speak in tongues, possess gifts of healing, etc. These expressions of spiritual power must, he says, be put to good use and not cause disunity amongst believers. Indeed the way to live as a member of this community is by the ethic of love. In the famous chapter 13 of the letter Paul tells of the 'more excellent way' of love.

> ... if I have prophetic powers, and understand all mysteries and all knowledge, and if I have all faith, so as to move mountains, but have not love, I am nothing. (13:2–3)

> So faith, hope, and love abide, these three, and the greatest of these is love. (13:13)

Love must be used to build up the Christian community of believers, a community which stands entirely on the basis of the death of Jesus for the sins of the world and his resurrection from the dead. If chapter 13 stands as the prime Christian expression of the ethic of love then chapter 15 is the foundation document for the Christian belief in the resurrection of Christ. We have seen how Paul said that he delivered to the Corinthians what he had received as far as the breaking of bread was concerned (11:23), we now find him saying that he also delivered to them 'as of first importance what I also received, that Christ died for our sins in accordance with the scriptures, that he was buried, that he was raised on the third day ... and that he appeared' (15:3–5). He appeared to Peter, to the Twelve, to five hundred or so others, and finally to Paul himself when he was converted on the road to Damascus, an account of which is given in the Acts of the Apostles (Acts 9:3–9). Paul ends his letter with some practical instructions on his hopes for future journeys and visits and shows how mobile and active were his plans as the apostle to the non-Jewish world of the first-century Mediterranean.

Christians at Rome

The letter to the Romans focuses on the similarity between the faith of Abraham expressing the heart of the Old Covenant and the faith of Christians in the New Covenant. God's deity is known through the created world (1:20) but mankind preferred idolatry to true worship, and idolatry involved immorality. God's wrath is stirred up by this human wickedness, a wickedness which becomes increasingly apparent through the Law of the Old Covenant which portrays God's righteousness at the same time as it shows mankind's sinfulness. All humans stand sinful before God until they are forgiven through having faith in Jesus. Through him peace comes to exist between believers and God, they are 'justified by faith' (5:1). God's initiative lies at the heart of this process of salvation: 'while we were still weak, at the right time, Christ died for the ungodly' (5:6). Paul compares Adam as the first man who sinned and Jesus as the second Adam who did not sin. The letter is full of opposites of this sort, as in arguing that believers were once enemies of God but now are friends, once they lived in sin but now they must live by the Spirit of God. He speaks of the old self which, as it were, has died along with Christ so that the new life of righteousness could begin. Even so the life of faith possesses a certain tension between the old life in the flesh and the new life in the Spirit: the good I want to do I cannot and the evil I do not want to do is exactly what I do (7:19). But God is on the side of such poor creatures and has 'sent his own Son in the likeness of sinful flesh ... to condemn sin in the flesh' (8:3). Even the universe itself groans under the power of evil and awaits a new day when God will transform it (8:22). The Spirit of God helps us in our weakness and by faith believers are convinced that nothing will separate them from God's love (8:39). Paul is sad that the great majority of his fellow Jews do not see that God has acted in Jesus to bring about the New Covenant, but even so he believes God has a plan that is inscrutable for he cannot see that God would ever reject the chosen people of Israel. The thoughts about God's ways bring Paul to poetic worship: 'O the depth of the riches and wisdom and knowledge of God! How unsearchable his judgements and how inscrutable his ways!' (11:33). This sense of God's great goodness draws from the apostle a call to believers to present their own bodies 'as a living sacrifice, holy and acceptable to God' (12:1). They are to be transformed in their thinking rather than conformed to the world, and they must show this in their obedience to human authorities (13:1), just as they do through their humility in welcoming those who are weak in faith (14:1), for 'We who are strong ought to bear with the failings of the weak, and not to please ourselves' (15:1). He ends his letter with various greetings showing how important human relationships were in the communities of early Christians

Romans in Christian history

This letter to the Romans has been of particular significance in practically every phase of the history of Christianity to date because of the way it influenced the spiritual development of several important church leaders and through them millions of others. Augustine, for example, was finally prompted in his conversion to Christianity in 386 CE by reading from the end of chapter 13, 'let us conduct ourselves becomingly as in the day, not in revelling and drunkenness ...' (13:13). So, too, with Martin Luther, whose work was basic to the Reformation. He lectured on Romans between 1515 and 1516, placing great emphasis upon the idea of justification by faith, and on the need for God to act in saving mankind from its wickedness. No amount of human religiosity could yield the kind of faith which leads to a person being justified; God alone can bring this about, as Luther makes clear in saying that:

> A monkey can imitate human actions beautifully but he is not a man because of this. Were he to become a man, this would happen without a doubt not by virtue of the actions by which he emulated man but by virtue of a completely different action, namely, God's. But, being made a man he certainly would perform human actions in the right way. (Rom 3:19–20)

In a similar way a person is justified not because the right actions are performed but because of a divine act which allows a person to believe in a way that matches the operation of divine grace. This idea of justification by faith was a freeing belief for Luther and has continued to be radically important in the life of Protestant Christianity. The best example of its influence came in the conversion of John Wesley on 24 May 1738 when he heard Luther's 'Preface to The Epistle to the Romans' read at a religious meeting in London when, as he put it, his heart was 'strangely warmed'.

In the modern world it was a commentary on Romans that the Swiss pastor and theologian Karl Barth (1886–1968) published in 1919 that triggered a new and creative period of theology. Turning his back on the liberal interpretation of Christianity associated with biblical criticism that had become common in the nineteenth century Barth believed that the transcendent God confronts men and women today through the divine Word present in Jesus, present in Scripture, and present in the preaching of the Christian message. He went on to write a massive study of Christian doctrine entitled *Church Dogmatics* which owes a great deal to biblical influence but which is a systematic and formal discussion of doctrine. His Romans commentary itself reads more like a sermon than a critical analysis of a text; it comes straight at the reader in the way that Barth believed God does address mankind, as is seen in this brief excerpt from his comments on part of chapter 8 and verse 10:

> The body is dead because of sin: but the Spirit is life because of righteousness.
> Christ is our freedom, our advance beyond the frontier of human life, the transfiguration of life's meaning, and the appearance of its new and veritable reality. In Christ is uttered the eternal decision that flesh is flesh, world is world, man is man – because sin is sin; that the existence

of the man of this world ... must become non-existence, must in fact, when it encounters God, die ...

Many other theologians have drawn extensively from the Bible but Romans has continued to stand out as a significant book while New Testament scholars have themselves seen the writing of a commentary on Romans as an important goal expressing their own maturity as a biblical commentator.

As with Romans so with practically every other book in the Bible; they have all attracted the attention of pastors, scholars, and church leaders, who have written commentaries on them. Biblical commentaries are valuable because they help shed light on the meaning of a text, they serve to inspire or encourage the reader in the life of faith, but they also show how scholars, in any generation, approach the Bible. In some Protestant traditions where the Bible itself is the major focus of religious knowledge many commentaries have played an important part both as an extension of sermons and also as a means of helping some ministers prepare their own sermons. John Calvin, for example, wrote extensive commentaries as a quite separate exercise from writing his formal theology, while John Wesley, late in his life (1754), wrote a commentary on the whole New Testament, aimed at 'plain, unlettered men, who understand only their mother-tongue, and yet reverence and love the word of God, and have a desire to save their souls'.

GOSPELS

Despite the fact that many of the letters were probably written earlier than the gospels it is still the gospels which are amongst the best known sacred writings of Christianity. This is probably because they give an account of the life of Jesus in a story form and because the religious teaching in them is often easy to grasp because of the story or parable form in which it is depicted. Stories like that of the Good Samaritan (Luke 10:29–37), who helped someone not of his own natural group who had been attacked and robbed and who had been left unhelped by those of his own background, have made the Christian ideal of service and care quite intelligible. Or, again, the account of the Prodigal Son (Luke 15:11–32) who claims his inheritance, leaves home, wastes his money, comes to ruin before coming to his senses and returns home to be met by his loving father and selfish brother.

There are four gospels. Three of them, namely Matthew, Mark, and Luke, are called synoptic gospels because they take a similar perspective on the life of Jesus and share such significantly large amounts of similar material that they could be organized in matching columns in a kind of 'synopsis'. John's gospel, by contrast, is not so similar and contains many passages, such as chapter 17, which are not in the other gospels and which express very definite and carefully composed theological ideas about the nature of Jesus.

CRITICAL STUDY OF THE GOSPELS AND BIBLE

The gospels have not simply been used as a means of feeding the public and private worship of Christians, they have also come under the scrutiny of biblical scholars. The striking similarities between Matthew, Mark, and Luke attracted detailed study by scholars in the nineteenth and early twentieth centuries who explored the relation-ships between these gospels to see whether, for example, Mark was the earliest gospel subsequently used by Matthew and Luke or whether perhaps some material in Matthew and Luke that is not in Mark might have belonged to an independent source, often called 'Q' and no longer known to us as an independent document. Some examples are the accounts of the temptation of Christ (Luke 4:2–13 and Matt 4:2–11), and some passages referring to John the Baptist (Luke 7:18–23 and Matt 11:2–6). All these questions are sometimes placed together and called the 'Synoptic Problem', constituting part of the total field of biblical analysis and critical scholarship. Other kinds of critical study have followed, concerning themselves with possible early traditions of Christianity from which particular arguments have been born, and also with the sociological conditions surrounding early Christianity.

Two other and rather different sorts of New Testament material are found in the Acts of the Apostles and the Revelation, or Apocalypse, of St John the Divine. They differ from each other quite considerably in that Acts is very much an account of events occurring in the world of everyday life while the Apocalypse is set in the realm of heaven and spiritual powers.

The Acts of the Apostles

The Acts of the Apostles is an interesting book because it is widely thought to have been written by Luke. The gospel of Luke ends with the risen Jesus telling his disciples that they must stay at Jerusalem until they are 'clothed with power from on high' (Luke 24:49), to enable them to be witnesses to the resurrection and to announce the message of repentance and forgiveness. Acts begins with a statement about the resurrection of Jesus and then focuses on the dramatic coming of this power from God:

> And suddenly a sound came from heaven like the rush of a mighty wind, and it filled all the house where they were sitting. And there appeared tongues as of fire ... resting on each one of them. And they were all filled with the Holy Spirit and began to speak in other tongues ... (Acts 2:2–4)

With this dynamic motivation the followers of Jesus begin to preach to Jews and then to non-Jews and move from Jerusalem out across the ancient world of Mediterranean culture. A firm picture is given of the apostle Peter leading the followers of Jesus, as on the day just mentioned when 'Peter standing with the eleven, lifted up his voice and addressed them ... and said repent and be baptized' (Acts 2:14, 38). This call to repentance came after he had outlined an Old Testament prophecy that God would one day pour out his Spirit on all people, proclaimed that God had already raised Jesus from the dead and, through him, had now given this powerful Spirit to mankind who needed to be baptized for the forgiveness of sins.

Acts portrays a community that sensed a deep unity of purpose as they 'devoted themselves to the apostles' teaching and fellowship, to the breaking of bread and the prayers ... and all who believed were together and had all things in common, and they sold their possessions and goods and distributed to all as any had need' (Acts 2:42, 44–46). One story tells of a flaw in this community as a man and wife, Ananias and Sapphira, sell some property and pretend they have given all the proceeds to the apostles while they have really kept part of it back for themselves, and both end up dead as a result of their deceit (Acts 5:1–11). The church community grows rapidly and an increase in organization occurs (Acts 6). Jewish opposition increases and the first martyr, Stephen, is stoned to death (Acts 7), in an event which introduces the figure of Paul to the story. Paul, or Saul as he still is called in his pre-conversion identity, sets out to persecute the Christians with full authority, but amidst his fervent activity he encounters the risen Christ in a vision while on the road to Damascus (Acts 9:1–31). He is radically converted and becomes the central figure for the rest of the Acts of the Apostles, figuring as a late entry to the inner circle of disciples who had known Jesus when he was still alive in his earthly ministry. Paul is the disciple of the resurrected Christ and is called to preach to the Gentile world. The distinction between Jews and Gentiles becomes critical in chapter 15 at the Council at Jerusalem where the apostles gather to discuss whether Gentiles need to observe the Jewish law or whether faith is a state of life that does not depend upon the former pattern of Jewish life. They come out in favour of faith as freeing people from responsibility to live according to Jewish tradition. Paul goes on to travel far and wide in a series of missionary journeys until he finally arrives in Rome as a prisoner for the gospel's sake. His travels provide the opportunity for the writer of Acts to produce sermons, speeches, and legal defences made by Paul in many different contexts all of which spell out many aspects of the Christian faith. A central point is the way in which the message concerning God's salvation, brought about through the risen Jesus, opens the love and forgiveness of God to all people, and not only to Jews. This message creates a new people; indeed, Acts pinpoints the fact in rather concrete terms: 'It was in Antioch that the disciples were first called Christians' (Acts 11:26). Acts ends with a typical speech in which Paul returns to the theme of the Holy Spirit and to the world-wide mission of the Christian Church: 'Let it be known then that this salvation of God has been sent to the Gentiles: they will listen' (Acts 28:28).

Apocalypse

The word 'apocalypse' is the Greek word for revelation, which itself means an unveiling. Apocalyptic literature pulls back the veil to show what will happen in God's plan and in God's own time. Jews were familiar with apocalyptic material from the book of Daniel, written about 170 or so years before the time of Jesus, a time of persecution of the Jews in which they needed encouragement and the belief that all was ultimately in God's hands no matter how bad things appeared to be on earth.

There are numerous apocalyptic books which were not given the status of Scripture by Jews, including the book of *Enoch*, the book of *Jubilees*, and the *Testament of the Twelve Patriarchs*. Against this background it is not surprising to find that one of the books, one that was not finally included in the canon or approved list of New Testament documents until after many of the others, is an apocalypse, Revelation.

This revelation claims to be given by Jesus, 'to show to his servants what must soon take place' (Rev 1:1). It begins in the form of a letter addressed to seven churches calling them to faithfulness despite the problems they are suffering. Then the author speaks of being caught up into heaven where he sees the throne of God and various supernatural beings about it including the 'four living creatures, each of them with six wings, and full of eyes all round and within, and day and night they never cease to sing, "Holy, holy, holy, is the Lord God Almighty, who was and is and is to come"' (Rev 4:8). Basic to these visionary insights is the image of Jesus as the Lamb of God lying at the centre of all God's activities, not least the judgements passed upon evil in the earth and upon Satan (Rev 12:9). The account of God's wrath being poured out on evil is occasionally interrupted with hymns of praise to God and to the Lamb for all these acts of power:

Just art thou in these thy judgements,
... for men have shed the blood of saints
and prophets, and thou hast given them blood
to drink. It is their due. (Rev 16:5–6)

Hallelujah! For the Lord our God
the Almighty reigns.
Let us rejoice and exult and
give him the glory. (Rev 19:6–7)

The Apocalypse ends with the vision of a 'new heaven and a new earth; for the first heaven and the first earth had passed away' (Rev 21:1). This brings a picture of heaven in which flows the river of the water of life, along with the tree of life whose leaves are for the healing of the nations. The ending is an ending of expectation as Jesus tells his followers that he will soon come to them: ' "Surely I am coming soon." Amen. Come, Lord Jesus!' (Rev 22:20).

APOCRYPHAL WRITINGS

Apocalyptic literature which reckons to tell of future things should not be confused with apocryphal literature which deals with 'hidden' (or apocryphal) things. There are numerous documents not included in the Bible which have the form of gospels or of epistles but which were not ultimately included in the Bible as it is known to Christians. Some of these have been discovered only recently as in the case of the *Gospel of Thomas*, which was discovered initially as some papyrus fragments in 1897 but which came into its own with major discoveries of more extensive records in 1945–46 in Egypt. It includes some sayings of Jesus not contained in the Bible such as 'It is not possible for a man to ride two horses, or to draw two bows'.

Authority, interpretation and study of the Bible

The fact that some apocryphal and some apocalyptic literature was not included in the official list of biblical books raises the important question of authority. As the central sacred text of Christianity, the Bible is viewed as authoritative in matters of religion and truth for a variety of reasons which some Christian traditions stress more than others. Protestant traditions emphasize the authority of the Bible because it is believed to have been inspired by God in its production. Those who wrote or composed its constituent parts as a sort of editor are believed to have been guided by God in some way. For these the Bible is sacred because it is the very word of God. Catholic traditions also value the Bible as the record of God's dealings with humanity and because the Church, in the sense of early Christian generations, accepted these writings as from God.

In the fundamentalist stream of Christian life this leads to a belief that there can be no contradictory material in the Bible, and that all should accept and believe what it says in a rather direct way. But those of a more liberal tradition see the Bible as a collection of human documents reflecting upon people's experience and insights about God and the way God works. These argue strongly that the context out of which the gospels, epistles, and other literature came influences what is said to a marked extent. What is then important is the question of interpretation, but interpretation, or hermeneutics as it is sometimes called from the Greek word for a translator – itself derived from the idea of Hermes as the messenger of the gods – is far from being a simple task. At the two ends of the wide spectrum of interpretation the fundamentalist prefers the plain meaning of the text while the liberal goes for a much wider meaning, giving full place to metaphor and analogy.

Another important difference surrounding the interpretation of the Bible concerns the Catholic and Protestant attitudes to the Bible. The Bible was a very important element in the Reformation period in the sixteenth century because Martin Luther and others argued that the teaching of the Bible should take precedence over the teaching of the Catholic Church in defining Christian doctrine. This led to a division between those who see the Bible as supreme in matters of faith and those who see the Church as central. The latter argue that it is Christian teachers, i.e. the Church, who actually interpret the Bible and therefore are ultimately more significant and authoritative. This tradition has grown to the point where the Pope, as the leader of the Catholic Church and as one who is believed to be St Peter's successor, is infallible when speaking officially and authoritatively on matters of doctrine. Protestants, by contrast, tend to argue that Christians sit beneath the words of Scripture and are formed by it, and in this sense it is scripture which is paramount.

The last two hundred years have witnessed an incredible growth in the study of the Bible by linguists, historians and theologians. It is almost certainly the one book that has been studied more than any other in the history of mankind, as is obvious from the thousands of commentaries that have been written on the Bible. Such biblical commentaries are an important source of study for many educated Christian people, especially ministers, priests, and other church leaders. Their very existence shows the importance of the biblical texts as foundation documents of all the Christian churches.

Scholarly opinion often offers its own account of how the biblical documents came together and, for some people, this kind of explanation which focuses on human processes of development has meant a decline in the intrinsic authority of the Bible. Even so, whatever the view taken of how the Bible came together in the first place, all Christian churches and movements use it in worship. This means that for many people, and in practical terms, the Bible carries a great power and is viewed as a sacred text. The proof of the status of the Bible lies in its place in worship and spirituality. This is an important point because it is sometimes easy to think that the proper use of the Bible lies in scholarly and critical study and not in the context of congregational worship and private devotion. But the prime purpose of the Bible was as a religious text and any proper appreciation of it should always bear this in mind. It came into existence to be used for the purposes of faith and not to be the basis for someone's academic career as a biblical or textual scholar. But, having said that, it must be recognized that the growth of the academic analysis of the Bible since the middle of the nineteenth century has led to an immense body of knowledge which forms a subject all of its own quite apart from the role the Bible plays in church life and the life of faith. Even so there is a great overlap between this academic study of the Bible for the sake of knowledge alone and the application of that knowledge within the religious life of church groups. The sacred Scriptures of Christianity exist in this double world of scholarship and piety.

In what is called Biblical Theology some of this knowledge of the structure and content of the Bible is used to construct a pattern of doctrine which describes what is in the Bible and tries to show how it may be applied within the Christian life. This is the task of theologians within the tradition of active church life. Biblical Theology starts with the assumption that the Bible is the vehicle by which God communicates with men and women, and tries to treat it in a way that is appropriate to its nature. Even so, different individuals and groups give different emphases to the text and arrive at varied patterns of belief.

There was a great fear in the nineteenth century that too many scholars wanted to analyse the Bible through the literary and historical factors that had influenced its growth. 'Source Criticism' and 'Form Criticism' were two examples of explanations that focused on the sources from which texts came, and the forms or types of literature into which various passage might be fitted.

Originally starting on the Old Testament, this sort of work extended into the New Testament in the early twentieth century. This form of study was elaborate and sophisticated and was open only to experts. In many ways the ordinary Christian was put at a distance from the Bible. Whereas the Reformation in the sixteenth century had brought the Bible close to ordinary Christians the nineteenth-century growth of critical scholarship took it away again. But there were several responses to this.

One lay in the new form of orthodoxy associated with the Swiss theologian Karl Barth, whose commentary on Romans we have already discussed as a new emphasis upon the dynamic entry of God into the human life. He called for an attitude towards the Bible in which the Bible brought believers to a kind of crisis, a creative judgement in which they came to see how God confronted them through the words of the sacred Scriptures. Three other responses include those of the fundamentalists, which we have already described in general but now need to set in a historical context, and those of Liberation and of Narrative Theology.

Fundamentalism

Academic interest in critical study of the Bible of this kind has not been universally accepted within Christian churches. At the beginning of the twentieth century there was a move on the part of a group of Christians in the USA to affirm very strongly their belief that the Bible was the infallible word of God. In a series of tracts beginning in 1909 some evangelical scholars placed great stress on certain doctrines including the atonement for sin won by Jesus as a substitute for sinners, on the imminent return of Jesus Christ, and on the personal need for salvation and an assurance of salvation. Their belief in the vital importance of the Bible for doctrine and in the inerrancy of the Scriptures were central convictions in what was to be called the Fundamentalist position. Fundamentalists tend to avoid interpretations of Scripture which depend upon ideas of social influence on texts. They speak of the direct and literal meaning of texts and avoid the critical and historical interpretation of the Bible. This way of approaching the Bible is useful for individuals without any extensive theological training since it enables them to see the Bible as the means by which God can communicate with them as individuals in a direct and immediate way in their private study of the Bible. In a similar way it allows preachers to approach the text with a minimum of scholarly intrusion into biblical passages.

Liberation and Narrative Theologies

Some fifty years after the first fundamentalist tracts and Barth's *Romans*, in the 1960s and 1970s, another approach to the Bible followed, alongside the growth of Liberation Theology in Latin America. Liberation theologians argued that ordinary people needed to work out their own beliefs as they lived and worked together along with Christian leaders and thinkers in the process of gaining justice and political freedom. The Bible was a powerful tool in their hands as they saw themselves as a part of the long history of God's people being set free in an oppressive world. As we showed in Chapter 1, Gustavo Gutiérrez's influential book *A Theology of Liberation* (1971) utilized the Bible in providing an understanding of history, justice, faith, and loving God by loving one's neighbour. Another very similar way of using the Bible which has extended this view has been called Narrative Theology; this encourages Christians to use biblical stories about God's dealings with humanity as the framework for their own church groups. In some ways this is a relatively simple task and it may be seen as a way of putting the Bible back into the hands of ordinary Christians so that it can be used for directing the life of faith. Some have seen the late eighteenth and the nineteenth centuries as a period when biblical scholarship became increasingly technical and so scholarly that ordinary people could no longer expect to understand what the Bible was about. Barth's neo-orthodoxy, along with Liberation and Narrative Theologies, have all tended to put the Bible back into the heart of ordinary church life.

Bible and worship

The Bible sits at the heart of congregational worship in Christianity in several ways. In the Liturgy of Orthodox, Catholic, and Protestant churches the Bible is chanted or read as part of the total pattern of the service. In many modern liturgies of major Christian denominations there are likely to be several readings, including one from the

Old Testament, one from the gospels, and one from other New Testament sources, especially the letters.

The emphasis on the importance of the Bible is often made dramatically clear in the reading of the gospel because in churches of a Catholic tradition all the people are likely to stand and face the reader and there may even be a procession of the clergy and others into the centre of the church carrying the Bible as the focus of activity; the priest may even kiss the book as a sign of honour. Instead of being read in an ordinary way the gospel may even be chanted or sung to indicate its special status, one that is greater than the readings from the Old Testament or the letters, which are likely to be read in a more ordinary style.

In churches of the Protestant tradition the authority of the Bible is portrayed through the sermon and the pulpit. The pulpit, from where the sermon is preached, can be located at a physical height above the people to symbolize that God's word of Scripture stands above mankind and comes down to us. Much time and care may be taken in the preparation of the sermon, especially if it takes the form of a biblical exegesis which is an explanation and interpretation of the meaning of the Bible for the congregation. In many Protestant churches the pulpit takes the place that is occupied by the altar in more Catholic churches. This is a dramatic expression of the primacy of the Bible over the Eucharist.

PSALMS IN HYMNS

Perhaps the single most influential part of the Bible as far as worship is concerned is the book of Psalms from the Old Testament. From early days Christians sang the psalms in a continuation of the practice of the Jewish synagogue. As time went on the psalms became especially important in the life of monks and nuns whose day and week composed a special pattern of worship. In the *Rule of St Benedict* all 150 psalms were divided throughout these services in such a way that all of them would be covered in the space of a week. In some churches the 150 psalms are collected into a separate book called a Psalter and are specially marked, or pointed as it is called, to make it easier for them to be sung. After the Reformation in the sixteenth century, when there was a great decline in the religious life of monastic houses, the psalms became more widespread in their use as lay people began to take them up. Metrical forms of the psalms were prepared in the sixteenth century to make the psalm into a patterned form that was easier to sing, and so it came to be a kind of hymn. They were widely used in this form by some of the churches of the Protestant Reformation, especially by John Calvin's church in Geneva from where the influence of metrical psalm-singing spread to Reformed churches in England, Holland, and Scotland. The increased popularity of psalm-singing that developed in English parish churches in the seventeenth century still has something of a presence at the parish level but in the twentieth century it is in cathedrals of the Anglican Church, especially in the Church of England, that psalm-singing has been developed into a distinctive musical form traditionally following a pattern which sings through all 150 psalms at Morning and Evening Prayer service during the course of each month.

It is probably also true that many Christians find the psalms of real benefit in their private prayer and devotion because they represent a wide range of human emotion and religious experience. Christians also tend to interpret them in the light of Jesus and his ministry which means that some psalms come to have a different significance from that of their Jewish context. The beginning of Psalm 22 offers a good example: 'My God, my God, look upon me; why hast thou forsaken me: and art so far from my health, and from the words of my complaint?' For a Christian these words, and much else in the same psalm, are likely to be read as a commentary on the passion and death of Jesus precisely because, in the gospels (Mark 15:34; Matt 27:46), these words are said to have been used by Jesus as he died on the cross. Later verses (17, 18) of the same psalm reinforce this Jesus-focus in its use: 'They pierced my hands and my feet; I may tell all my bones: they stand staring and looking upon me. They part my garments among them: and cast lots upon my vesture.'

Hymns as general songs for lay people to sing probably began in about the thirteenth century but it was from the sixteenth century on, with the birth of the Reformation, that hymn writing and hymn singing became a fundamentally more central part of Christian worship and life. The Methodist Revival in Britain in the eighteenth century marked a vitally important change as hymns, alongside sermons, became a central means of expressing doctrine and faith. Developing from metrical psalm-singing, hymns expressed the doctrines of new religious outlooks in language that could be deeply biblical but could also use non-biblical expressions to great effect.

Many hymns took biblical ideas and presented them for use in this new form of popular worship; this was especially true in the nineteenth century, which was the century when hymns fully entered the life of the great majority of churches in Britain, as we show in a different context in Chapter 6.

It is very nearly possible to find hymns enshrining texts or stories drawn from every part of the Bible as this brief list of biblical texts and the hymns based on them shows:

Genesis 1:3: 'God said, "Let there be light": and there was light.'

> Thou whose almighty word,
> Chaos and Darkness heard,
> And took their flight;
> Hear us we humbly pray,
> And where the gospel-day
> Sheds not its glorious ray
> Let there be light.

Exodus 23:19: 'The first fruits of your land you shall bring into the house of the Lord your God.'

> Fair waved the golden corn
> In Canaan's pleasant land ...
> Like Israel, Lord, we give,
> Our earliest fruits to Thee,
> And pray that, long as we shall live,
> We may Thy children be.

1 Samuel 3:9: 'If He calls you you shall say, "Speak Lord for your servant hears."'

> Hushed was the evening hymn,
> The temple doors were dark;
> The lamp was burning dim,
> Before the sacred ark;
> When suddenly a voice divine
> Rang through the silence of the shrine.

Isaiah 49:15: 'Can a woman forget her sucking child.'

> Hark my soul it is the Lord ...
> Can a woman's tender care,

Cease towards the child she bare?
Yes, she may forgetful be,
Yet will I remember thee.

Matthew 3:1: 'John the Baptist preached.'

On Jordan's bank the Baptist's cry
Announces that the Lord is nigh.

Romans 8:35: 'Who shall separate us from the love of Christ?'

The saviour died, but rose again,
Triumphant from the grave ...
Nor death nor life, nor earth nor hell,
Nor time's destroying sway,
Can e'er efface us from His heart,
Or make His love decay.

But, although many parts of the Bible have served as a basis for hymns, none can overtake the psalms in popularity or frequency of use. They stand out as the bedrock of Christian hymnody as this short list of hymns indicates:

The Lord's my Shepherd, I'll not want	(23:1)
Lift up your heads, ye mighty gates	(24:7)
As pants the hart for cooling streams	(42:2)
A safe stronghold our God is still	(46:1)
O God our help in ages past	(90:1)
O worship the Lord in the beauty of holiness	(96:9)
Unto the hills around do I lift up	(121:2)

Although the Bible has been a major source of inspiration for hymns and for the worship and doctrine of the mainstream Christian churches, and in that sense has helped unite Christians in worship, it has also been the cause of disagreement amongst Christians on points of doctrine. This is one of the problems of written texts as they come to have a life of their own, often separated from their original context, and certainly made to apply to later and very different situations.

Bible for all

The Reformation of the sixteenth century brought the Bible out from the control of priests and scholarly church leadership and made it widely available for ordinary men and women to read. As time went on the consequences of this shift were dramatically significant. Not only could ordinary church members study the Bible as part of their own religious devotion, but they could also question its meaning. More than this, the Bible sometimes seemed to impress particular individuals with a religious message that differed from that of the traditionally established churches. Believed to be sacred Scriptures, the Bible gave to some creative, yet often relatively uneducated, people ideas that were new and exciting.

Sometimes these ideas grew and developed and formed the basis for a new religious movement. This was especially the case with parts of the Bible that were not immediately intelligible and seemed mysterious in some way. The books of Ezekiel, Daniel, and Revelation, for example, have all been interpreted in distinctive ways by groups believing the end of the world to be near. Both the eighteenth and nineteenth centuries were periods when many such millennial movements were born. These groups read with interest those passages that spoke of Christ returning to earth and setting up a divine Kingdom.

It has often been the case that leaders of new religious movements have interpreted the Bible in ways that diverged quite dramatically from established patterns. Such people often believe that they have been given special gifts from God enabling them to interpret Scriptures in a true way that is hidden from recognized church leaders. One major example focusing on the Mormons will show how important the Bible has been as a pattern of divine revelation and source of authority.

The case of Mormon churches offers an important insight into the power of sacred Scriptures in moulding religious life. Joseph Smith, who founded the Church of Jesus Christ of Latter-day Saints in 1830, believed God had granted him access to a written history of early American civilizations that had initially originated in the Holy Land. He was given power to translate this and published it as *The Book of Mormon*. Divided into named books of particular prophets, very much like the Old Testament, and also into chapters and verses just like the Bible, it contains many answers to religious issues current at the time of Joseph Smith. Instead of engaging in debates over points of doctrine and rites such as infant baptism, early Mormons could use *The Book of Mormon* for an authoritative judgement. So it was that Mormons came to view this book as an additional witness to the Bible and to use it as a source of religious teaching and spiritual fulfilment. In all practical terms this is also a sacred text and of great significance in ordinary Mormon life. This shows how the idea of a sacred text can be extended to embrace other scriptures and to impart a sacred character to them.

Another branch of the overall Mormon Restoration movement is called the Reorganized Church of Jesus Christ of Latter Day Saints which is not based in Utah and is led by a descendant of the prophet Joseph Smith. It also uses *The Inspired Version* of the Bible which Joseph Smith is believed to have partly translated from the King James Version of the Bible by special divine power which enabled faults and errors that had crept into earlier translations to be rectified. A further volume of writings used by both the Utah Church and the Reorganized Church is *The Doctrine and Covenants*, containing what are believed to be revelations given to the prophet by God. A distinctive difference between the Utah Church and the Reorganized Mormon Church lies in the fact that while the Utah version contains only early prophecies, the Reorganized Church adds to its *Doctrine and Covenants* each year new revelations that come to their living prophet. Here again is another kind of sacred writing believed to have divine authority.

Many other groups have highly valued key books or, as in the case of the Jehovah's Witnesses, their own version of the Bible. So, for example, Mary Baker Eddy (1821–1910), who founded the Christian Science Church in the 1870s and 1880s in New England, produced *Science and Health with Key to the Scriptures* as an explanation of the Bible as she understood it in relation to healing through a process of thought which she called mental healing. In this case, as in that of the Mormons and numerous other groups with a strong Protestant cultural background, the idea of an authoritative book is very powerful.

Translations of the Bible

The great majority of the writings now in the Old Testament were originally written in Hebrew, but several centuries BCE these Hebrew scriptures were translated into Greek for the use of many Jews in the largely Greek-speaking Mediterranean world. This translation is called the Septuagint (often shortened to LXX) because of a tradition that it was written by 72 translators. It was this version of the ancient Jewish Scriptures that the early Christian Church possessed. The LXX had added to it some books not in the Hebrew scriptures; these form the Apocrypha in the English Bible.

Numerous, though not all, of those authors whose epistles and gospels would come to form the New Testament used the LXX when quoting from the 'Old Testament'. Very occasionally this led to slight shifts of meaning, as in Matthew 1:23 which quotes from Isaiah 7:14. Christians are familiar with the words 'a virgin will conceive and bear a son', a translation that came about because the LXX used the Greek word for 'virgin' to translate a Hebrew word for a young woman of marriageable age. The Hebrew in Isaiah does not intend any idea of a miraculous virgin birth, but early Christians interpreted the birth of Jesus in the light of their knowledge of the Greek Septuagint text which did say 'virgin'. Many of the early Church Fathers used the LXX as their standard Old Testament reference book. The first printed editions of the complete text were published between 1514 and 1517.

A Latin version of the Bible, commonly called the Vulgate, was produced by Jerome during the late fourth and very early fifth century. Jerome came to see the superiority of the Hebrew texts of the 'Old Testament' and increasingly worked from them rather than from the Greek Septuagint. The first actually printed edition was not published until 1456 and is called the Gutenberg Bible.

These dates of publication of the Septuagint and Vulgate translations of the Bible mark the beginning of European printing in the fifteenth and sixteenth centuries. The invention of the printing press coinciding with the emergence of the Reformation marked a dramatic change in European communication and debate. The Reformers wanted people to possess the Bible in their own language. This led Luther in the early sixteenth century to translate the Bible into German and to set a new trend in a more modern style of German language.

William Tyndale published an English New Testament in Germany in 1526, and a complete English Bible was published by Miles Coverdale in 1585 in England. William Caxton had had a printing press set up at Westminster in London from 1477 but religious and political aspects of the Reformation often led to Protestant material being published on the Continent before appearing in Britain. It was, for example, in a New Testament published in English in Geneva in 1557 that the text was first divided into verses. Perhaps the best known of all English Bible translations is that of the Authorised Version, prepared under the authority of King James I and VI and published in 1611. It became all the better known because this was the version used as the basis for all the readings from the epistles and gospels in the Book of Common Prayer of 1662. This is a very good example of Bible translation, in a language understood by the general population, being combined with a book of worship intended for all the people of a nation. Interestingly the psalms in that Prayer Book were kept in the Coverdale translation.

With the growth of scholarship and biblical knowledge over the eighteenth and especially in the nineteenth century it was inevitable that new translations should be sought. The Revised Version was one important outcome of that desire, and represented the work of some of the greatest of English biblical scholars of the nineteenth century; the New Testament section was published in 1881 and the Old Testament in 1885. Numerous other translations have followed in the twentieth century including the American Revised Standard Version, and the British New English Bible, which aim at a direct yet more conservative style of language, unlike Today's English Version or the Good News version which uses language of an even more vernacular style. All these translations demonstrate Christianity's conviction that the Bible is a vital component in understanding God and that the life of faith is intimately connected with its sacred Scriptures.

Further reading

Barr, J. (1973) *The Bible in the Modern World*. London: SCM Press.

Barr, J. (1981) *Fundamentalism*. London: SCM Press.

Coggins, R. J. and J. L. Houlden (eds) (1990) *A Dictionary of Biblical Interpretation*. London: SCM Press.

Rogerson, J. W., C. Rowland and B. Lindars (1988) *The Study and Use of the Bible*. Basingstoke: Marshall Pickering.

5. Sacred place

Christians have many sorts of sacred places including cities, geographical territories, and churches which they regard as deeply significant. Some of these are pilgrimage centres, places where miracles are believed to have happened. Most are actual geographical locations as with Jerusalem, Rome, or the local church but some, like heaven, belong to the realm of belief, imagination, and hope. It is very easy to discuss sacred places that can be located on ancient or modern maps, but it is much more difficult to talk about those 'places' that are often described as though they exist in a physical way but which belong essentially to the world of faith and certainly cannot be visited today. The Garden of Eden and heaven might be two obvious examples.

When Christians talk about these 'places' they use language in a special way, often without realizing it. This can be a problem because it touches the way different Christians interpret the Bible and talk about their faith. The major difference is between those who hold a literal interpretation of the Bible and those who bring to the text various other means of interpreting it and who, for example, are happy to see parts of the Bible as poetic, metaphorical, or theological expressions of belief.

This is not a particularly new problem in Christianity since Augustine in the early fifth century CE devoted chapter 21 of Book 13 of his remarkable work *The City of God* to the question of whether the Garden of Eden stories in Genesis should be interpreted in allegorical terms to refer to 'spiritual meanings' or in a more literal sense to refer to a real place. He concluded that it was perfectly proper to use the stories to derive additional meanings 'provided that the history of the true and local ... paradise ... be firmly believed'. Augustine was happy with the idea that Eden could represent the bliss of the saints or could stand for the Church itself, or that the four rivers flowing from Eden could be seen as the four gospels, but whatever else was said he believed that Eden was an actual place where actual people lived. For him Eden lay at the heart of human history and the dealings of God with humankind. Some modern-day Christians would agree with him, but many other believers, who accept the modern world-view grounded in evolution, read the Genesis stories as theological truths about God and humanity rather than as literal accounts of human origins.

Jerusalem and Babylon

One of the best examples of this literal and metaphorical interpretation of sacred places focuses on Jerusalem, a city which makes its appearance in the Bible as the capital of Judah, and the site of the Temple or holy place of the Jews. As such it plays a vitally important part in the history underlying the Old Testament and the account of God leading the Jews into the land divinely promised to them. In the sixth century BCE it was overcome and many of its citizens were deported to Babylon. Psalm 137 expresses the hopelessness of the exiles in Babylon:

> By the waters of Babylon we sat down and wept,
>   when we remembered thee, O Zion.
> They that led us away captive required of us a song,
>   and melody in our heaviness, saying,
> Sing us one of the songs of Zion.

They find themselves quite dispirited as they ask 'How shall we sing the Lord's song in a strange land?' In this poignant question Babylon symbolizes alienation from the sacred place of Jerusalem or Zion. After the exile Jerusalem was rebuilt with its second Temple which served as an important centre for worship and a focus of Israel's identity. Yet further political disaster led to this temple being profaned in the second century BCE. The third Temple was established only in the generation before Jesus and plays a significant part in the New Testament accounts of his life. This Temple, in its turn, was destroyed by the Romans in 70 CE, an event which marked the end of any centralized Jewish sacrificial worship. Although these temples were interpreted by the Jews in terms of their faith as important sacred places for the worship of God they all actually existed in a physical location. To this very day Jews in Jerusalem regard the 'Wailing Wall' as part of the remains of Solomon's Temple, and it serves as a sacred place for prayer and lamentation over the downfall of Israel's temples.

This site of the last Jewish Temple is now partly covered by the Dome of the Rock, a sacred place for Muslims who believe that it covers the rock from which Muhammad ascended to heaven. This kind of interpretation shows how places come to play an important part in the practical life of religions even if beliefs associated with them cannot be proved historically or even in terms of the actual world in which we live. The idea of a heavenly Jerusalem in Christian thought offers a dramatic example of the way an actual place comes to function symbolically as an expression of faith and hope.

Heavenly Jerusalem and heaven

In the book of Revelation, placed at the very end of the New Testament, there is a vision of 'a new heaven and a new earth', and of 'the holy city, new Jerusalem, coming down from God out of heaven' (Rev 21:1–2). This image united together two features of Old Testament thought. The one spoke of the sky as heaven (Gen 1:8), and also as the abode of God (Eccles 5:2), while the other depicted Jerusalem as the earthly city where God dwelt in some symbolic way.

By the first century CE heaven is widely seen as the place where God reigns and the faithful find their ultimate life (Matt 5:12). Numerous other references occur in the New Testament (e.g. 2 Cor 12:2–4), and are perhaps best summarized in the very opening words of the Lord's Prayer as presented in Matthew's gospel: 'Our Father who art in heaven' (Matt 6:9).

The link between the Christian idea of heaven and the image of Jerusalem is one of the strongest marks of the fact that Christianity emerged out of Judaism. It was developed by later Christians to the point where heaven came to be viewed as the actual place into which people passed after death. This belief is enshrined in many Christian liturgies, hymns, and prayers.

The biblical image of the descent of Jerusalem from heaven was, for example, taken by Bernard of Cluny in the twelfth century as the basis for his hymn 'Jerusalem the golden'. For him the heavenly Jerusalem – with milk and honey blessed – reflects the promised land of the Old Testament. He speaks of 'those halls of Zion, all jubilant with song', of 'the throne of David' surrounded by a triumphant 'martyr throng' of Christians who have 'conquered in the fight'. Christ is there as their Prince, surrounded by 'many an angel', while the daylight is serene and the 'pastures of the blessed are decked in glorious sheen'. Bernard ends his hymn with a prayer which says much about a type of popular Christian piety that probably extends from the days of the first disciples to the present:

O sweet and blessed country,
The home of God's elect!
O sweet and blessed country,
That eager hearts expect!
Jesus, in mercy bring us
To that dear land of rest:
Who art with God the Father,
And Spirit ever blest.

Very similar thoughts come from Thomas à Kempis in the fifteenth century who is reckoned to have written 'Light's abode, celestial Salem'. This hymn speaks of heavenly Jerusalem as an image which serves as a vision that brings peace to the believer. It is a place of unending worship, as befits the dwelling of God, and in it the human body will ultimately be transformed:

O how glorious and resplendent,
Fragile body, shalt thou be,
When endued with so much beauty,
Full of health, and strong and free,
Full of vigour, full of pleasure,
That shall last eternally!

This hymn, like many other hymns of heaven, can help believers think about themselves by providing a framework for reflecting upon contemporary experience and giving life a sense of direction. At certain periods in the history of Christian movements, especially during times of evangelism and revival, the idea of heaven as a real

123

place seems to become increasingly important to people. This was true in many parts of Britain and America during the later nineteenth and early twentieth centuries. *Sacred Songs and Solos* was one famous hymnbook that grew out of that period of largely Protestant evangelism and was used by many different Christian denominations. Of its approximately 1200 hymns more than a hundred are devoted to the idea of heaven and to a heavenly life after death. The general outlook of many such hymns is expressed in one that runs 'There's a land that is fairer than day, And by faith we can see it afar, For the Father waits over the way, To prepare us a dwelling place there'. A chorus takes up this hope in the repeated refrain, 'In the sweet by and by, We shall meet on that beautiful shore'. Many of these hymns contrast the hardship and pain of life on earth with the joy and pleasure of heaven in quite a literal way.

Heaven on earth

It is quite easy to see these hymns as examples of a heavenly reward following earthly hardship or, as the popular expression puts it, as 'pie in the sky when you die'. It is probably true that many Christians and converts who have sung these hymns with gusto have had relatively low standards of living. What is interesting is that heaven as a future place is practically ignored in the Charismatic form of evangelism that emerged in many parts of Britain and the USA from the 1960s onwards, and which involved a kind of religious revivalism amongst people of relatively high standards of living. In *Songs and Hymns of Fellowship*, published from the late 1980s and much used by enthusiastic Christian groups, practically none of its 600 items deals with heaven as a place. Instead tremendous emphasis is placed upon today's experience of God and the powerful presence of the Holy Spirit.

Another historical period, that of the Industrial Revolution in Britain, illustrates a similar yet slightly different attitude towards the idea of Jerusalem as God's special city. During the period of approximately 1750–1850 Britain shifted from being a largely agricultural to an industrial society. There were many consequences of this and one of them involved uncertainty and fear resulting from rapid change in customs and social habits. The change of the century in 1800 was one trigger to some people's imagination and caused them to wonder if it heralded some portentous event such as the Second Coming of Christ and his thousand-year reign on earth as part of the establishing of the kingdom of God. These millennial movements often took the idea of a new Jerusalem as a dominant theological motif. At just this time, in 1804, William Blake published his poem *Milton* which includes the section entitled 'Jerusalem'. This was, much later, set to music by Hubert Parry and has come to be one of the best known of all English songs, ending with the strident affirmation:

> I will not cease from mental fight,
> Nor shall my sword sleep in my hand
> Till we have built Jerusalem
> In England's green and pleasant land.

Here the Jerusalem of the Old Testament combines with the Jerusalem of Christian hope to fire and motivate an attitude to the land and society of England. Blake sets Jerusalem against the image of the 'dark Satanic Mills' of the Industrial Revolution and in doing so he echoes a recurrent theme in Christian thought about the world as a sacred place. The issue focuses on contradiction between the belief that God is perfect, powerful, and responsible for creating this universe and the actual human experience of life as flawed and problematic. The world is both wonderful and terrible. It is aweful in the two senses of the word, it both strikes terror into us and draws our profound admiration. To explore this theme of the dividedness of the world we turn to the accounts of creation in Genesis.

THE GARDEN OF EDEN

The myths of creation presented in the first book of the Bible (Gen 1:1 – 2:3, and 2:4bff.) raise many themes founded on the basic belief that God made the universe and everything in it. God is said to have looked upon all that he had made and saw that it was good (Gen 1:31), but this picture of perfection, of the whole world as a sacred place, is soon fractured and flawed through human disobedience. As discussed in Chapter 3, this act of human wickedness is often called the Fall, and is depicted in Genesis as having both moral and physical consequences for humanity. The mythical figures of Adam

125

and Eve become ashamed of themselves before God (Gen 3:10). Eve is told that she will have pain in bearing children (Gen 3:16), and Adam is similarly told that only through the sweat of his labour will the ground yield any harvest. God curses the very ground because Adam disobeyed the divine command not to eat from the forbidden tree growing in the Garden of Eden (Gen 2:15–17).

The Genesis story of Adam and Eve soon comes to a critical climax as the guilty pair are thrown out from this place of perfection which now comes to be protected by the heavenly creatures, the cherubim, and by a similarly supernatural flaming sword which guards the way to the tree of life (Gen 3:24). All these features, events and characters are described in strongly mythical language and spell out the fact that God is responsible for the creation of the universe, that God is the source of commands that must be obeyed, and that humanity is imperfect and responsible for imperfection.

THE PROMISED LAND

The book of Genesis continues its stories of Adam and Eve after their expulsion from Eden; the great flood is one episode through which God condemns evil. But God also establishes a covenant with certain chosen individuals, and with Abraham in particular God establishes a covenant and promises to give him and his descendants a land as their home and inheritance (Gen 12). As the narratives of the biblical story progress the descendants of Abraham come to feature as those who inhabit their promised land, who go into captivity in Egypt, who leave in a great exodus and wander as pilgrims in the desert before settling fully in their promised land. That land of Canaan comes to be viewed in some way as a sacred place.

Christianity, emerging as it did from Judaism, and inheriting the Jewish Scriptures, also inherited these images of divine covenant and promise. But in the process of time these motifs of faith were elaborated and developed into more abstract ideas. The promised land of the Jewish people is transformed through metaphor to become an image of heaven. Life on earth is taken to be a pilgrimage through a wilderness to the promised land of life after heaven.

One of the hymns to emerge from the creative work of William Williams in Welsh Christianity in the eighteenth century is entirely grounded in this image of pilgrimage to heaven as the promised land. 'Guide me O Thou great Jehovah, pilgrim through this barren land' pray the worshippers who acknowledge themselves to be weak and in need of God's powerful hand. The images of the Old Testament are then brought into play. The fire and cloudy pillar that led the Israelites through the wilderness (Exod 13:21), and the supernatural rock that was the source of water, these must now succour the believer, as must the 'bread of heaven' or the manna that God provided (Exod 16:15). The hymn-writer then uses the image of the river Jordan to symbolize death and asks that God will calm him, 'bid my anxious fear subside', and bring him safe to heaven, 'land me safe on Canaan's side'. This hymn typifies the Christian experience of life as transitory, as a pilgrimage, as a movement to heaven and to God. In the New Testament this is most clearly expressed in the Letter to the Hebrews where many of the themes we have already considered are closely linked.

The writer of Hebrews roots Christian understanding deep in the Old Testament, painting a picture of Abraham and Sarah as journeying to the land of God's promise but dying before they had attained the final goal, a goal which Hebrews sees as heaven itself, a better country which is itself symbolized by the heavenly city (Heb 11:16). In one verse Hebrews unites these images, as Christians are encouraged and exhorted in their faith because 'you are come to mount Zion, to the city of the living God, the heavenly Jerusalem' (Heb 12:22).

In all these texts and hymns there is a kind of supernatural geography, a territory of faith, in which believers see themselves depicted as part of the great community of believers down the years all moving towards God's final sacred place. But on the way they encounter and are encouraged by actual and local sacred places which help them to their goal. But what are sacred places in Christianity? How did they originate? What purposes do they serve? In answering these questions we also explore the rich diversity of Christian ideas of the sacred in sacred places.

Holy people and sacred places

The first three hundred years of Christian history were marked by sporadic persecutions which resulted in the deaths of many individuals who were regarded as martyrs. Their tombs were held by the faithful to be places of special significance and even of religious power. The anniversary of a martyr's death was often celebrated at the tomb as a kind of 'heavenly birthday'. A *martyrium* was a special building set up as a shrine for the site of death or for the body of a martyr; they often resembled the mausoleums which pagans built to honour their dead. It was only after Christianity became the official religion of the Roman Empire in the early fourth century under the authority of Constantine that believers were able to express and practise their religion in a more public way. This included an increased access to martyrs' tombs. In later centuries they would become important for pilgrimages.

RELICS

What made these sites especially significant were the actual physical remains of a martyr's body. These relics were often treasured as the central possession of a church and marked, in some physical way, the continuity of the faithful with those who had given their lives for their faith in Christ. At the level of popular religion these relics were often reckoned to possess special powers which could, for example, heal people. In twelfth-century Europe relics played an increasingly important part in popular religious life; indeed it was the century of relics, many important churches kept lists of the relics they owned and which they obtained either as gifts or through exchange with other churches. These relics not only reckoned to include pieces of the bodies of martyrs but embraced an extremely wide variety of things including, for example, 'Our Lord's shoe, his swaddling clothes, blood and water from his side, bread from the feeding of the five thousand and the Last Supper ... the rods of Moses and Aaron, relics of St. John the Baptist' (Bethell, 1972: 67).

While some relics of saints and martyrs may have been genuine it is probable that very many were not. But genuine or not the relic could serve as a concrete expression of the faith of past believers and as a focus for the faith of the living. This tradition became particularly important in the Roman Catholic Church where until the present day it became customary for every new altar to have a martyr's relic within it. It even became customary for the priest to begin the Eucharist with an acknowledgement of the relic's presence by kissing the altar. The importance of relics to the faith of the twelfth century was linked with the fact that the Crusades led to many relics being brought back to Western Europe.

Relics are widely significant in the Greek Orthodox tradition. So, for example, a special cloth containing a relic in one of its corners is placed on new altars as part of the total process of consecrating a church. Relics in general play an important part in Orthodox life and in some ways function like an icon, as a medium through which a saint or other sacred person may influence the living in some benficial way. The Second Council of Nicaea held in 787 established the importance of icons and pronounced an anathema, a denunciation or formal curse, on anyone who denied the significance of relics. That council made relics necessary for the consecration of a church. So a Christian sacred place was intimately associated with sacred persons through their relics.

Relics still play a part in many religious and social activities in Orthodox and Catholic contexts. St Spyridon, for example, died in the middle of the fourth century CE. He is said to have suffered and survived the persecution of the Roman Emperor Diocletian and to have taken part in early Christian councils. Various miracles were also associated with him including the delivery of the island of Corfu from its enemies. His whole body is now kept as a relic on Corfu and on the Saturday before Easter Day it is carried around the streets of the city in a religious procession before being returned to the church where it normally remains. Thousands queue to kiss the feet of St Spyridon and to gain the benefit of so doing.

SACRED PLACES FOR BURIAL

Churches built over the martyred remains of the faithful served as points of attraction for Christians, not least as far as their own burial was concerned. It became desirable to be buried near to a saint or a relic for a variety of reasons, including the hope of gaining some sort of protection from them. To cope with the increased demand many churches were expanded in size to accommodate the burial of larger numbers of Christians within their walls. As time went on churchyards and cemeteries immediately outside the church building took on the nature of sacred places for the burial of the dead.

The idea of consecrating ground specifically for the burial of the faithful emerged from the original desire to be buried near to a saint or relic whose very remains consecrated an area. Indeed the first formal ritual for consecrating a church as a church, apart from the earliest practice of simply holding a eucharistic service there, came with the bringing of a relic to place in the new altar of a church. By the eighth and ninth centuries this pattern was established and in many respects it is based on the model of a burial. The symbolic 'burial' of a relic in the altar established the church as a sacred place for Christian worship, and for the subsequent burial of Christian people.

One of the most interesting examples of death in relation to sacred places is currently found in British crematoria. Crematoria have only become popular in Britain since the 1960s so that by the 1990s approximately 70 per cent of dead people are cremated. The crematoria themselves are not built, owned, or run by the churches but largely by local authorities. Still, funeral services are conducted in them, usually by ministers of religion, and research shows that increasing numbers of people say that they think crematoria are sacred places. This sense of sacredness seems to be associated with the dead and the rites performed for them. As individuals gain experience of crematoria by attending funerals at them so they regard them increasingly as sacred places. In some respects this resembles the early Christian experience of building churches over the tombs of the celebrated dead.

HOLY RITES MAKE SACRED PLACES

Baptisteries provide another example of sacred space to emerge very early in Christian history. Baptism was the major ritual for entering the Christian religion and was interpreted as a form of death to an individual's old way of life and entry to the new life of faith. The octagonal architectural form of baptisteries in the fourth and fifth centuries often followed that of a mausoleum and this was often intentional, as in St Ambrose's fourth-century church in Milan. Symbolically speaking, this was because the baptistery, as a place of spiritual rebirth, was also a place of death to the old nature.

Ritual often works in a way that adds many layers of meaning to objects used, to actions performed, and to the places where rites take place. The architectural significance of the baptistery as a form of grave is repeated in the water of baptism as representing the waters of the Red Sea through which God's chosen people were delivered from captivity, just as they are waters of cleansing, and waters of birth. For Christians the underlying significance both of baptism and of death lay in the death and resurrection of Jesus Christ. In theological terms the font of baptism represented death because it stood for the death which Christ had undergone just as it also represented the tomb from which he rose from the dead.

Just as baptism unites believers with the death and resurrection of Jesus, so burial associates them with his death in anticipation of their resurrection on the pattern of his rising again to life. This demonstrates the important theological point that in Christianity sacred space is predominantly Christ-focused.

MIRACLES MAKE SACRED PLACES

Some places become sacred because it is believed that something miraculous took place there, as with the Holy Land, given that name because Jesus was born and lived there. Several important holy sites in Europe resulted from appearances of the Virgin Mary in visions to the faithful.

One of the best known is Lourdes in southern France. There the Blessed Virgin is believed to have appeared to a young peasant girl, Bernadette Soubirous, in 1858. In fact there were some eighteen appearances in all, lasting over a period of five months. When the girl asked the apparition who she was the Virgin identified herself as the 'Immaculate Conception'. Some of the faithful interpret this title as rather miraculous in itself since it was only four years earlier that the Pope, Pius IX, had formally announced the doctrine of the Immaculate Conception of the Blessed Virgin Mary, a doctrine that some think would hardly have been known to a poor miller's daughter in rural France.

Whatever was the case, the girl believed that she was commanded to build a church, and that the Virgin's appearance was marked by a miracle in the form of a spring of water. After a difficult period when she was, inevitably, questioned about all these beliefs, Bernadette's claims were widely accepted, so much so that Lourdes has become a major sacred place where many come for healing to the waters of that miraculously occurring spring. The Roman Catholic Church authorities also accepted the account of the visitation by canonizing Bernadette in 1933.

Pilgrimage and sacred places

Today many thousands of people travel to Lourdes each year as pilgrims. As we have already said, one major reason for so doing is in the hope of being healed from physical complaints through the miraculous waters. But for many of those who are not healed other benefits are obtained, not least a sense of an increase or strengthening of faith. And, when people travel in groups, they also often sense a depth of unity with one another.

The desire to visit sacred places involves many reasons and touches deep desires in human life and religion. One important dimension in the pilgrimages of Catholic religion lies in the belief that merit can be gained through pilgrimage. The hardship of the journey along with the devotion shown in the worship at shrines along the way and at the final pilgrimage centre all bring merit to the individual. And this merit can be set against their load of sin as far as the final judgement is concerned, an idea fostered in medieval Catholic life because pilgrims were able to procure indulgences from the Pope in respect of their pilgrimage. Various sacred sites were ranked in order of priority according to the merit gained from them. So, for example, two visits to St David's in Pembrokeshire in Wales were equal to one visit to Rome. Other major sacred sites of European pilgrimage included Canterbury where the Archbishop Thomas Becket was murdered in 1170 after being in confrontation with King Henry II. Many miracles were recorded in relation to his shrine and he was, in fact, canonized in 1173. Chaucer's *Canterbury Tales*, written in the late fourteenth century, show how popular pilgrimage was at that time.

MODERN CHRISTIAN PILGRIMAGE

One of the most popular modern pilgrimages in Britain is to the Shrine of Our Lady of Walsingham. It was believed that the Virgin appeared in 1061 to the lady of the manor at that village in Norfolk and commanded that a replica be built of Mary's house in Nazareth.

Popular tradition adds that this house was built with the help of the angels. A priory was later built on the site incorporating the house and near to miraculous wells of water. Walsingham became not only one of the leading British shrines but also one of Europe's most important pilgrimage centres, but it was destroyed in 1538 by Henry VIII who had himself visited the shrine. One suggestion is that he was disappointed because he had not received the male heir to the throne which his visit and prayers had requested. Despite centuries of neglect Walsingham has risen again in the twentieth century as a place of pilgrimage for both Anglicans and Catholics.

Another dramatic origin is described for the pilgrimage centre of Fatima in central Portugal. Three local children reckoned to have seen a lady appear on some five separate occasions in 1917. She called herself 'Our Lady of the Rosary', and requested that a chapel be built there. Subsequently many people have been drawn to that spot and have experienced a strengthening of their faith as a result of their visit. This, along with many other sites such as Santiago de Compostela in Spain, where St James is supposed to be buried, still serve as sacred places where pilgrims go in hope and with many motivations. For some the desire is for physical answers to physical needs as in sickness, for others the need is to be associated with the saints of the past and their perspective on life. The church of St Francis in Assisi in Italy is one example of a less dramatic saint who himself found his life changed after his own pilgrimage to Rome where he was touched by the poverty of some people there. He died in 1226 and was canonized in 1228. Many who visit Assisi as tourists will have in mind this man who lived simply and in harmony with nature. They are reminders of the fact that there was something of the tourist in the medieval pilgrims, just as some modern tourists may, occasionally, have a pilgrim spirit.

POWER, MERIT, AND SACRED PLACES

But for the pilgrim proper there is always the underlying belief that sacred places are places of power. Standing out from other spots they focus the piety and faith, power and merit, of Christian saints of the past, and trigger a faithful response in living Christians. In this way sacred places afford a concrete expression of the idea of the Communion of Saints, the view that all believers of all ages and places, and whether dead or alive, share together in the life of God. In a vague way people sometimes talk about places having a special 'atmosphere' or a power that enables them to express their faith and hope in a way that makes sense to them. This kind of 'power' has been widely discussed in the study of many different religions and seems to be an expression of human nature at large. Gerardus van der Leeuw used the experience of power as the basis for his extensive and influential study *Religion in Essence and Manifestation* (1967).

In theological terms sacred places are special because they speak of the power and grace of God that was evident in the lives of past believers. The stress is on God rather than on the individual saint. But in terms of practical religion amongst people at large, particular saints and particular places do come to have a special relevance of their own; the individuality of saints or of miracles comes to the fore and attracts the faithful of today. Here, once more, the relationship between formal theology and the piety of folk-religion is complicated and many individuals will bring their own interpretation to sacred places. This is perfectly understandable since experience is a very personal thing even if the church or group to which someone belongs tries to lay down a pattern for experience and faith. This is especially important as far as salvation is concerned.

Christianity is a religion of salvation. It teaches that God shared in human life through the person of Jesus of Nazareth and that he died to save human beings from the consequences of their sin. Salvation means that the individual is caught up into this divine work of love and mercy, though different Christian traditions explain and interpret how this is done in various ways. Some have taught that merit which influences personal salvation for good can be gained through pilgrimages and worship at particular shrines. This was an important feature of Catholic Christianity in the medieval period. Part of the outlook of the Protestant Reformation lay in a fundamental objection to special merit being gained in such ways.

As described in Chapters 1 and 6, similar debates took place amongst the Orthodox, focused on the Iconoclastic Controversy, which resulted in the retention of icons as part of faith and worship. The Protestant Reformation, involving many political and economic reasons alongside religion, sought to remove these external sources of religious power and merit and to replace them with a doctrine of faith that lay in a personal and interior attitude towards God. The dissolution of the monasteries in England under Henry VIII in the

1530s brought to an end a whole world of monks, sacred places, relics, and pilgrimages. The influence of the Puritans in the early seventeenth century reinforced and extended these objections to a priestly way of life and control of popular religion. But, despite this, the human attraction to sacred places remained, albeit in a transformed fashion.

Protestant sacred places

The 'sacred places' of Protestant Christianity obviously involved churches, just as amongst the Catholics and Orthodox, and these will be described in detail in the next section. Here we return to a theme raised at the beginning of this chapter to discuss 'places' which are mentioned in the Bible and which function in the imaginative realm of faith, in particular the places associated with the life, and especially, the death, of Jesus. Having already considered the symbolic significance of Eden, Babylon, Jerusalem, and heaven, we now focus on Calvary, and the places of Christ's passion.

Although the Protestant Reformation retained the basic sacraments of baptism and the Eucharist along with an official ministry to lead the Church, its basic stress lay on preaching and the Bible. Excessive emphasis on the lives of the saints, miracles, pilgrimages, and sacred places gave way to a rediscovery of the stories of the Bible and the significance of the Bible for understanding God, the Christian religion, and personal dimensions of faith.

The death of Jesus lay at the heart of Protestant religion. His life was interpreted as morally perfect and as a preparation for him to be the sinless sacrifice for the sin of the world. But equally important was the fact that God had become a particular individual in the process of identifying with humanity. And that one person was a man who lived in Palestine. He inhabited the holy land and was associated with the landscape of the Old Testament. He was, in other words, part and parcel of the sacred places of the Bible.

The Incarnation, the process of God incorporated with humanity through the flesh and blood of Jesus, brought an added quality of the sacred to the established location of the holy land. His passion and suffering in the garden of Gethsemane, and his crucifixion on the hill of Calvary, added even more to their sacredness. And preaching developed this vision of God's acts in time and place and sought to

135

catch up modern believers in those events. The sacred places of Protestantism were based on the locations of Christ's life taken up into the imagination of believers through these sermons, Bible stories and, as time went on, especially in hymns. These are sacred places of a spiritual geography.

Religious experience underlies such spiritual geographies just as it does any physical sacred space. The Protestant stress on conversion involved a psychological sense of freedom from guilt and release from sin. It emphasized the crucifixion as the scene of salvation and encouraged the sinner to identify with the death of Jesus on the cross. Many hymns reflected on the experience of salvation from sin by describing the place and event of the crucifixion.

Mrs C. F. Alexander's children's hymn written in the mid-nineteenth century has become very popular also with adults. Its familiar lines tell their own story: 'There is a green hill far away, Outside a city wall, Where the dear Lord was crucified, Who died to save us all.' This and many other hymns ask the believer to imagine Christ's death and to enter sympathetically into his pain. The hymn replaces the relic as an object of meditative adoration, as it also replaces the icon as a medium of obtaining religious benefit. In the hymn 'When I survey the wondrous cross on which the Prince of glory died', written in the early eighteenth century, Isaac Watts speaks of counting his richest gain as loss and as pouring contempt on all his pride when he considers the pain suffered by Christ. The imaginative mind sets to work through the lines: 'See from His head, His hands, His feet, Sorrow and love flow mingled down', and brings the hymnwriter to decide that 'Love so amazing, so divine, Demands my soul, my life, my all'.

One of the most direct expressions of the retrospective hymn is by J. R. Wreford and Samuel Longfellow:

When my love for Christ grows weak,
When for deeper faith I seek,
Then in thought I go to thee,
Garden of Gethsemane.

There I walk amid the shades,
While the lingering twilight fades,
See that suffering, friendless one,
Weeping, praying there alone.

When my love for man grows weak,
When for stronger faith I seek,
Hill of Calvary, I go
To thy scenes of fear and woe.

Other hymns make similar points and show the attractive power of the poetic description of sacred places in the devotional life of believers. So even in churches where there would have been no pictures or stained glass windows giving an artistic portrayal of biblical scenes, those scenes would be created in the mind's eye of believers as they sang and as they heard sermons describing the death of Jesus. Their own experience of forgiveness would often be intimately linked with those images and, in many respects, that experience would help give a sense of the sacred to the picture. Their own awareness of God in the present would feed back through their belief to give the sense of God's influence in that picture of the passion of Jesus centuries ago.

These experiences of many Protestants would have taken place in religious buildings. Those buildings may have been devoid of Christian art and bare of ornament but, as we have suggested, they were filled with imagery through hymns. The power of music to fill a building and add yet another dimension to words must never be ignored when considering sacred places in Christianity. This is especially important for those situations where believers argue that their building is not sacred in any special way. Statements about the ordinariness of religious buildings raise an important theoretical problem in religious studies precisely because certain ideas such as ritual and sacredness carry particular meanings for some religious practitioners which differ significantly from those used by scholars of religion.

The sacred and ritual in theology and religious studies

Some Protestant groups, for example, identify ritual and sacred places with Catholic theological ideas from which they want to distance themselves. In practice such a group might carry a Bible in a procession and give it a place of great honour but would strongly deny any suggestion that this constituted a ritual. For them ritual is something that Catholics or other people do, and which does not belong to true religion. To the anthropologist or student of religion anything can be a ritual, because for them the word bears no theological overtones. This obviously raises a technical problem in religious studies which will be considered below.

It is, in fact, an intriguing fact that some Christians are extremely happy to say that their meeting places are sacred while others strongly deny it. We have already given the example of Catholics and Orthodox incorporating relics into their altars as one way of consecrating – or making sacred – their churches. By stark contrast there are contemporary groups of Christians, especially those who are said to belong to House Church Movements, who specifically use for worship buildings originally built for quite different purposes. One contemporary group meets in a disused cinema and specifically tries not to put religious signs or symbols into the building. For them the idea of a sacred place does not make much sense, they see the group of believers as the real focus of God's activity through the Holy Spirit and not the place as such.

One key to understanding the difference between Christians happy with having sacred places and those unhappy with the idea lies in the sacraments and the emphasis placed upon sacraments and upon an authorized priesthood trained to administer them. We saw much earlier in this chapter how sacred places emerged in Christianity in relation to martyrs and dead believers, and how baptism soon led to special buildings being used by Christian groups. Similarly the early rise of the Eucharist as a central Christian ritual meant that churches emerged as places invested with a distinctive significance. Alongside these rites of baptism and death there emerged a formal priesthood of people whose task it was to conduct the ceremonies and to minister to the congregations associated with the church. When these factors are taken together it is easy to see how the church building as the place for sacraments and priesthood came to be viewed as different in some respects from other public places.

But in addition to these ritual elements the experience of the members of the congregation cannot be ignored. There is some strong evidence from social anthropology to suggest that experience and ritual are closely related through a kind of awareness that comes from ritual and which grows and develops through practice and throughout life (Sperber, 1975). Such 'symbolic knowledge' influences the emotional life of people and supports a pattern of moods which particular religious traditions favour. If people find that through particular rites within a church they gain a sense of God's presence and activity it is to be expected that the place itself will be viewed in a special way as a place of encountering God. Many religious rituals are rites of intensification where the same behaviour is repeated over and over again on a regular basis; a particular building is likely to enhance and foster this pattern of feeling. People may even become so attached to a particular place and to the sacredness of it that they are unwilling to change their behaviour for fear that their experience will suffer.

Another dimension of human life closely related to patterns of experience concerns personal identity. One theory suggests that things which help confer a sense of identity upon individuals are themselves highly valued in return (Mol, 1976). They may be valued to such an extent as to be sacralized and given a status beyond the normal range of mundane significance. When this occurs over long periods of time the dimension of history comes to be added to personal identity and individual experience, giving a place particular cultural significance and making it very sacred.

The sense of identity people gain through religious and cultural life comes through many channels but their own religious tradition is likely to focus it for them in some very particular way. Catholic theology has traditionally stressed the sacraments while Protestant and Reformed outlooks have emphasized the Bible and its teachings. One of the consequences of these differences lies in the way churches have been organized as far as their sacred dimensions are concerned.

Churches as sacred places

Because Christianity was from the beginning a congregational religion it engaged in church-building to provide meeting places for members as soon as was practicable and publicly possible. This has continued in the great majority of Catholic, Orthodox, Lutheran, Anglican, and Reformed traditions as well as amongst many independent and sectarian forms of Christianity.

The actual theological and symbolic significance attached to these various buildings has differed quite considerably. Where the liturgy of the Eucharist has been central, as in sacramental forms of the religion in Catholic, Orthodox, Lutheran, and Anglican traditions, the altar has been set apart and has become the most sacred part of the church building. With time the area around the altar came to be set apart as a specially sacred area sometimes called the sanctuary. It is worth remembering that the word 'sanctuary' has been used not only for this area but also to describe the place reserved for the clergy, and also for a church as a whole. This indicates that the idea of a sacred place can vary depending upon circumstances and context.

The altar itself has occupied several different positions in Christian churches. When churches are built as rectangles facing the east it has often been the case that altars, their sanctuaries, and the preferred place for burials have been at the most eastwards part of the building, often interpreted in relation to the rising sun and the symbolism of the resurrection, but this is only one partial explanation. 'The eventual triumph of the east end has yet to be fully explained in either architectural or liturgical terms' (Colvin, 1991: 128). In practical terms the eastward sanctuary of churches in many parts of Europe often allowed the nave, or the large central body of the church, to be viewed as less sacred and to be used for all sorts of non-religious purposes. In fairly recent centuries the naves of some churches have been used for meetings and even sporting activities.

But altars have also been placed in the centre of churches both in some early Christian buildings of a basilica pattern derived from pagan buildings, and in modern churches such as the Roman Catholic Cathedral at Liverpool. When this is done the church becomes a much more obviously sacred building with relatively little scope for other activities unless the altar is portable. In churches of a strongly sacramental character, including Roman Catholic and Anglican churches, the consecrated communion bread or host is sometimes kept in a special tabernacle placed above the main altar or else in a Lady Chapel. Where this occurs it provides a central focus for piety and devotion and constitutes the centre of the sacred place because it is believed that the real presence of Christ is located within that host.

The Lutheran tradition has retained the central focus of an altar but it also places a stress on the pulpit for the preaching of sermons which are focused upon the teaching of the Bible. The Anglican Church has also focused on the altar as the central sacred spot in a church even though its Reformed strain of thought led to pulpits being added to every Church of England parish by law in 1604.

In the Reformed Protestant traditions of the more Calvinist perspective the Bible and the preaching of God's word have assumed paramount importance; it is the pulpit and not the altar that assumes pride of place, as in the Church of Scotland and many Non-conformist churches. Often the pulpit is placed centrally, with a high vantage point, and above the table that is used instead of an altar for the Eucharist. In the earliest Christian congregations it appears that sermons were given from the bishop's chair which was itself centrally placed and marked off from the rest of the building.

So we see that the Reformed tradition does not speak of a building as intrinsically sacred even though the preaching and reading of the Bible are treated with great respect, and hymn and psalm singing are given an important place in worship.

CHURCHES SACRED OR NOT?

This difference between Christian groups over the idea of the sacred presents an interesting problem because religious studies regularly uses the category of the sacred in its analysis of religious behaviour. There are at least two ways of dealing with this issue.

First, by not using the category of the sacred for those Christian groups who have no theological need for it or who specifically avoid it. Their churches could simply be described as locations of ritual, and the very term sacred space be avoided altogether. In many respects this is exactly what tends to happen in the social anthropology and sociology of religion where the idea of sacred spaces and sacred places is largely ignored when analysing religious behaviour.

Second, it is in the phenomenology and history of religions that the idea of the sacred is most often used when describing religious events. It is possible to retain this perspective by defining sacred places in a strictly descriptive way to apply to places where people gathered for religious ritual irrespective of how those people define their own places. On this basis the former cinema in which a religious group now meets is as much a sacred place as an ancient cathedral. The terms are used by the scholar and not by the participant. As long as terms are defined and clearly used there is little danger of making a major error of judgement over this question of method. This example clearly illustrates the fact that serious study of religion involves an understanding of how the scholar's criteria of analysis relate to the way practising believers think about their religion.

The holy Eucharist in sacred and secular places

The case of the Eucharist provides another good example of the need to be precise over the categories used to analyse religious behaviour. In the phenomenology of religion the temples of many religions are often interpreted as representing the centre of the world, or the point of axis and contact between the world of everyday life and the realm of the deity. Such places are reckoned to be sacred precisely because they are the point of contact between God and humanity.

This scheme can be applied to Christianity in several ways. The Eucharist, for example, is a strong candidate for being a ritual that links heaven and earth. In the rite the central history of the faith is recalled and focused in the life and earthly ministry of Jesus. Then in the prayer of consecration the priest asks that by the power of God's Holy Spirit the bread and wine may be to the worshippers the body and blood of Christ. As Chapter 6 shows in more theological terms, in the medieval period the doctrine of transubstantiation was developed to give a philosophical explanation of how the elements of bread and wine actually came to be the body and blood; in modern life many Christians would not accept that kind of explanation but still find a deep sense of being at one with God through this rite. Although this ritual normally takes place in a consecrated church, it can be carried out anywhere by a suitably ordained priest, whether in someone's home or in a field or factory. In some churches it may even be conducted by someone who is not formally ordained. The significant point is that in this service believers are drawn both into the presence of God and into the history of the life of Jesus. The group celebrating the Eucharist comprise the sacred community of believers without having to be in any church building. In other words it is the community of believers that marks off a sacred territory rather than the other way around. In terms of popular theology this is often argued by saying that the church is people and not a building. As one Christian hymn expresses it:

For Thou within no walls confined
Inhabitest the humble mind.
Such ever bring thee when they come,
And going take Thee to their homes.

But preaching is also seen by some, especially in the Lutheran tradition, as providing a moment of communication between God and the congregation. When the preacher addresses the people it is God, they say, who addresses them through the words of the sermon. So the sacred place is the place where the divine word is spoken.

A final example of the sacred place which changes the meaning of the word might be that of self-sacrificial service to one's neighbour. The Christian tradition of care in hospitals and schools and other agencies is an expression of the belief that to serve another human being is to serve Christ. A few Christian groups have seen it as necessary to turn away from formal religious buildings and traditional religious behaviour and expressions of faith in order to pursue a 'secular' meaning of the faith. The German theologian Dietrich Bonhoeffer, who was killed in 1945 because of his part in a plot to kill Hitler, is often seen as a pastor calling other Christians to live fully in a secular world as their Christian duty: 'Before God and with God we live without God.'

The decade of the 1960s was very much a period when phrases such as the 'secular gospel' were popular. The American theologian Harvey Cox's influential book *The Secular City* (1965) went so far as to say that the Jewish–Christian tradition was the root cause of secularization. Once Christian faith argues against petty forms of superstition then it is only a step away from denying any distinctive and particular significance to religious buildings. Here we see the two poles of Christian views of the sacred. The one accepts that sacred places exist as distinct from the rest of life, the other says that all life is equally sacred because God in Christ has become part of it. The one elaborates and develops ritual as a way of focusing on God, the other abandons special Christian places so as to make all places Christian.

This diversity is part of the challenge to religious studies to do justice to what devotees of a religion say while also describing their behaviour from a non-committed perspective. As a final example we try to do this for one less familiar religious group, The Church of Jesus Christ of Latter-day Saints. In this example we also incorporate many of the central topics introduced throughout this chapter on the sacred in Christianity.

Sacred places in Mormon life

Perhaps the best example of sacred places developing in nineteenth- and twentieth-century advanced societies is found in the Mormon religion. Joseph Smith, as the first Prophet of this movement, believed God had restored fundamental truths to mankind which had been lost since the early days of Christianity. Because of this Mormons called their church a Restoration movement. Its central message called men and women to serve God according to these freshly restored truths and religious rites or ordinances in a new land of promise in America. And it is here that the first idea of a sacred place appeared in Mormonism as the Saints believed that Jesus would soon return and set up his kingdom. This would be a kind of New Jerusalem or Zion and would be in America. Thousands of Europeans emigrated to the USA in response to this message, and the hymn 'Come, come, ye Saints' gave voice to their hopes and served as an anthem for what were, in effect, migrant pilgrims as they journeyed to their land of promise.

> Come, come, ye Saints, no toil nor labour fear;
> But with joy, wend your way.
> Though hard to you this journey may appear,
> Grace shall be as your day.
>
> Tis better far for us to strive,
> Our useless cares from us to drive.
> Do this and joy your hearts will swell.
> All is well! All is well!

As time went on and the nineteenth century came to a close without the Second Advent of Christ Mormons came to accept that the Kingdom of God would not take the form of a miraculous divine appearance but of a steady growth of the Mormon Church throughout the world. At the same time Mormons placed increasing stress on buildings they called temples in which special rites were performed. They already had several temples in Utah, notably the temple at Salt Lake City, and as the twentieth century unfolded they began building temples in each continent across the world. As Mormons acknowledged that a geographical Zion was unlikely in the near future their temples assumed this role of being pure and sacred places within an otherwise corrupt world. Sacred buildings replaced the idea of a sacred land.

In the 1990s there are some 44 Mormon temples distributed throughout the world where members may perform a wide variety of religious rites which cannot be carried out anywhere else. The temple is distinguished from ordinary churches and chapels of Mormonism by being closed to the general public and open only to Mormons who receive special permission to enter them because they live up to the expectations and rules of their faith.

The temple is distinguished from the local chapel or 'stake-house' in a way that many non-Mormons initially find difficult to grasp. This difference is absolutely crucial to understanding the temple as a sacred place and is grounded in the distinction Mormons make between time and eternity. Ordinary chapels exist in time and any rites that take place in them last for the period of life on this earth. So, for example, a marriage conducted in a local Mormon chapel is 'for time', or as it might be expressed in more traditional Christian language, 'till death do us part'. But (as we will describe in greater detail in Chapter 7) in the temple things are different. Rites performed in temples are 'for eternity', their effect is for ever and extends into the heavenly domain. So, a marriage that is performed, or 'sealed' in a temple as the Mormons put it, lasts not only for time but for eternity as well. And this applies for other rites as, for example, in the Mormon practice of being baptized on behalf of the dead.

The temple shares in the world of eternity quite closely and is a kind of point of contact between eternity and time. It is not surprising, then, that some Mormons speak of experiencing God, and sometimes their departed ancestors, in more intimate ways in the temple than elsewhere. In this sense the temple is a clear example of Mircea Eliade's analysis of sacred places as centre points of religious significance where earth and heaven intersect.

What this also indicates is the fact that for Mormons the life after death involves another sacred place, that of heaven. In Latter-day Saint understanding heaven is divided into several domains and it is only in the highest one, which they call the Celestial Kingdom, that the fullness of eternity and of encounter with God is possible. And the opportunity for this is available only for those Mormons who have been married for eternity in earthly temples.

We can now see a variety of ideas of sacred places in the history of Mormon religion. There is the idea of an American Zion in which Jesus Christ will appear in his Second Coming, then there are the temples which enshrine eternity, and finally there is the heavenly domain for those who have fullness of life after death.

Another distinctive teaching of Mormonism was that human souls lived in heaven before this human life, and would ultimately return to that realm after death to be with both God their heavenly father and a heavenly mother. The famous Mormon hymn 'O My Father' expressed this truth and was important in conveying it to many new converts who would not have met that idea in the churches from which they came. The hymn speaks of God as having 'withheld the recollection of my former friends and birth', and of believers occasionally feeling that they are strangers on earth. The idea of heavenly parents is put in the form of a question: 'In the heavens are parents single? No, the thought makes reason stare! Truth is reason, truth eternal Tells me I've a mother there.' The hymn continues:

When I leave this frail existence,
When I lay this mortal by,
Father, Mother, may I meet you,
In your royal courts on high?

Then the hymn ends by saying that Mormons will return to live forever with their heavenly parents, having accomplished all they had been sent to earth to do. For many Mormons this hymn takes on special significance in relation to Mormon temples where important rites take place on behalf of the dead.

THE SACRED IN RELIGIOUS PLACES

When people criticize Mormons for the secrecy surrounding their temple rituals they often reply by describing the rites as 'sacred not secret'. This shows the depth of feeling Mormons have towards rites that mean so much to them. It also reflects the much wider religious phenomenon that believers often focus their cherished beliefs on some particular place. The sacred involves the personal and corporate significance of a place which enshrines and focuses vital beliefs, even beliefs that God can be known, worshipped, and served at all times and in all places, as the next chapter shows in greater depth.

Further reading

Biran, A. (ed.) (1981) *Temples and High Places in Biblical Times.* Jerusalem: Jewish Institute of Religion.

Davies, J. G. (1982) *Temples, Churches and Mosques.* New York: Pilgrim Press.

Davies, J. G. (1986) *A New Dictionary of Liturgy and Worship.* London: SCM Press.

Sperber, D. (1975) *Rethinking Symbolism.* Cambridge: Cambridge University Press.

Turner, H. W. (1979) *From Temple to Meeting House: The Phenomenology and Theology of Places of Worship.* The Hague: Mouton.

6. Worship

Closely related to sacred places and sacred writings, worship emerges as the human response to God's greatness, both in creating the universe and in providing salvation for humanity. In worship, men and women become aware of themselves as finite creatures on the one hand and as morally limited beings on the other. In the Christian tradition, growing as it did out of Jewish backgrounds, this moral element is as vitally important as the sense of wonder before the creator. Creation and salvation stand side by side as the Jewish–Christian foundation for worship so that worship integrates and echoes a dual framework, of the moral perfection of God and imperfection of humanity as one perspective, and of the greatness of God in creating the universe as the other perspective. This is the major reason why confession followed by absolution from sin is central to Christian worship, and often precedes expressions of God's glory revealed in the created order.

But the distinctive feature of Christian worship is the focus on Jesus Christ as shown in so many prayers which end with the formula 'through Jesus Christ our Lord, Amen'. Christians believe that through Jesus, God became part and parcel of humanity. The Christmas carol 'Behold the great Creator makes himself a house of clay' expresses this fundamental Christian conviction that the creator has become part of the creation to bring salvation to humanity. When Christians say 'Amen', they use a Hebrew word meaning 'truly' to emphasize that it is through Jesus as the Jewish Messiah or anointed one – 'Christ' being derived from the Greek word for 'anointed' – that their worship takes place.

In theological terms, worship is based on the idea of God as a Holy Trinity comprising Father, Son and Holy Spirit. With this pattern in mind, it is often said that worship is offered to the Father, through the Son, by the power of the Holy Spirit. Even so, in different churches and at different times the emphasis placed upon the Father, the Son, and the Spirit, can differ to quite a degree.

From its first days as a new religion, Christianity has been a community of worshipping people. In very many respects worship came before theology, prayer before doctrine. An old Latin phrase, *lex orandi lex credendi*, refers directly to this fact of Christian history that the law of prayer establishes the law of worship, or in other words, that what is to be believed emerges from prayerful worship.

The priority of worship is perfectly understandable, given the fact that the earliest followers of Jesus were Jews whose established religious practice was grounded in local synagogues and also, to a more limited extent, the Temple at Jerusalem. For centuries Jews had regularly come together to worship God and to hear the words of their sacred scriptures. Jesus was, himself, thoroughly grounded in this practice, and it is perfectly natural to read in the Bible of him being taken to the Temple as a boy (Luke 2:41–50), of reading the Scriptures at the synagogue (Luke 4:16), and of teaching in synagogues (Mark 1:21).

Early in the Acts of the Apostles we read of Peter and John going to the Temple to pray, and of Paul arguing his Christian cause in the synagogue at Corinth during one of his visits there lasting some eighteen months (Acts 18:4–17). One of the profound issues that arose in the development of Christianity during the century after the death of Jesus was the break-away of Jewish Christians from their Jewish synagogue base as they established their own gatherings for worship, where they were joined by Greeks or others who had become Christians.

Temple and Jesus

There are several points in the New Testament where the status and significance of Jewish places of worship, especially the Temple at Jerusalem, are called into question. There is a well-known story in the gospels where Jesus visits the Temple at Jerusalem and drives from it merchants and stall-holders (Mark 11:15–17). In the version written in John's gospel (and it comes very early in that gospel as though to emphasize the significance of the point being made) Jesus is asked on what authority he drives out these sales-people, or what sign he can give to justify doing it? The text then runs:

> Jesus answered them, 'Destroy this temple and in three days I will raise it up'. The Jews then said, 'It has taken forty-six years to build this temple, and will you raise it up in three days?' But he spoke of the temple of his body. When, therefore he was raised from the dead, his disciples remembered that he had said this; and they believed ... the word which Jesus had spoken. (John 2:18-22)

These words hint at one strand of early Christian belief in which Jesus was believed to be so important in the relationship between God and humanity that his resurrection provided a more significant focus of faith than any sacred building ever could, even the Temple at Jerusalem which was initially the resting place of the Ark of the Covenant. A person had replaced a building, just as a new covenant had replaced the old. There is a full-scale discussion of this replacement of the Temple by Christ in the Letter to the Hebrews, a discussion made all the keener by the fact that Jerusalem's Temple was destroyed in 70 CE (a devastating blow as far as Jews were concerned).

Jesus is interpreted as both the high priest (Heb 9:11) and the sacrificial victim (Heb 9:26) who through his resurrection has entered into heaven, which is the true sacred place (Heb 9:11–12), to serve as both priest and victim. Earthly things are reckoned, in this epistle, to be but shadows of the heavenly reality. The Christians addressed in this letter are called to the kind of life of faith which sets its mind on the ultimate realities of heaven and not upon transient aspects of earthly life.

> Therefore let us be grateful for receiving a kingdom that cannot be shaken, and thus let us offer to God acceptable worship, with reverence and awe. (Heb 12:28)

BODY AS TEMPLE

This emphasis on worship is repeated later in the Letter to the Hebrews to stress the fact that Christians exist not to participate in the sacrifice of animals in earthly temples but to 'continually offer up a sacrifice of praise to God', a sacrifice which is the 'fruit of lips that acknowledge his name' (Heb 13:15). Such sacrifices to God are also said to include doing good and sharing what they had (Heb 13:16), so that worship embraces the wider meaning of ethical aspects of life as well as narrower practices such as singing or the like. A very similar picture emerges in the Letter to the Romans where Paul appeals to believers to present their bodies as a living sacrifice to God for this very thing is their 'spiritual worship' (Rom 12:1). Here worship is seen as a way of describing the Christian life as a whole and not simply as one part of it restricted to the congregational activity within a particular building. This is expressed in a slightly different way when Paul writes that Christians should see their own bodies as a 'temple of the Holy Spirit' (1 Corinthians 6:19). This brings worship down to a very personal level as the individual believer is seen as the true focus of worship of God since, through the Spirit, God indwells each person. This view of the relation between the Spirit and the individual transforms the idea of sacred space and sacred architecture.

In fact, the history of worship within Christianity involves a constant relationship between the inwardness and the outwardness of worship, between those who say true worship of God is an inward attitude of the individual believer, and others who do not deny that inwardness but who also stress the outward acts and context of worship.

The period of Jewish history into which Jesus was born involved, in Palestine, strict obedience to the commandment against making 'any graven image, or any likeness of anything that is in heaven above, or that is in the earth beneath, or that is in the water' (Exod 20:4). Early followers of Jesus were likely to have held a similar outlook, but with time, and as many non-Jews also became Christians, ideas changed. From the second century on, pictures emerged in Christian contexts, as in the catacombs, and grew in religious significance. One important aspect of this development lay in the Christian belief that God had become part and parcel of humanity in Jesus of Nazareth. This belief came to be enshrined in the doctrine of the Incarnation and changed the way Christian believers looked at the world.

ICONS

The doctrine of the Incarnation meant that, instead of God being beyond the material realm, there was now a sense in which God had entered into material reality. Through the process of salvation in

Jesus, the stamp of divine approval had been placed upon created things in a new way. This led to Christ, his disciples and martyred followers, along with many aspects of human life, being portrayed in art forms. In Eastern Orthodox religion this ultimately led to the growth of icons. As described in Chapter 1, icons are paintings of Jesus, of the Virgin Mary, and of various saints. They may be simple paintings or highly decorated with precious metals, but whether simple or elaborate they are believed to be a special medium through which spiritual benefits may be derived. In the most fundamental sense icons are symbols, they participate in that which they represent, they are a vehicle for the power of the person depicted upon them to come through to the pious worshipper. In Greek and Russian Orthodox Churches icons play a very significant part in the piety of ordinary believers, who often pray before their icons.

Religious interest in icons grew increasingly in the Eastern Mediterranean world until, in the eighth and ninth centuries, there was a flare-up of feeling both for and against their use in the Greek Church. This has been called the Iconoclastic Controversy from a Greek word for image-breaker. Icons had become increasingly widespread, and some felt that they had become far too significant within popular church life, and it was when some of the Byzantine Emperors adopted this view that the issue reached epidemic proportion. Despite the strength of opposition the right to use icons was won in 842 CE so that, in practice, icons would continue to be a significant part of Eastern Christianity.

Western Christianity had its own problems over the use of images at a later date. It was during the period of the Reformation in the sixteenth century that Western Christians argued over images in churches and took different views. Roman Catholics retained the use of images in the form of crucifixes, statues and paintings, as did, to a certain extent, the Lutheran churches. But the increased emphasis, both upon the personal inwardness of religious experience and, perhaps even more importantly, on the Bible and preaching as the source of knowledge of God, led to the more Calvinist streams of the Reformation making their places of worship increasingly bare in an artistic sense. The Puritans in England in the early seventeenth century objected to any form of church decoration, ritual and the symbolic vestments worn by clergy in church. Several church denominations, including the Presbyterians, Baptists and Independents, were influenced by this outlook and continued to be simple in their church life as far as artistic representations were concerned. But, though the walls of these churches would be bare of all images, these developed a rich tapestry of images within hymns. The tremendous growth of hymns following on from the Reformation generated a form of pictorial poetry which fed the pious through their congregational singing in a way that pictorial images had done for earlier generations.

Eucharist as worship

One major focus of worship in the Christian tradition which has long occupied a central place in Christian life is the Eucharist, the ritual in which the faithful gather together to bless, share, eat and drink bread and wine. It is sometimes called the Liturgy, especially in Greek Orthodoxy where it stands as the uniquely central vehicle for expressing the doctrine and theology of that tradition. In the Roman Catholic Church it is called the Mass, while in Protestant and Reformed Churches it is called by a variety of names including the Lord's Supper and the Holy Communion.

The Eucharist is traced back to the Last Supper held by Jesus for his disciples before his death as recorded in different ways several times in the Bible (e.g., Matt 26:17ff.; Mark 14:13ff.; Luke 22:8ff.; John 13:1ff.; 1 Cor 11:23ff.). At first it seems to have been a meal shared by all the faithful, then the action changed in the middle of the second century to focus on the bread and wine over which special prayers were said. The gathering has also switched from an evening to an early morning rite. The great increase in church membership following the Roman Empire becoming nominally Christian led to the Eucharist being increasingly associated with the clergy, as fewer of the total Christian population were involved in it. Its ritual and symbolic meaning were greatly elaborated in different parts of the Christian world.

WORSHIP AND SACRIFICE

One unifying feature in the theology and language of the Eucharist in both the Eastern and Western Christian traditions lay in the free use of ideas of sacrifice and offering. As outlined in Chapter 1, in the medieval period the Western Church developed the doctrine of *transubstantiation* to explain the belief that Christ's body and blood were somehow realized in the sacramental bread and wine. As such they could be offered to God as a re-presentation of Christ, or as a re-offering of the sacrifice Christ had once made of himself. The technical arguments used to define just how the divine presence came to be in, or associated with, the bread and wine were often quite complex and tied up with the way philosophy at that period explained matter. The important point is that the Eucharist was seen as a kind of sacrifice and that the worship of God was inextricably bound up with the life and death of Jesus as a sacrifice.

DEVOTION TO THE BLESSED SACRAMENT

In the Roman Catholic tradition this belief led to an important form of faith focusing on devotion to Christ as present in the consecrated bread or host. The 'Blessed Sacrament' was kept after the Mass and placed in a special receptacle called a Tabernacle. This was and is a central feature of any Catholic church, representing the constant presence of Christ as a focus for worship and prayer. Often it would be near the high altar as the key focus in a church, or else placed in the Lady Chapel where private prayer and worship could be conducted at any time. From about the thirteenth century on, it became customary at some services to display the reserved sacrament to the people in a container called a monstrance. As time went on, monstrances became increasingly decorated and consisted of a little circular window through which the consecrated host or wafer could be seen, and with precious metal used, for example, to depict radiating rays of the sun coming from the host. Over the centuries a separate service emerged called Benediction in which the host was displayed in its monstrance, and incense was used along with prayers, hymns, and silent adoration. This was especially the case in the nineteenth century as Benediction was used as a special evening service. From the mid-twentieth century Catholics have increasingly held major Masses as evening services, which has led to a decline in the service of Benediction. This whole process is a good example of how the rise of a doctrine, that of transubstantiation, fostered a rite which later declined as the rite on which it depended, the Mass, changed its own place in the weekly flow of worship celebrating Christ's sacrifice.

154

In Eastern Orthodoxy this practice never emerged, partly perhaps because of the emphasis on Christ's resurrection rather than on his death. But the death of Jesus as a sacrifice for sin in saving the world was absolutely central to the theology of the Reformation in the West although it was interpreted in a different way, leading to intense disagreement between Protestants and Catholics over the meaning of the Eucharist and especially over the idea of the eucharistic sacrifice. Once more the debate between the inwardness and outwardness of religion in Christian faith came to the surface. For most Protestants the emphasis was placed on the faith of the believer in relation to Christ, and not upon any change in the bread and wine itself. For Catholics, as for the Lutherans to a certain extent, the sacramental bread and wine remained important as a means of interacting with the presence of Christ. The Anglican Church hotly debated the issue and, as a Reformation movement, went theologically for the stress on the faith in the one receiving the elements, and on the ritual as a memorial of the sacrificial offering made by Christ himself. Most Protestant churches retained the Eucharist in some form, often calling it the Lord's Supper, or the Holy Communion, while stressing the aspect of a memorial of Christ's death.

From the later nineteenth century the Eucharist has come increasingly to the centre of worship in Catholic churches on the Continent through the Liturgical Movement as lay people have been encouraged to use it as a means of fostering their faith. The Second Vatican Council of the mid-1960s further encouraged this by insisting that the Mass should be said in the language of each country and not in Latin. So too in the Anglican Church, where the Parish Communion movement from the 1930s strove to establish each parish as a congregation focused on the Eucharist. But other Protestant churches have also increased their emphasis upon the Eucharist in the latter part of the twentieth century.

One interesting feature of the Eucharist is the fact that in the Greek Orthodox Church even very young children are allowed to have the sacred bread and wine once they have been baptized, Roman Catholics permit them to do so after their first confession but before the rite of confirmation, while most Anglicans have resolutely held confirmation as a necessary qualification for taking the Holy Communion. Most Protestant churches also stress the adult self-conscious awareness of members before they are admitted to Holy

Communion. This can be compared with the fact that children, and even the unbaptized, are allowed to sing hymns and otherwise take full part in services in these churches, which shows that even within acts of worship divisions are drawn between who may and may not take full part in them.

Music, mass and oratorio

To talk of hymns is to come to music as one channel of worship which is practically universal in Christianity. Irrespective of their theology, churches have used musical forms to chant portions of Scripture, to sing old and new hymns, and to be the medium for all sorts of services from the earliest days of the faith. The liturgies of Eastern and Western Christendom as well as the hymns and psalms of Protestantism bear witness to the power of music as a vehicle for worship.

In the medieval period chant combined with the Latin text of the Mass to give a form of worship that would influence Western culture from Bach to Beethoven and on to Andrew Lloyd Webber in the 1980s. In similar ways, the Mass has been set to music under local cultural influences in Africa, South America and other countries. In addition to the Mass various biblical passages have been set to music in oratorios such as Handel's *Messiah* or Haydn's *Creation* and have taken religious themes into the world of more popular culture.

HYMNS AS WORSHIP

But it is in hymns that the greatest number of people encounter music in worship. As general songs for lay people, hymns probably began in about the thirteenth century, though it was from the sixteenth century on, with the birth of the Reformation, that hymn writing and hymn singing became a fundamentally more central part of Christian worship and life. The Methodist Revival in Britain in the eighteenth century marked a vitally important change as hymns, alongside sermons, came to be the central means of expressing doctrine and faith, as in the first book, *Hymns and Sacred Poems*, published by John and Charles Wesley in 1739. Developing from metrical psalm-singing, hymns expressed the doctrines of new religious outlooks in language that could be deeply biblical but could also use non-biblical expressions to great effect. The freedom to use ordinary language to mirror and echo biblical turns of phrase was a powerful means of stimulating piety among the faithful, as in Luther's famous hymn 'A safe stronghold our God is still, a trusty shield and weapon'. Many hymns took biblical ideas and presented them for use in this new form of popular worship. This was especially true in the nineteenth century which was the century when hymns fully entered the life of the great majority of churches in Britain, a shift that was marked by the publication of *Hymns Ancient and Modern* in 1861.

It was in the Protestant tradition that hymn singing came to be a central and vitally important aspect of worship during the eighteenth and especially the nineteenth century. During this period all the major Protestant churches, including the Church of England, had shifted the centre of gravity of worship away from the Mass or Eucharist to services where the Bible was read, sermons preached, and hymns sung. Because this period was one of astonishing missionary expansion, carried out by members of various European countries establishing Christianity in their numerous empires and dominions, hymns were exported as a fundamental component of Christianity itself.

From the earliest period of the Reformation Martin Luther's hymn 'A safe stronghold' conveys a clear picture of God as a castle set against the attacking Devil:

A safe stronghold our God is still,
A trusty shield and weapon;
He'll help us clear from all the ill,
That hath us now o'ertaken.
The ancient prince of hell
Hath risen with purpose fell,
Strong mail of craft and power
He weareth in this hour;
On earth is not his fellow.

But one of the most prolific and influential hymn writers was Charles Wesley (1708–88), one of the founders of the Methodist movement, who had over 200 hymns in the *Methodist Hymn Book*, a book which symbolizes the vital importance of hymnody in this Protestant Church. The following examples have been chosen to illustrate the theme of Christian worship and to show how diverse strands of human experience and life feed into the central nature of worship.

In 'O for a thousand tongues to sing my Great Redeemer's praise' Wesley takes the theme of salvation as the basis for his praise of God. The triumphs of God's grace have, in Christ, reached into the darkened life of the sinner as into a locked cell:

> He breaks the power of cancelled sin,
> He sets the prisoner free;
> His blood can make the foulest clean,
> His blood availed for me.

The emphasis on Jesus as the atonement for sin, and as the basis for the life of the forgiven sinner, is a dominant chord in Protestant worship as this hymn stressed in its final verse: 'See all your sins on Jesus laid: The Lamb of God was slain, His soul was once an offering made, For every soul of man.' For Wesley there is a certain wonder and a trigger for worship in the mystery of God's goodness in taking on the problem of human wickedness. The hymn 'And can it be that I should gain an interest in the Saviour's blood?' involves a profound reflection on the dual theological theme of God's love expressed in the death of Jesus on the one hand, and the human transformation brought about by forgiveness on the other, as these few phrases show: 'Amazing love! How can it be that Thou, my God, shouldst die for me! 'Tis mystery all! The immortal dies: Who can explore His strange design?'

Horatius Bonar (1808–89) explored this same experience of forgiveness in his hymn 'Not what these hands have done', as he says, 'Not what I feel or do, Can give me peace with God; Not all my prayers, and sighs, and tears, Can bear the aweful load.' This sense of sin as a weight bearing down upon life, or as chains holding people captive is a powerful one in the spirituality of Protestant religion. It is experienced as part of that total process of conversion or of being 'born again', as someone passes from the oppressive sense of sin to an awareness of forgiveness from God, an awareness often spoken of in terms of light, freedom, or peace. Bonar continues his hymn in exactly this way by shifting his attention from himself first to Christ and then to God:

Thy work alone, O Christ,
Can ease this weight of sin;
Thy blood alone, O Lamb of God,
Can give me peace within.

Thy grace alone, O God,
To me can pardon speak;
Thy power alone, O son of God
Can this sore bondage break.

Wesley's emphasis is thoroughly Christ-focused and rooted in the belief that God's love to humanity is fully revealed in Jesus whose Incarnation brings God into the very arena of human life. Human nature itself is perceived as sinful and in need of transforming conversion through God's grace so that men and women may themselves become loving. One of his best known hymns, now widely sung as a Christmas carol, 'Hark the herald-angels sing', uses all these ideas and uses them as the basis for the worship of Christ.

Christ by highest heaven adored,
Christ the everlasting Lord,
Late in time behold him come,
Offspring of a virgin's womb.
Veiled in flesh the Godhead see,
Hail the incarnate Deity,
Pleased as man with man to dwell
Jesus our Immanuel.

Mild he lays his glory by,
Born that man no more may die,
Born to raise the sons of earth,
Born to give them second birth,
Hail the heaven-born Prince of Peace,
Hail the Sun of Righteousness,
Light and life to all he brings,
Risen with healing in his wings.

Through hymns like this, more than through any formal teaching, millions of people have come to absorb aspects of theology and have been led into worship. It is quite easy to use Wesley's hymns alone as a means of covering the life of Jesus and the nature of God as these representative titles show:

O Love divine what hast thou done? (Cross)
Christ the Lord is risen today. (Resurrection)
Hail the Day that sees him rise. (Ascension)
Entered the Holy Place above. (Heavenly Priest)
Rejoice the Lord is King. (Kingly Rule)
Lo he comes with clouds descending. (Second Coming)
I want the Spirit of power within. (Holy Spirit)
Father in whom we live. (Holy Trinity)
When quiet in my house I sit. (Bible)
Sinners turn why will ye die? (Conversion)

Spirituality and worship

Throughout Wesley's hymns there is a sense of inner peace, certainty and assurance which is typical of an important strand of Protestant religion. It is also the hallmark of those described by William James in his important book *The Varieties of Religious Experience* (1902) as the 'twice-born' type of religious believer, those who undergo a sense of striving with sin and guilt until they feel born-again through God's power that comes to them. These people James distinguished from the 'once-born' type of individual who accepts religious ideas and grows in them without any marked stage of conversion or transformation.

ONCE-BORN AND TWICE-BORN WORSHIP

Though it would be quite wrong to distinguish between Protestant and Catholic forms of religion on the basis of the twice-born and once-born categories, it would also be wrong to ignore these different styles of religious outlook and attitudes. It would, of course, be easy to find once-born people in Protestant churches and twice-born individuals in Catholic and Orthodox communities. But, even so, the style of all these churches is influenced by their theology, and Catholic and Orthodox theology emphasizes the pattern of sacraments through which a person enters the faith and passes through life by means of that scheme of sacraments. History, too, influences theology and worship, and this is certainly the case in this Protestant example of Methodism.

160

The early Methodist stress on conversion as the foundation for the life of faith comes out in some of the hymns already mentioned. But hymns, as part of worship, form part of a whole which includes prayers, Bible-reading and sermons. Worship for twice-born individuals offers an opportunity to reflect on God's work as they have experienced it in their own lives. Entry into worship involves a reflection on their own past. This framework for life is an important part of worship because individuals are given a sense of place, an awareness of where they fit into the actual history of the world as understood by their religion. And this is done not simply in a rational and logical way, by some sort of a theory of history, but in a much more personal way through their own experience. Music and songs serve as the vehicles for this process of self-understanding. People sing themselves into Christian history and into the meaning of their own lives. The worship of God and a growth in self-understanding furnish two aspects of the total process of the life of faith and the growth of personal identity. One favourite hymn of nineteenth- and early twentieth-century Protestant church groups has the chorus 'At the cross, at the cross, where I first saw the light, And the burden of my heart rolled away; It was there by faith I received my sight, And now I am happy all the day.' Many hymns of this sort have been used in worship. When their content is scrutinized it is slightly surprising to find that instead of focusing on God and recounting the wonderful nature of the deity they dwell very largely on human life and the changes that have come about in it. In hymns we see how closely human identity is linked with the worship of God.

Worship is also intimately linked to the worshipping community because it is in and through the group that individuals gain this sense of their own identity and have a chance to reflect upon it. This is especially true of twice-born people. The identity they once possessed in everyday life is now overtaken by the new sense of themselves as God's specially chosen people. In some Protestant churches there are special occasions when people can talk about their religious experiences and develop their knowledge of how God works in individual lives. Early Methodism held 'Experience Meetings' for this very purpose, and many Evangelical groups allow people to 'give their testimonies'. At such meetings people talk about their former life as unforgiven sinners and about their new life following their conversion. Their sense of gratitude for this change of outlook motivates and influences their worship to a considerable extent. This provision of a context for life and for understanding existence is also true for those who are once-born Christians, but the way their churches explain reality is different.

Religious life and everyday life

The Catholic and Orthodox traditions of Christianity have strong theological explanations for the history of the world and for the place of the Church within it. The use of the sacrament of baptism to make people into members, along with the other sacraments – of confirmation, marriage, absolution, and last rites – to accompany them throughout life, provides a pattern through which people can gain a view on the world and grow in their appreciation and knowledge of God. These churches also use music in their worship and have done so from the early centuries of Christianity.

In the case of Orthodoxy, only vocal music in the form of chants is used, the music of organs or other accompaniment being avoided. It was decided at the Council of Laodicea (367 CE) that the congregation in general should take no part in the singing of services in order to keep the purity of the music and ritual. Only the clergy, a special singer or cantor, and a choir are allowed to sing. And all services are sung, an important point since Orthodoxy is quite the opposite of Protestant worship where, apart from hymns, which are strongly congregational, no part of worship services would be sung. The Anglican and Lutheran traditions stand out, in the sense that parts of their liturgies are sung by priest, choir, and people.

The growth of chants and hymn-forms of religious poetry from the fourth century into the Middle Ages was especially important, fostered as it was through Catholic monastic houses with their set canonical hours forming a regular pattern of daily worship. Prayers, hymns, and readings, formed the basis of worship which, in the summer months, started at 1 a.m. and proceeded through some five services interspersed with reading and work until bed at about 8 p.m. This constant round of prayer was an important phase in the history of Christian worship and marks out the belief in the worthwhileness of particular people giving their lives specifically for the service of God through formal religious services of worship, as well as through prayer, study, and sometimes service to the community at large. For

162

practically a thousand years Western Christianity gave special emphasis to this form of religious life of monks and nuns, a life-style which exalted celibacy as the ideal way of life for worship.

As we have already mentioned, from about the thirteenth century hymns were introduced in the ordinary language of people, a change that was in marked contrast to the traditional church use of Latin. This shift into the vernacular was to become dramatically important with the Reformation, as monasteries were increasingly abandoned and as the ideal form of Christian life moved from celibacy to marriage. This change is deeply important as far as worship is concerned because the holy is no longer seen as separate and isolated from everyday life. One need not be a monk or nun in order to give God true and full worship. Worship can take place in the ordinary flow of life with its duties and obligations. Such a 'this-worldly' orientation of faith and worship is enshrined in Wesley's hymn 'Forth in thy name O Lord I go, My daily labour to pursue, Thee, only Thee, resolved to know, In all I think or speak or do'. An even more famous example is given in the hymn by George Herbert (1593–1632): 'Teach me, my God and King, In all things Thee to see; And what I do in anything, To do it as for Thee.' Herbert emphasizes the spiritual nature of ordinary existence in the verse, arguing that if a believer does something for God's sake, then even 'A servant with this clause Makes drudgery divine; Who sweeps a room, as for Thy laws, Makes that and the action fine.' The belief that drudgery may be divine is closely linked with the idea of the Protestant work ethic which reads religious worth into everyday activity and calls people to be good stewards of their daily work because they work to serve God and not to please others. Their very calling as Christians is worked out through everyday work and duties and not only in formal worship of God.

Worship, sacred languages and society

It is no accident that the prayer book of the Church of England after the English Reformation came to be called The Book of Common Prayer (1549), for it was the book to be shared in its use by the whole community, minister and people alike. This book, like the service books of the Roman Catholic and Orthodox churches along with most mainstream Christian denominations, gives a form and pattern for worship. Such books help provide an established pattern of worship over many centuries and over wide geographical areas. In many respects it is just such books that help reinforce the idea that the religious ritual of worship is extremely conservative and changes very little over time. This can be true, but it is also the case that when change comes, as it did in the Roman Catholic Church from the mid-1960s, after the important Vatican II conferences on religion and the faith, it comes dramatically and rapidly. Instead of the Mass being said in Latin in the great majority of countries of the world it was now said in local languages. In this the Roman Catholic Church was doing what had been done by the Protestant churches at their birth in the Reformation some four hundred years before, namely, putting the worship of the congregation into the everyday language of the people.

In terms of the history of Christian worship the issue of language had been vital from the earliest days of the Church. The first followers of Jesus probably worshipped at their local Jewish synagogue using the Aramaic language, while at Jerusalem's Temple Hebrew would have been used and understood only by those specially educated in it. In other parts of the Mediterranean world where Jews lived and worked they used Greek in their synagogue life. As far as new Christian congregations were concerned, worship followed the local language. In Rome, for example, the liturgy was initially in Greek because Greek was so widely used as a common language by those of the lower social class groups who constituted the largest group from which converts were drawn. This changed as time went on and, by the third century, most Christians spoke Latin and so the liturgy shifted to its Latin base. Later, in the seventh century, Greek came into use again as more Greek-speaking merchants and others came to be in Rome. As time went on Latin returned to become the dominant language used. Latin went on to become the language of the Roman Empire and many would have had some knowledge of it as a popular tongue. But, with the passage of time and the rise of the more modern European languages, Latin became increasingly a language for literature and scholars, leaving the mass of people ignorant of it, and of the liturgy of the Church.

This distance between ordinary believers and the form of worship of their Church was dramatically reversed in the Reformation as we have already indicated. What is interesting is that the Eastern Orthodox churches had their liturgies in local languages from the outset. But languages are dramatically open to change, and what is vernacular in one era can easily come to be less than intelligible in another. Some of the churches that originated in the Reformation have liturgies that are some three to four hundred years old and which are not completely intelligible in the present day. Because most contemporary Christians favour worship that is understandable and direct, some churches have sought to modernize their service books. The Church of England is a good example of this having published the Alternative Service Book (1980), to be used alongside or instead of the 1662 Book of Common Prayer.

To compare and contrast some passages from these books is to see not only how language has changed but, even more important than this, how social ideas, conventions, and theological outlooks, lying behind the text, have changed. The place of social influences upon the texts of worship is easily overlooked but remains radically significant.

The 1662 book assumes a form of society with the monarch as its powerful head followed by layers of people in authority. In the Prayer for the Queen's Majesty in the service of Morning Prayer, God is said to be 'high and mighty, King of kings, Lord of lords, the only Ruler of Princes', who from his throne beholds all the dwellers upon earth. In the service of Holy Communion, there are prayers for the monarch, 'that under her we may be godly and quietly governed', as well as for the monarch's 'whole Council, and all that are put in authority under her, that they may truly and indifferently minister justice to the punishment of wickedness and vice'. The whole service presumes a strongly hierarchical sense of society moving from God through the monarch and those in power down to the humble believer. The theology of the Holy Communion service follows in this line of thought and sees God as the one whose wayward servants have offended against him. God is the merciful Father who forgives his humble and penitent servants because of the sacrificial death of his dearly beloved Son, Jesus Christ. True worship follows from a restored relationship with the offended God, and from a life of obedient service.

The 1980 book views the world differently. Its Holy Communion service begins by saying 'The Lord is here. His Spirit is with us.' The scene set is of a democratic community of friends rather than a hierarchy of master, monarch and servants. God as Spirit takes precedence over God as mighty ruling Lord. Even the prayer involving the monarch asks that every nation may be directed in the ways of peace that 'men may honour one another, and seek the common good'. Once more equality replaces hierarchy, and salvation involves a strong sense of community membership, and not only the forgiveness of sins. These subtle differences between the two books show how changes in society influence changes in theological expression and, through that, of the way worship takes place.

History does not stand still. There are many modern influences at work and not simply those originating hundreds or thousands of years ago. One major new development in church life and worship belonging to the latter part of the twentieth century that has affected Catholic as well as Protestant and Anglican churches, is that of the Charismatic Movement. Its importance demands special consideration.

Charismatic worship

A major feature of mainstream Orthodox, Catholic, Anglican, and Protestant church worship is a fixed and written liturgy which is followed through in the service conducted by authorized ministers and priests. The sermon and some of the intercessory prayers offer a degree of freedom for leaders to introduce thoughts of their own but, by and large, there is a fixed expectation of what will take place. Worship is organized.

We have already spoken about once-born and twice-born styles of worship, and these remain important for Charismatic worship since Charismatic activity often takes place within the overall framework of a traditional religious service. This is especially true in Catholic and Anglican traditions.

The Charismatic Movement gets its name from the *charismata* or gifts of the Spirit mentioned in the Acts of the Apostles and in the First Letter to the Corinthians. At the beginning of the twentieth century some revivalist churches emerged in the USA which stood in the Protestant and Evangelical tradition, stressing the importance of conversion. These Pentecostal churches, as they were called, went further than this, to talk of the need for individuals to have an additional experience of the Holy Spirit which brought them to a new level of Christian awareness. As their name suggests these churches read the story of the early Christians in the Acts of the Apostles, of a wind coming from God and inspiring the apostles to preach the gospel, and also giving them the ability to 'speak in tongues'. This form of inspired utterance or glossolalia was regarded as a special sign of the presence and power of the Holy Spirit, and a sure mark that an individual had received an additional blessing or renewal from God.

In the 1960s a very similar kind of religious enthusiasm emerged in the United States of America and quickly spread to Britain and across the world. It, too, emphasized the gifts of the Spirit, especially glossolalia or speaking in tongues, seeing that gift as one of a number of signs that an individual had received a renewal of spiritual life. One important feature of this Charismatic or Renewal Movement, as it was also called, was that those influenced by it tended to remain within their original denomination or church rather than come out to create new churches. At least this was the case for much of the 1960s and 1970s, with the result that many congregations of the main Christian churches came to have Charismatic members. A relatively small but significant number of clergy, Protestant and Catholic, were also influenced and experienced a revitalization of their spiritual lives. This led to some churches having services which included period of Charismatic worship set amidst the traditional liturgy. Some also added new 'praise' services to their list of ordinary events.

The word 'praise' came into its own as a description of Charismatic worship when individuals might lift their arms up into the air while singing or as an expression of adoration of God. Some would speak in tongues or even sing in tongues as the whole group stood and swayed to the music. As with many periods of religious enthusiasm and creativity the Charismatic Movement gave birth to hundreds of new hymns, to much new music, and to a distinctive ethos or mood of spirituality. This is typified by a sense of the immediate nearness and power of God through the Holy Spirit. Anything might happen, and God might decide to say something to a group through someone speaking in tongues or, perhaps, through a revelation. The centre of gravity of worship was in the present. The meaning of life was immediately available. A sense of expectation in worship was connected with gifts of healing that many believed to be given to the Church by God.

Many of the new hymns expressed these thoughts. One called 'For I'm building a people of power' is interesting in that it begins in the

167

first person singular as though Jesus was giving a direct message through a prophetic utterance: 'For I'm building a people of power, And I'm making a people of praise, That will move through this land by my Spirit, And will glorify my precious Name' (Dave Richards). The second verse then gives the response of believers to this message as they say: 'Build Your Church Lord, Make us strong Lord', and they go on to ask the Lord to join their hearts in one and give them unity in Christ's Kingdom.

Another dimension to this excitement in divine activity was a belief, held by some charismatically inclined Christians, that evil spirits were also active in the world and might even possess people. In some churches, ministers and priests conducted exorcisms to expel spirits from individual lives. Another hymn echoes this aspect of religion: 'For this purpose Christ was revealed, To destroy all the works of the Evil One.' The hymn then divides with lines for men and women to sing separately before they reunite to say that in the name of Jesus they stand and claim victory because 'Satan has no authority here, Powers of Darkness must flee, For Christ has the victory' (Graham Kendrick). A feature of many Charismatic hymns, as in the hymns of the Pentecostal churches of the twentieth century, is a repetitive chorus sung after each main verse. This is characteristic of songs in religious groups where the democratic unity of all members is stressed. So it was that worship of God came to embrace a wide variety of intense experiences and beliefs.

While many Charismatics remained in the mainstream churches, others left to found house churches, making the House Church Movement a significant point of religious growth in later twentieth-century Britain. These also developed patterns of emotional worship of a charismatic type and often used buildings of a non-traditional church-style for their meetings. By using, for example, a redundant cinema as a church such a group expresses its belief that true worship of God does not require architecture or symbolism of a traditional Christian kind. Sincerity of faith is what matters for true worship to be given to God, and not any particular sacred place.

Adaptability of hymns in worship

It is precisely because hymns are very often taken for granted in most branches of contemporary Christianity that we have emphasized their significance in this book, especially in Chapter 4. Once hymns became established in eighteenth-century Protestant religion as a means of expressing doctrine and religious experience they opened up new possibilities for new religious movements. New content could easily be put into the traditional form of a hymn, or new words could be sung to a familiar tune.

The Salvation Army, initially founded in 1865 on the model of an army whose task was actively to convert people to Christianity, established brass bands rather like military bands to accompany singing in public places. The founder, 'General' William Booth, encouraged hymn singing to well-known and popular music on the basis that 'the Devil should not have all the best tunes'. In terms of Christian worship, the Salvation Army is one of the best examples of Christians expanding the meaning of worship to include service to the community. Uniform-wearing members put their faith into action by helping the poor, deprived and distressed in society through active social welfare programmes. In their citadels, services are held on different occasions for those who are actively committed members of the Army and for members of the general public. Unlike practically all other churches within the Christian tradition, the Salvation Army do not hold services of Holy Communion. Singing, Bible reading, prayers, sermons and the giving of personal testimony to the work of God in their personal lives form the basis for services of worship.

If popular tunes helped people think about the Christian message, as with the Salvation Army, so it is very likely that patterns of worship based on hymn singing, Bible reading and prayers helped others already familiar with one church to move to others. Familiar patterns of behaviour ease the passage of converts as they leave their former religious base and become members in new churches. Many groups, including Christian Science, Jehovah's Witnesses, Seventh-Day Adventists and Mormons, all used hymns as part of their own religious worship.

Sacred places and religious habit

We have already mentioned the tension in Christianity between those who value special places for worship and those who do not. The weight of emphasis has, historically, always fallen on the need for religious buildings precisely because Christianity is a group-focused and congregationally-based religion. Sooner or later a group of Christians requires somewhere to meet. Many new groupings of believers would like to keep their faith free from the impediments of buildings and materialistic concerns. It is often argued that people become too attached to particular places of worship and value the place more than the purpose for which it exists.

In practice worship is a habit-forming activity. From its earliest days Christianity has been organized for frequent worship, often of groups of people meeting together. Such regularity fosters commitment to a particular place. When people have particular experiences in particular places they associate the one with the other, and over time they can come to be firmly wedded together. Someone may worship in the same church building for many years and may even sit in the same seat. In many traditional societies, where relatively few left their home village or town to live and work elsewhere, many of their memories would be associated with the church building. Moments of joy and moments of sorrow would be connected with that one building. From the theological standpoint of ministers or priests, this situation can easily be interpreted as unfortunate or childish, especially if they have had the wider experience of worshipping in many different places and living in many towns. But the fixed residence of long-term inhabitants gives them their own sense of continuity and habit.

Some sacred places, whether actual buildings like cathedrals, or places of pilgrimage such as Rome or Jerusalem, develop their significance over thousands of years. The habit of many generations is the framework for each new pilgrim or visitor. Some people speak of the 'atmosphere' of some sacred places as positive and beneficial to their own prayers and worship. While it is difficult to describe exactly what is meant by an atmosphere of worship, it marks the readiness of people to pray and worship within a particular church or place. Readiness for worship is probably associated with the traditional triggers for prayer in a culture, not least a certain organization of space, light, smell and sound.

Human beings have probably engaged in worship for as long as archaeological evidence is available, and it is certainly the case that all known religions (including folk-Buddhism) contain some aspect of worship directed to their supreme focus. In terms of Christian theology this is explained as the human awareness of creatureliness.

In broader terms it probably involves the human drive for meaning in the face of a universe and a life that is both beautiful and terrifying. Reason takes us into the world of theology, philosophy and science where arguments help explain the universe and the place of people within it, but such rational explanations often seem to leave the emotional depths of life untouched.

In Christianity these two dimensions of reason and emotion come together in the worshipping life of the Church. In worship Christians do not simply think about the meaning of life, they also respond to the meaning of life. Through theology they learn that God is both the creator of all things and also the one who undertakes to love mankind and to bring meaning to the relationships in which people live. Through worship these ideas are not merely entertained as thoughts but are expressed as worship.

Worship: its nature and dynamics

So, theologically speaking, worship is a response. People worship because they are aware of something. In Christianity this is an awareness of God's self-revelation in creation, in redemption through Jesus, in the life of the Church, and in personal experience. Worship is the grateful response for these loving acts of God, the response of the creature and of the redeemed servant. The important nineteenth-century Danish theologian Søren Kierkegaard (to whom we return in greater detail in Chapter 8) spoke about the 'first wonder' that humans encountered through nature, a wonder that was lost in despair and which can come to be replaced by a 'second wonder' or consciousness of God as the individual is confronted by God in realizing the nature of sin and of faith. This is a clear example in the Christian tradition of the double knowledge of God in creation and salvation, and of the two sources of worshipping response.

A further understanding of worship as a human activity can be gained by shifting from a theological to a more sociological outlook, focusing on questions of meaning and identity already hinted at. In terms of meaning, worship is an expression of satisfaction at having discovered truth, it involves commitment to the explanation of life furnished by a particular religion. Knowledge of a religion does not simply involve philosophical, historical, and textual study gained in an academic way; there is also a kind of knowing that comes from active participation in the life of a worshipping church community. Such worship can provide a context where other forms of reflection gain a greater significance.

IDENTITY AND WORSHIP

Closely aligned with the meaning gained in worship is the sense of identity that worship helps individuals to gain for themselves. Identity is a complex idea but it refers to those things that give individuals a sense of their past, of who they are and of where they belong in life. It includes the language people speak, the history they share with others, the land where they belong, the kind of music, dance and social occasions that they enjoy. But identity also comes from a particular way of understanding and responding to God. At the community level of particular regions or countries, shared worship can help bind people together into a unified group, but it can also help keep people apart from others whose way of worship, even within the overall world of Christianity, is different from their own. So at the human level of relationships, worship can serve as the focus for wider religious differences that divide people.

One of the sharpest examples of this is the Eucharist itself, since it is a major division between Roman Catholics, Greek Orthodox, Anglicans and other Protestants. This service and its theology, along with those authorized to conduct it, enshrines the history of debate between these churches and ensures that historical differences are perpetuated. Many Christians see this as shameful, since worship should unite believers and not divide them, and since worship is a form of relationship between the human and the divine which belongs to the essential nature of life. This relationship can be perverted if something or someone replaces God as the very centre of adoration, for then worship becomes idolatry. But in the proper ordering of human life, the setting of worship is a powerful context for learning about God, both through acts of worship and also through sermons or other forms of instruction.

CHANNELS OF WORSHIP

Worship flows through several channels. Traditionally the emphasis is placed upon the church or sacred building, but many Christians engage in private prayer in any setting. When praying, individuals explicitly set themselves in relationship to God in several ways. Very often human language is used as the basic means of addressing God. This can be a formal or a less formal style of language, it may be spoken, intoned, or sung, conducted jointly with others in common prayer or else be private. The substance of prayer may be adoration of God, but may also involve confession of sin, petition for something that is desired by the worshipper.

In terms of posture there is great variation both among and within traditions. Some stand to pray, others kneel or sit, while at the Catholic ordination service the new priests lie full length upon the ground in prostration before God. Eyes may be closed, when there is an inner focus on God's presence, while eyes may be left open if an icon or statue or other form of religious art is part of the total process. Human hands also play a vital part in worship since they may be placed together making the body symmetrical and balanced, or one hand may be used to make the sign of the cross as believers identify themselves with the cross of Christ, and increasingly, the return of the dance to Christian worship involves the whole body.

The history of Western culture is full of sacred music, largely as the vehicle of the Eucharist and its worship, but also in oratorios such as Handel's *Messiah* where biblical words have been set to music to tell the story of salvation or of some detailed biblical period. At a more general social level bells have played an important part in making public 'noises' signalling the worship of God.

But worship can take place in silence and some traditions of Christianity have favoured silence, even for the congregational gathering of believers, as the context in which to wait for God to encounter them. The Society of Friends started by George Fox (1624–91) believed in the 'Inner Light' which involved a prompting of the Holy Spirit in worship (Dandelion, 1996: 162). Their alternative name, the Quakers, indicates another aspect of their religious life in which they trembled or shook as a result of divine influence. Movement as a form of worship was characteristic of the Shakers who developed in Manchester in the mid-eighteenth century under the influence of some French Protestant refugees called

Camisards. After some Shakers emigrated to America their number grew as they formed and lived in communities. In the nineteenth century they developed complex group dancing as a form of worship. In quite a different religious climate some present-day Christians in the mainline denominations have explored liturgical dance as one form of worship. This, along with all the other patterns of worship we have sketched, shows how varied worship can be as different sorts of people at varied times and places respond to the mystery and revelation of God and, in some measure, share in it.

Further reading

Davies, J. G. (ed.) (1986) *A New Dictionary of Liturgy and Worship*. London: SCM Press.

Dix, G. (1945) *The Shape of the Liturgy*. London: Dacre Press.

James, W. (1902) *The Varieties of Religious Experience*. London: Longman.

LeFevre, P. D. (1956) *The Prayers of Kierkegaard*. Chicago: Chicago University Press.

Otto, R. (1924) *The Idea of the Holy*. Oxford: Oxford University Press.

7. Rites of passage

Within the context and experience of worship Christianity has, over the course of its 2000-year history, changed from being a small sect of Judaism to a religion with branches in most countries of the world where local customs have influenced Christianity just as, it, in turn, has helped fashion local ways of life. This is especially true in terms of the human life-cycle (Turnbull, 1984). Christianity has brought its own rituals and interpretation of life to bear upon periods of birth, adulthood, marriage and death in extensive ways.

These events are often discussed through the concept of rites of passage which first emerged as a technical term in social anthropology early in the twentieth century. It describes the ritual process accompanying the movement of people from one social status to another, as from being a boy to a man or from being a married woman to becoming a mother. This we explore throughout this chapter recognizing that social changes can also be closely linked to deep changes within personal experience.

Life and change

Behind the idea of rites of passage lies the fact that the whole of human life is marked by change. Babies are conceived, born, grow, mature, produce offspring and finally die, all as part of the biological facts of life. Biological and social facts of life combine in theories of ageing and changes in the 'life-course' which show how social value is added to the biological facts through various celebrations (Spencer, 1985).

Religious ideas also enter into the value brought to changes in life through both teaching and rituals. The passage from birth to death has also been extended into another dimension as the dead are reckoned to enter into a life after death. Divine help is often invoked to give power or protection to those undergoing these changes.

As a concept 'rites of passage' was first developed in 1908 by the Belgian anthropologist Arnold van Gennep. Though used extensively in the study of preliterate and tribal societies it has also been extended to complex modern societies. Van Gennep saw rites of passage as organized events in which, as it were, society took individuals by the hand and led them from one social status to another, conducting them across thresholds and holding them for a moment in a position when they were neither in one status nor another. He distinguished between three phases of these rites: the first separated people from their original status, the second involved a period apart from normal status, and the third conferred a new status upon the individual. By comparing rites of passage with moving from room to room within a house van Gennep described these three phases of rites of passage in terms of the Latin word *limen* meaning 'threshold' or 'doorstep'. He spoke of the three phases as (1) pre-liminal, (2) liminal, and (3) post-liminal.

LIMINALITY

In more recent years the British anthropologist Victor Turner (1969) took up this middle phase and developed the idea of liminality by exploring the quality of relationships people have with each other during periods of change in social status. He suggested that during liminal periods individuals experience what he called a sense of *communitas* or intense awareness of being bound together in a community of shared experience. But Turner was also very much aware that ideas applicable to tribal and preliterate peoples traditionally studied by anthropologists are not easily transferred to modern and urban societies.

With this caution in mind Turner (1982) still thought there were aspects of preliterate and modern life that were similar and could, with some appropriate modification, be compared. The most significant modification came when he coined the word 'liminoid' to describe periods in modern society when the ordinary system of organized activity is put aside to enable people to share in a sense of the common oneness of human existence. This is important for this book because many of these events are set within Christian contexts.

HIERARCHY AND *COMMUNITAS*

Turner's thought works on the assumption that for much of the time societies operate a system of hierarchical and structured life where people exist with seniors above them and juniors below them and even with a degree of formal respect for their equals. But, periodically, this life of hierarchy and formal structure is interspersed with non-hierarchical and informal interaction as though the underlying nature of being human breaks through to bring people together. He coined the term *communitas* to describe this feeling which people might have whilst in a liminal state. Just as hierarchy divides so *communitas* unites in many different sorts of activity. With this in mind Turner (1978) studied the place of pilgrimage, festivals, holidays, and of various celebrations in Christian cultures as examples of liminoid activity, as well as suggesting that monks, nuns, and some others live a kind of permanently liminal life.

But it is also important to see that many examples of liminoid periods in modern societies take place outside religious institutions as with sport and entertainment. One of the most interesting and extensive liminoid moments of world history came in July 1985 with the Live Aid concert organized by the pop musician Bob Geldof as part of an attempt to raise money and express concern for poverty stricken areas of the world. The concert was shared by literally millions of people all over the world through the medium of satellite television. His own account of his experience at the Wembley Stadium concert in London on that night provides a direct description of a liminoid quality of relationships:

> Everyone came on for the finale. There was a tremendous feeling of oneness on that stage. There had been no bitching, no displays of temperament all day. Now everyone was singing. They had their arms around each other ... everyone was crying. Not the easy tears of showbiz but genuine emotion ... (On the way home) ... people walked over to the car and hugged me. Some cried, 'Oh Bob, oh Bob', not sneering, not uncontrollable, just something shared and understood. 'I

know', was all I could say. I did know. I wasn't sure what had happened in England, or everywhere else, but I 'knew'. Cynicism and greed and selfishness had been eliminated for a moment. It felt good. A lot of people had rediscovered something in themselves. (1986: 310)

In Turner's terms this was a moment when the underlying humanity of many individuals was shared as distinctions of fame and celebrity faded into insignificance behind their common human nature. It was an example of that *spontaneous communitas*, described below, and shows that even when societies change and become very modern under the influence of extensive media coverage and management the dynamics of human nature can still have a powerful effect.

RITES AND EXPERIENCE

Another dimension of rites of passage directly concerns the issue of personal experience or circumstances in relation to socially defined categories. Van Gennep was, for example, very clear on the fact that a gap might exist between personal circumstance and socially defined identity as in his example that in some societies boys and girls may be deemed adult either before or after they are biologically and sexually adult. In Christianity the sacraments announce the status or calling of individuals whilst recognizing that it may take some time for their self-identity and status to match each other.

STRESSING THE GOAL

Not only did van Gennep think that rites of passage had three component rituals built into them but he also thought that one of these three components would be emphasized depending upon the overall purpose of the ritual. So, for example, some funeral rites stress the pre-liminal aspect of separation from the land of the living, the consecration of monks or nuns might focus on a liminal existence apart from ordinary life, while confirmation emphasizes the post-liminal world of incorporation into a new family-like group of the church.

Having said that, it is important to remember that rites of passage are often quite complicated and can have a variety of emphases within them. In the example of a funeral the ritual can stress the incorporation of the deceased into the heavenly realm of the departed while, as far as the mourners are concerned, the stress may lie on their separation from the dead.

Kinds of *communitas*

Turner identified three sorts of *communitas* which he called *spontaneous*, *ideological*, and *normative*. Spontaneous *communitas* occurs when people suddenly find themselves caught up in a shared sense of oneness. This may be because of a joy in triumph in battle, in sport, or even in a musical event like the Live Aid concert just mentioned. Moments like this can become part of a tradition of a movement or group so much so that it becomes an ideal. That is how Turner sees ideological *communitas*, as an ideal which reflection on past events and the wisdom of hindsight brings to a focus as a prized value. The case of the Day of Pentecost can be understood in this way as an account of an experience which can come to be an ideal of Christian life which present-day congregations might seek to emulate. This is the point where ideological and normative *communitas* overlap, for normative *communitas* refers to attempts at building the ideal of spontaneity into contemporary life. Societies or groups might, for example, seek to live according to that unity of purpose outlined in a sacred text. In the Christian case the wish to get back to the biblical form of fellowship expresses a desire for authenticity and truth which has motivated many protest movements in Christianity over the centuries. Other groups realize that history cannot be relived in this way but might still wish to express the value of the ideal.

Status and identity

It is important to realize that there is a distinction to be made between status and identity, a difference that van Gennep also recognized. At its simplest status can be viewed as coming from society, as something which is accorded to an individual either because of their birth-right or else through personal achievement. Identity, by contrast, reflects the more internal process of becoming what one is supposed to be. It often takes time for the internal change to match the externally granted position. The importance of identity within transition rites is reflected in the baptismal names given to Christians or in new names given to those becoming monks or nuns.

As already mentioned, van Gennep was aware that a rite of passage, as a social event, might not always be timed to correspond exactly with biological maturity or particular psychological states of individuals. This is a significant point, especially if we add to it a religious dimension and say that official church ritual does not always directly reflect the inner state of faith of an individual. In terms of sacraments, for example, a rite may express some theological truth outwardly which, at that particular moment, does not correlate with the inner life of an individual. In some Protestant groups people are not admitted into full membership until they are able to assert that some inner transformation or conversion has taken place, for more Catholic traditions it is enough to assert the ideal of a change through a ritual performance.

 ## Baptism–confirmation

Baptism is the most fundamental Christian rite of passage. It is one of the additional rituals which Christianity brings to the catalogue of rites performed by humanity in the normal course of human life. By the use of water and in the name of the Holy Trinity a person becomes a member of the Church. The natural substance of water, which is the ordinary medium of washing and cleansing, comes to have several layers of theological meaning when it becomes the water of baptism. The New Testament presents a command of Jesus to the disciples to 'go and make disciples of all nations baptizing them in the name of the Father and of the Son and of the Holy Spirit' (Matt 28:19–20). John the Baptist appears in all four of the gospels preaching a baptism of repentance for the forgiveness of sins and the coming of God's chosen one. Jesus is then himself baptized by John, an act interpreted by Christians as being not for the forgiveness of sin but to mark the commencement of Jesus' own ministry as God's chosen one who will save people from their sin and who, in baptism, identifies himself with all people. Paul, one of the most notable early converts to Christianity from Judaism, is himself baptized (Acts

9:18) and is a firm witness to the importance of baptism among early Christians (1 Cor 1:13ff.).

Just as circumcision had been a mark of membership in the Jewish nation as God's people, so baptism comes to be the defining mark of people being Christian. Many additional meanings were associated with baptismal water. Not only does it remind Christians of the river Jordan in which Jesus was baptized, in his rite of passage into his active public ministry, but it can also represent the Red Sea through which God's people had been delivered from slavery in Egypt. By additional metaphors it stands for the deep waters of death through which Christ was delivered in his resurrection to life, for in baptism the Christian dies to sin and is born again to holiness. Baptismal water can also gain significance in that just as the waters of the womb bring us to our first and natural birth, so the waters of baptism bring us to new birth by the grace of God.

Practically all subsequent Christian groups continued the use of baptism as the basis of membership even though it came to assume different forms and to have varied theological meaning. In the Orthodox, Catholic, Lutheran, and Anglican traditions, the sacramental nature of baptism stresses the divine act of God's grace in forgiveness. Here baptism involves washing from sin, a passage from death to life, a statement of God's covenant established with God's chosen people. This perspective involves what is called sacramental regeneration, which means that the rite itself brings about the desired goal. Some Christians, especially amongst Protestants, view sacramental regeneration as too mechanical and too dependent on the work of the priest and the ritual, and insufficiently related to the heart-felt personal faith of the individual. So, for example, in the Baptist Church, originating in the seventeenth century, and in many evangelical Christian churches, great stress is placed upon the faith of the individual who is to be baptized. For this reason baptism is called believers' baptism and is not administered to babies. In this tradition it is important that individuals should be of an age of discretion – old enough to know what they are doing, aware of the truth of Christianity, and having experienced the forgiving love of God in Christ in their own lives. The service of baptism by immersion allows individuals to acknowledge publicly their faith in Christ before being admitted into the visible body of believers which is the Church. Baptism does not of itself change these individuals in the sense of adding any divine power or grace to them. In terms of rites of passage this self-conscious commitment to Christ, which the adult undertakes in the presence of the congregation of believers, is a rite of incorporation into full membership of the group. Although faith is internal the testimony of faith is external.

During the first five hundred years of Christian history, church leaders developed the practice of baptism in some quite complex ways. In Western Catholic Christianity baptism usually took place at Easter or Pentecost. There was a period, traditionally that of Lent, when candidates were formed into a group called the catechumenate and were taught the Christian faith. They worshipped with the congregation but were not allowed to remain and witness the actual Eucharist of the faithful. Before Easter they underwent rituals of exorcism prior to their baptism on Easter Sunday. After baptism in water and in the name of the Holy Trinity they would be vested in white clothes and taken from the baptistery into the body of the church where the bishop laid hands on them and anointed them with oil to receive, and be sealed by, the Holy Spirit. Only then were they fully part of the Church and able to share in the Eucharist. This scheme follows the threefold process of rites of passage involving separation from the old status, a period of transition, and a rite of incorporation into the new status. By the Middle Ages, when baptism was increasingly administered to babies, largely because of the theological idea that unbaptized babies would not go to heaven, these rites were compressed and the baby was made a catechumen at the church door before being admitted to be baptized at the font.

In the Eastern Orthodox Church the idea of baptism covered a wider sweep of behaviour than it did in the West, focusing not only on the water rite but also on anointing with oil and the laying on of hands. One major difference emerged between Eastern and Western Christian traditions as time went on and this was that in the West a separation emerged between the use of water and the laying on of hands in the initiation ritual for Christians. In the West the water rite came to be administered by local priests, while the laying on of hands for the conveying of the Holy Spirit took place later and was restricted to the office of the bishop. In the East the priest took over both functions, which meant that the pattern of the earlier tradition was retained to a greater extent than in the West. Eastern rites have also been compressed into shorter periods, but the ritual still retains a phase for the making of a catechumen, involving being breathed on by the priest, blessed with the sign of the cross, exorcisms, the renunciation of evil, and the profession of faith. Baptism proper follows after the water has been blessed and after oil has been blessed and placed on the candidates. Baptism is by total immersion and afterwards the new Christians are dressed in white and receive what is called the sacrament of chrismation, involving anointing numerous parts of the body with chrism and the laying on of hands for the 'seal of the gift of the Holy Spirit'. This sacrament of chrismation is the equivalent of the Western rite of confirmation. The distinctive difference is that it follows immediately after the water rite and is part and parcel of the total rite of baptism.

In the West, as is the case in the Church of England, baptism became quite separate from confirmation for two reasons. On the one hand it was due to the fact that priests performed the first and bishops the second (bishops were also far fewer in number than were priests), but on the other hand there emerged the tradition that baptism was largely performed on babies and confirmation on children from the age of about seven, as preferred by some Catholics, or the teenage period which became popular in the Anglican Church. This sharp separation of baptism from confirmation runs counter to the earliest Christian tradition where, as we have seen, they formed part of an overall initiation rite. But an equally important point is that confirmation came to be a distinctive rite, not only gaining the official status as a sacrament in the Roman Catholic Church at the Council of Trent in the late sixteenth century, but also serving in some countries as its own sort of rite of passage.

In many parts of Great Britain, as also in the Lutheran Church of Sweden, for example, it was customary for younger teenagers to join a confirmation class and to be 'prepared for confirmation'. Separated from ordinary Sunday School children and teachers, they were 'prepared for confirmation' by the parish priest in what was a liminal period, prior to confirmation and incorporation into full church membership at their first communion service. In terms of social history, it appeared odd in Britain when mature adults of thirty or forty years of age increasingly presented themselves for confirmation from the 1970s thus breaking the social pattern of confirmation as a teenage rite of passage into full church membership. This reflects the fact that many babies are no longer baptized and that those who, as adults, come into church membership do so much more in the fashion of early church converts for whom baptism and confirmation as one rite is far more appropriate.

In terms of religious studies it is interesting to see how churches developed theologies to explain changes that occurred in their ritual for non-theological reasons. The split between the water rite and the rite of laying on of hands was closely related to the division of labour between priest and bishop. We have seen how the Eastern Orthodox kept the two rites together within the total process of baptism performed by the priest, while, in the major Western churches, the rites were split and attempts were made to develop a theology of confirmation as a distinctive sacrament. Recent theological debates in Catholic, Anglican, and some other churches have tried to focus more on baptism as the major rite of passage into membership of the Church and to see it as the basis for taking a full part in the Eucharist. In the Church of England, for example, unconfirmed children are not, officially, permitted to receive the Holy Communion bread and wine despite the fact that they have been baptized. There is a certain lack of theological logic and pastoral insight in this, for some people think that since full participation is part of the very process of developing a knowledge and awareness of God, the children who are prevented from participation are hindered in their spiritual development. From the perspective of rites of passage, as far, for example, as the Church of England is concerned, the status of being a baptized member has shifted from being a post-liminal to being a liminal ritual, with the confirmed status being the post-liminal status of a fully participating member.

Eucharist

The Eucharist itself is sometimes described as a rite of passage in a way that is not entirely appropriate, but it is worth mentioning here as a good example of an occasion that is better described as liminoid than liminal. It is not a rite of passage in the formal sense because it does not conduct a person from one social status to another. What it can do is take people out of their normal everyday and hierarchical form of life and place them for a moment within a context of shared equality together and with God.

One reason why some people make the mistake of seeing the Eucharist as a rite of passage is because it does possess something of a threefold pattern. An initial period of confession and absolution from sin separates worshippers from the everyday world of evil and then places them into the transitional phase of worship. While in the liminoid phase they may feel a sense of unity of purpose and fellowship. The theological stress on the Holy Spirit in many modern liturgies reinforces this interpretation of the event, as does the 'sharing of the peace' in an emotional way, as described elsewhere in this chapter. With this sense of unity in mind, the Eucharist can be interpreted as involving a liminoid period. Turner described liminoid events in modern society as normally lying outside central political and economic processes as moments when a sense of community is experienced. The Eucharist, Mass, Holy Communion, or Lord's Supper, does very largely lie on the margin of everyday life and takes place in leisure time, and it can provide a sense of community. Not all members of a church may interpret the Eucharist in this way, for some will see it as a time of private and personal worship rather than as a phase of collective and emotional unity. At the end of the service the people are returned to everyday life in a kind of ritual of reincorporation to normality. In one Anglican form, in the Alternative Service Book, the service ends with the people praying together 'Send us out in the power of your Spirit to live and work to your praise and glory'. They are then told by the priest to 'Go in peace to love and serve the Lord'. This example of the Eucharist shows the care needed in using the idea of rites of passage to interpret ceremonies taking place in modern societies, and in particular to draw a distinction between rites which actually alter someone's status and rites that, perhaps, simply alter their mood and quality of relationships with others for a short period.

It is also possible to use other ideas to describe these rites in order to draw out different goals attained. So, for example, we could speak of the Eucharist as a rite of intensification, when basic beliefs and sentiments are focused upon and experienced anew. Many repetitive rites of a society foster such an intensification, as in the case of renewal of baptismal or ordination vows. Another way of talking of such ceremonies is to see them in terms of what I call 'accessive' rites, ritual occasions when particular beliefs and cultural values are made explicit and people are given distinctive access to them through the arousal of particular moods. The main distinction between rites of passage and rites of intensification is that most people undergo a rite of passage only once, as in confirmation, but they repeatedly experience accessive rites of intensification such as the Eucharist. Periodic festivals celebrating Christmas, harvest, birthdays, and anniversaries are all examples of repetitive rites that are not rites of passage (except for some birthdays when the age of majority is attained) but which may well include a liminoid sense of unity and oneness.

Thanksgiving, blessing, and naming

Those Protestant churches where baptism takes place in adult life, or where parents choose not to have their children baptized as infants, often undertake a service of thanksgiving for the child. A good example may be found in the Church of England's new Alternative Service Book (1980), which included a special service of Thanksgiving for the Birth of a Child. This Anglican service is interesting as far as religious studies are concerned because it has undergone a series of changes indicating shifts in theological emphasis and in social conditions. From a brief historical perspective we can see the service change, starting from a medieval service for the 'Purification of Women' after childbirth (in the 1549 Prayer Book). This ritual for the purification of mothers focuses more on the woman than on the child and was a thanksgiving for her safety during childbirth. In England this took place about a month after the baby was born; in one medieval rite she was met by the priest at the church door, sprinkled with holy water, and then led into church. In the 1552 Prayer Book the service is called 'The Thanksgiving of Women after Childbirth commonly called The Churching of Women'. By the time of the Alternative Service Book, the service has become one of thanksgiving for the birth of a child.

In terms of rites of passage, a switch has occurred from a focus on the woman and her return to ordinary social life to that of the child and thanksgiving for its birth, It is likely that the older rite for the Purification of Women readmitted them to normal social activity after the birth of a child, for pregnancy has often been viewed as a liminal period in which the woman, especially if she was childless, moved into the status of motherhood from that of simply being a wife. The difference also mirrors the fact discussed in Chapter 10 that, in earlier centuries, women would have given birth to many babies, some of which would probably not survive for long, while today the stress and value placed upon the one baby is incredibly strong.

186

Children are themselves blessed and sometimes given their Christian name at these services of thanksgiving, as they are in the rite of baptism. Such name-giving is an important moment, marking as it does the fact that the child is given a social identity of its own, Babies are often dressed in special white robes or dresses for thanksgiving or baptism services. Such 'christening robes' continue to express the traditional Christian practice of initiates being dressed in white at their baptism to symbolize the freedom from sin brought about through the baptismal washing. In terms of popular religion they often reflect family tradition with the same robe being used for generations.

Marriage

Being a major life event in terms of changed social status marriage would be expected to involve rites of passage. In this case the passage is from a variety of unmarried states to the one married state. This is obviously the case in that prior to the marriage individuals may be single, divorced, or bereaved as widows or widowers. After marriage they are husbands or wives. Most present-day Christian churches practise marriage rites and the image of, for example, the Church of England's marriage service, with bells, organ, vicar and choir, all set within an ancient building, has become an established part of British cultural life. But Christian churches have not always conducted marriages and, compared with baptism, the Eucharist, and death rites, marriage is a slightly relative newcomer to Christian ritual.

The pre-liminal phase involves separation from purely single and unattached life. In Britain this is an informal and personal period but does involve a change when young men and young women no longer fill their leisure time in the company of a group of same-sex friends. A couple going out together on a regular basis is the informal mark of a pre-liminal phase which is formally marked with the giving of an engagement ring. The engagement is the liminal period when the couple are no longer single and unattached but neither are they formally married. In the state Church of England their transitional status is expressed in the reading of the banns, which takes place over three separate weeks preceding the marriage in the parish church where the individuals live. Only with the marriage ceremony, either in a church or else in a civil register office, does the liminal phase end and the post-liminal status of married life begin. Sometimes there is an engagement party, but there is nearly always a formal social celebration to mark the marriage.

As far as the wedding ceremony is concerned, especially in church, the ritual very interestingly expresses the change in status that now occurs. The bride and groom are formally separated for a day before the wedding. They will probably celebrate with their single-sex friends in a stag-night or hen-party a day or so before the wedding. He is not supposed to see her on the wedding day, nor even see her wedding dress until she appears in church. He will have gone there with his best man and entered in an unceremonious way. The bride enters very formally, accompanied by her father who is, tradition-ally, said to 'give her away'. The bride's family and friends sit on one side of the church and the groom's family and friends on the other.

Generally speaking there are two dimensions to wedding rites; on the one hand there is a legal ceremony in which promises are made between bride and groom, and on the other, a religious blessing of the couple with prayers for their future life. In Eastern and Western Christendom these elements are stressed in quite different ways. In Western Catholic and Protestant Christianity the marriage rite is actually performed by bride and groom rather than by the priest. They are the heart of their own rite of passage into marriage as is clearly shown in, for example, the Anglican rite where the bride says 'I ... take thee ... to my wedded husband', and also, when the man says 'With this ring I thee wed, with my body I thee honour, and with all my worldly goods I thee endow'. The priest pronounces that they are man and wife only because they have made each other so. The prayers that follow bless them as husband and wife but do not make them husband and wife.

In Eastern Orthodox Christianity there is also a betrothal of each to each, as a form of natural human bond, but this is then taken up into a sacramental rite in which the priest crowns the husband and the wife as a central feature of the wedding. This expresses the hierarchy of the Holy Trinity extended into that of husband and wife. They share in drinking wine together as a symbolic expression of their unity, and they go in procession within the church to express the unity they possess within the mystical fellowship of Christ which cannot be broken, even by death. This contrasts sharply with the Western tradition and its stress upon the contractual nature of marriage which exists 'till death us do part'.

Marriage was a relatively late ritual to be taken up by the Christian churches. In their early history churches had prayers for blessing those who had married by the normal rules of their society, but it was only in the eleventh century in the West that the church became a central and dominant focus for marriage for almost the next thousand years. Civil marriage in Britain was firmly established only by the Marriage Act, passed by Parliament in 1836. By the late 1980s, just about half of all wedding ceremonies took place in church and half in a register office. Slightly more detail shows that nearly 70 per cent of all first marriages took place in churches of some denomination but, by contrast, some 76 per cent of all second marriages, which include divorced people, took the form of civil marriages, This shows a continued preference for the church form of ceremony for the first wedding. Even some of those whose second marriages take place in register offices then go to church for a service of blessing. Such a service of blessing a marriage is, as we have seen from the history of marriage rites, quite logical given the nature of marriage in European culture, where the first major focus is on the partners marrying each other before the Church pronounces a blessing on the union. Remarriage brings to an end the period as a bereaved or divorced person, two statuses that need to be considered in their own right.

DIVORCE

Divorce is a problem because churches argue that marriage is for life. So, for example, in the traditional wedding service of the Church of England both bride and groom are asked if they will have the other as their marriage partner to love, honour and keep in sickness and in health, 'so long as you both shall live'. Then, in the actual statement where each one takes the other as a spouse the fact of death is clearly mentioned, as in the words the man says to the woman: 'I ... take thee ... to my wedded wife, to have and to hold from this day forward for better for worse, for richer for poorer, in sickness and in health, to love and to cherish till death us do part, according to God's holy ordinance.' The woman then makes a very similar statement to the man, In both statements marriage is assumed to be for the whole of their earthly life and for no longer. For many reasons the union between husband and wife does not always last this long. Traditional Catholic teaching has argued that once a real marriage union exists it cannot be dissolved by any human power. If separation comes this line of thinking leads to attempts at showing that no proper and full marriage existed between people. The Orthodox tradition, even though it has a high idea of marriage as a relationship in Christ that transcends death, has accepted the idea that a marriage can die and a divorce be granted. The Protestant and Reformed tradition has stressed that marriage ought not to be dissolved, but has also accepted divorce for particular reasons, usually those of immorality.

The Church of England, representing within itself elements both of Catholic and Reformed traditions, has generally accepted the reality of divorce but has largely objected to the remarriage of divorced people in church while the divorced partner is still alive. This explains why some clergy are prepared to hold a service of blessing on a second marriage that has already taken place according to a civil rite. Divorce is an increasingly common status in modern society and comes about through legal procedures and not through religious rites. The status of being divorced has no formal rites of passage associated with it.

BEREAVEMENT

In some respects bereavement resembles divorce while in others it differs significantly. Bereavement begins for most people with the funeral of the deceased; thereafter the surviving spouse is a widow or a widower, and children are without father or mother but do not have a distinct status because of that unless they become orphans at the loss of both parents.

In some Christian cultures, especially Orthodox and Catholic ones where church rites have become intimately associated with the traditional practices of a people, there are formal celebrations of anniversaries of the death which help locate the widow as a member of the community. But in many modern Western societies fixed periods of mourning are not widely practised and there is no settled convention as to the identity and status of widows and widowers. In terms of rites of passage, some bereaved people seem to be in an extended period of liminality with no settled position in society. This is the case because, for example, a widow may remain a widow or may marry again. The status of widowhood is a slightly variable one, and in this it resembles divorce. Sometimes divorced and bereaved people speak in similar ways about their sense of identity as one which is difficult for other people to handle. A central issue lies in the fact that in many modern societies married couples engage in leisure activity together along with many other couples. Once a person ceases to be one of a couple they fit less easily into the leisure world of social life. But human societies are adaptable and some people join groups or clubs for the divorced or widowed which help provide an arena for leisure and many have to learn to live on their own.

Similarly, some individuals carry out a kind of private rite of passage which is significant for them. A bereaved woman might, for example, decide to remove her wedding ring or to wear it on a different finger from that on which the ring was placed at her wedding. In the same way, a divorced person might decide to bury or otherwise dispose of the wedding ring as a sign that the old relationship was now finished.

These examples throw light on the power of firmly established rites of passage to help guide individuals in their ordinary life. When human behaviour changes fairly rapidly a gap emerges between tradition and the way present life functions, a gap that is problematic for many people. It is likely that new customs may emerge to furnish rites of passage for new situations.

MARRYING FOREVER: ETERNAL RITES OF PASSAGE?

If some people are glad to have divorce as a legal act that serves as a rite of passage into the single state, some others do not even wish to accept the death of a spouse as the end of their relationship. In the broad Western Christian tradition of theology death ends marriage. A saying of Jesus in Mark's gospel is often taken to focus the issue: 'When they rise from the dead they neither marry nor are given in marriage but are like angels in heaven' (Mark 12:25). In some popular Christian views the idea of life after death has been extended to embrace the idea that husbands and wives, indeed whole families, will be together in heaven. In terms of formal doctrine, one religious movement has taken this idea as central to its view of life and possesses distinct rites of passage to express it. The group is that of the Church of Jesus Christ of Latter-day Saints, commonly called the Mormon Church (Arrington and Bitton, 1980).

The Mormon Church believes that through the power of the priesthood, restored to mankind through the founding Prophet, Joseph Smith, men and women may be sealed together forever. Marriages performed in ordinary Mormon churches or in register offices are 'for time' and life in this world only, but marriages sealed in one of the Mormon temples are also 'for eternity'. In terms of rites of passage and of Mormon thought, a temple marriage brings the mark of eternity to bear upon what otherwise belongs only to time. Couples sealed in the temple will remain together for all eternity and may also have their children sealed to them in a similar temple ritual. In fact, the Church of Jesus Christ of Latter-day Saints sees the extended family as the fundamental basis of eternal life and of salvation, so much so that, through another rite of passage, living family members are baptized on behalf of dead family members who did not know about Mormon doctrine and its way of life. This 'baptism for the dead' offers a means of incorporating ancestors into the Mormon family for eternity.

These particular Mormon rites are interesting in that they are vicarious, undertaken on behalf of someone else. Many Mormon rites can be performed in this vicarious way, which explains how Mormons interpret the text from Mark's gospel which has already been quoted, saying that there is no marriage in heaven. This text might, initially, seem quite contradictory to Mormon ideas of marriage as the basic unit of celestial existence. Mormons agree that there is indeed no marriage in heaven, but in the sense that there are no marriage rites performed in heaven. In order to be in a married state in the eternal world one needs to have been married through the power of the priesthood within a Latter-day Saint temple on earth, either personally or vicariously.

Death

We have already considered changes in status for those who are bereaved. But, for Christian theology, death primarily focuses on the change of status of the person who has died. As the twentieth century has proceeded, funerary customs have changed quite significantly in many countries and the process still goes on, which means that any description of funerary rites must acknowledge changes that are still occurring. The major change in Britain, and in some parts of Europe, lies in the rise of cremation, and crematoria as the place where the body meets its end, and also in the rise of funeral homes as places where the body is kept rather than in the domestic setting of the house of the deceased.

From the earliest days of Christianity the death and funerals of believers have been linked with the death and resurrection of Christ. The ritual of the last rites in the Catholic tradition involved confession of sin, absolution by the priest, anointing with oil, and communion. The idea was to prepare the dying for the journey to God which was about to follow; the communion part of the rite was even called the *viaticum*, a Latin term for the provisions for a journey.

After death came the preparation of the body for burial, followed in most church traditions by a service marking the movement of the dead from the realm of the living. This brief ritual takes place on the day of the funeral at the home of the deceased, at a special funeral home where the dead person has been kept, or else at the reception of the dead body into the church the night before the funeral. On the day of the funeral this short service precedes the journey which leads the body away from its human home to the church, to the cemetery, or to the crematorium, where the main service takes place. There is variation here, since sometimes a church service precedes a service at the crematorium while at others there is no service at church, and in yet other circumstances the main service is at church with very little ritual performed at the crematorium.

Wherever the major rite occurs it serves as a liminal period where the dead body stands between the world of human social life and that of its final eternal destiny. The Christian doctrine of the resurrection of Jesus deeply influences the funeral service because the dead are buried or cremated in the hope of a future life brought about through a divine act of resurrection. Just as Jesus was raised from the dead so the dead Christian will be brought to a new existence through the creative power of God. God is thanked for the life that the person led, the congregation is reminded of the mortal nature of human life and all are encouraged to lead their own earthly lives in the light of this knowledge. The dead person is then given back to the earth, or to the fire, on the understanding that we come from the natural elements and to them we return until God's new creation, symbolized in the resurrection of Jesus.

The service ends with the dead being given a new status, incorporated into the eternal world. No longer part of the living world, the dead now take their place among the Communion of Saints in the care of God. This shift of status is associated with what happens to the mortal remains. The shift from living status to the status of being dead takes place either when the body is buried in a grave or else when the body is burned and the ashes buried or scattered in some sacred or significant place.

This picture of a rite of separation in the first service at home, a rite of transition in the major service, and a rite of incorporation into the other world through burial of remains is, however, slightly too simple, for the reason that many contemporary Christians place greater significance on the immortality of the soul than on the resurrection of the body. For such people the soul is believed to leave the body at death and go into the nearer presence of God; but the body continues to represent something of the identity of the deceased and its final burial or cremation indicates the end of the public life of that person in this world. Even so, in terms of Christian theology the idea of a body, or more properly, of a resurrection-body, has played an important part in the idea of continuity of identity between a person in this earthly life and the same person in heaven. The nature of the relation between the two produced some interesting speculation, including St Augustine's belief that in the resurrection God would give perfect bodies to those who had some deficiency in their earthly body, just as he would ensure that those who died as babies would be resurrected full grown: 'I say they shall not rise with that littleness of body in which they died, but that the sudden and strange power of God shall give them a stature of full growth' (*City of God*, Book XXII, ch. 14).

Ideas about the body and the soul run parallel in much practical Christian thought with several consequences. In the Catholic tradition the liturgy for the dead refers to the journey the soul undertakes as it moves to God and is welcomed by the saints. Sometimes a special Requiem Mass is said for the dead as a means of benefiting them in the afterlife through the offering of the Mass and the prayers of the Church. The funeral service is sometimes set within the context of a Requiem Mass, and such masses are also used on the occasion of anniversaries of death. The Protestant tradition has been far less ready to talk about and assume any knowledge of what awaits any particular individual; for this reason the prayers for

194

the dead which are central to the Catholic tradition are largely missing among Protestants.

AGAINST CREMATION

While many churches of the Protestant tradition came to accept cremation relatively early in the twentieth century, the Roman Catholic Church did so only in the 1960s, while the Orthodox churches have continued in their opposition. The Orthodox example is interesting for it shows perhaps the most traditional of ancient Christian approaches to death, and also enshrines a fundamental commitment to the resurrection of Christ as a dominant aspect of its theology and liturgy. The forms of service differ depending upon whether the dead is a child, lay-person, or priest. The general pattern follows the threefold distinction between service at the home, in church, and at the grave. The overall scheme is that of a journeying procession. One prayer that is sung in each phase is an ancient prayer for the dead which addresses God as 'God of spirits and of all flesh, who has trampled down death and overthrown the devil and given life to the world'. This reflects the Christian sense of death as the triumph of God over evil through Christ and his resurrection.

The coffin is placed in the church in such a way that the face of the dead looks towards the altar; the coffin is normally open. The hymns and Scriptures sung are the same as for Holy Saturday, the day before Easter Sunday, symbolically expressing the fact that this day is the day of awaiting the resurrection. In terms of rites of passage the funeral day is truly a liminal period between the old life of this world and the life of the world to come. A further section of the service reminds the living of the mixed nature of life where joys and sorrows intermingle; then the soul of the individual is addressed and told that a place of rest awaits it. Finally, the congregation gives the kiss of peace to the corpse to symbolize that it is still part of the total fellowship of the Church in Christ.

At the grave earth is placed on the coffin in the form of a cross and the grave blessed to receive the body, then all are dismissed. At this final moment all sing a prayer enshrining the Orthodox idea of 'memory eternal': in Orthodox theology this refers to a belief that it is Jesus who keeps the dead alive in the memory of God.

In the Mediterranean village contexts of Greek Orthodox life, the dead are not simply left in the grave forever. It has been traditional for the bones of the dead to be removed from the grave between three and five years after the burial and to be placed in the village ossuary. During this period it is customary for women from the village who have been bereaved to visit the graves where they continue a kind of relationship with the dead. For such women the total rite of passage of death takes the shape of a rite of separation, marked by the total funeral ending in burial, then a very long liminal period during which the body of the dead decays, and when they increasingly come to accept the death in terms of their own psychology, then finally as the bones are removed from the earth and incorporated into the village ossuary the women fully enter into their identity as a widow. Against that style of burial rite it is quite understandable why Orthodox religion objects to cremation, even in terms of the practical processes of grief and accommodation to the single life. More important still, however, is the theological stress placed upon the final resurrection of Christ and on the part played by that belief in many other parts of Orthodox thinking and practice.

Ordination and priesthood

Ordination is one rite of passage that has affected a small but significant group of people within Christendom for many centuries in that, from the earliest period of church history, certain individuals were set apart to lead the believing community. By about the fourth century there is a discernible pattern of bishops, priests, and deacons, each having a recognizable function, especially in worship. Bishops and priests were set apart by the laying on of hands, a rite that continues to this day. Other minor orders in the early Church period were those of doorkeeper, reader, exorcist, and acolyte, but they have ceased to be of widespread significance in later periods.

As church traditions developed and diverged so did the more detailed nature of ordination; even so the pattern of bishop, deacon, and priest was retained in Orthodox, Catholic, Anglican, and Lutheran traditions, even when their precise theological significance was altered. Many Protestant churches largely abandoned this threefold order and have focused on a non-priestly minister of the word as a central figure who tends to share leadership along with a group of non-ordained laypeople.

In contemporary life the rite of passage of ordination follows an identifiable pattern. The first period is one of separation from a purely lay status through a process of selection and choice on the part of the Church. It is marked by the distinct identity of ordinand, one who has been selected and is now in training for the sacred ministry. This period will often take three or so years and may be longer. On the one hand it is a time of education in theology, church history, and pastoral matters but, on the other, it is also a time of spiritual formation and development in prayer and worship.

Even this period of training is not the end of the process of preparation, which is taken a step further when the individual is made a deacon for a period, of perhaps a year, before actually being ordained priest. Being made deacon marks the beginning of the fully liminal period, for in many respects the deacon represents the status of being between laity and priesthood; although dressed like priests, deacons may not celebrate the Eucharist.

In many traditions this long period of training and diaconate is symbolized and comes to an end in a retreat prior to the actual ordination to the priesthood, when liminality ends and the individual is incorporated into the status and office of priest. The ordination service itself throws into sharp focus the fact that the individual's life is now dedicated to the service of God and God's people. The tasks of ministry are spelled out and objects appropriate to that ministry are given. In some traditions this involves a copy of the holy Scriptures, priestly vestments, and eucharistic vessels. It is made clear that the dedication and promises involved are lifelong. This was traditionally reinforced for the threefold order in the Catholic Church, and in the case of bishops in the Orthodox Church, by admitting only single men to these offices, indicating a kind of marriage to the office of ministry.

MINISTRY AND PRIESTHOOD OF ALL BELIEVERS

There is a major difference between the idea of priesthood in the Orthodox, Catholic, and some strands of the Anglican traditions on the one hand, and in the Protestant Reformed traditions on the other. The former see priesthood as affecting an individual for life, and in some traditions even imprinting an indelible priestly character upon the very being of the individual concerned. This tradition also stresses sacrifice and mediation between humanity and God as a major function of the priest – the priest sacrifices on behalf of, and to mediate for, others. From the period of reform initiated by Martin Luther in the early sixteenth century, the Protestant tradition repudiated these dimensions and developed the doctrine of the priesthood of all believers by right of their baptism. All God's people, it is argued, are priests in the sense that they represent themselves before God and have no need of any sacrifice because Christ sacrificed himself and is the great high priest of all Christians. For the purpose of good church organization some believers are chosen to exercise their priesthood as a ministry for a particular church community. This representative function of priesthood may only last for a particular period in a particular place, and the office focuses on the preaching and teaching of the word of God in Holy Scripture.

If many Protestant churches developed their ministry through the doctrine of the priesthood of all believers in such a way that a few people served as ministers for many, one Western religious movement, that of the Church of Jesus Christ of Latter-day Saints, or the Mormon Church already mentioned above, has popularized priesthood in the opposite direction. All Mormon males hold an office, first within the Aaronic Priesthood with its three grades of deacon, teacher, and priest, which extend from the twelfth to the nineteenth year of age, and secondly within the Melchizedek Priesthood, composed of all worthy males from their early twenties onward. Their duties vary depending upon grade but all are ordained for their tasks and help form a firm church organization. Ordination is usually by the laying on of hands with prayer, and is one means of impressing young people with the seriousness of their religion and encouraging in them a sense of identity as part of a greater system of priesthood, one that is ultimately shared by God in the Mormon understanding of reality. Many rites of passage are experienced by Mormons as they move from one grade of priesthood to another and this encourages a sense of development and progression throughout life, something that is in accord with the Mormon idea of eternity as an ever-developing scheme of reality.

Religious orders

From relatively early times some Christians have felt called to serve God by living in religious communities as monks and nuns. A distinctive feature of this way of life is celibacy where people remain single to devote themselves to a life of prayer and of various kinds of service to the world. Entry into religious orders such as the black-robed Benedictines, whose history extends from the sixth century, or the Franciscans and Dominicans, which originated in the thirteenth century, usually involves very distinct rites of passage. As a postulant, candidates enter a phase of separation from the world at large, often of several months' duration. If successful they become a novice in a probationary period under the guidance of a senior member of the order. This liminal period is usually symbolized by being clothed in the distinctive robes of the order while not having been fully admitted to it. If finally successful, candidates are incorporated as full members of the order in a ritual of solemn profession which resembles a marriage, and which explains why nuns are sometimes seen as brides of Christ and wear a wedding ring. In addition to the vow of chastity, vows of poverty and obedience are also taken.

Koinonia and *communitas*

For ordinary Christians such a separate existence is not possible and may not even be viewed as desirable. What is important in theological terms is that Christians have a sense of belonging together in a community of believers as the people of God. Sometimes this ideal is simply stated, but at other times it becomes a much more tangible awareness.

On a small scale, a sense of unity and fellowship can be reproduced for periods of Christian mission and worship, especially during periods of religious revivalism such as occurred, for example, in South Wales in 1904. Many village communities, both industrial and rural, experienced periods when the power of God seemed to transform individuals. People repented of their sins in public worship and were caught up in hymn-singing as they felt themselves to be born again as new people (Evans, 1969).

It is often the case that music, singing or other corporate vocal activities serve to integrate and unite people in liminoid moments as in the joint speaking in tongues of the Day of Pentecost (Acts 2). Turner's idea of *communitas* helps interpret that example where, for a short period after the day of Pentecost, the early Christians are described as sharing in fellowship with the apostles and with each other as they sold their goods, and worshipped and ate together. The divisions of society, not only in terms of hierarchy, but also the distinction between Jew and Gentile, were to be overcome in the early life of the emerging Christian Church, so well attested in the Acts of the Apostles. This suggests that the Greek word for fellowship and for having things in common, *koinonia*, reflects Turner's idea of community and oneness expressed in his term *communitas*. But such moments as these do not last. As time goes on, the very human tendency towards organized and hierarchical forms of life re-establishes itself, so much so that, in the First Letter to the Christians at Corinth, Christians need to be reminded of their status as one with another and with Christ and to be called to live accordingly (1 Cor 1:10ff.).

Victor Turner appreciated the fragile quality of *communitas*, just as many Christians recognize the fact that a sense of unity and love which is sometimes experienced in worship, religious gatherings, conferences, or missions does not often last for long. As we have already seen, Turner not only interpreted human life in society as a kind of pendulum swing from organized hierarchy into *communitas* and back again, but also defined several types of *communitas* to cover the responses people make to these switches in experience. His scheme is quite useful when interpreting aspects of Christian ritual and theology.

One interesting historical example of spontaneous *communitas* occurred in the Moravian Church gathered on the estates of Count Zinzendorf at Herrnhut in Germany in 1727. The congregation, coming to church on 13 August, felt a sense of unity and love that was quite overpowering. After the service the Count sent food to some of the homes of church members and they ate what came to be called a Love Feast together in this atmosphere of unity. Subsequent Moravian communities have held love feasts to celebrate many kinds of church activities, and in these that historical moment of spontaneous *communitas* is reflected in the normative style of *communitas* contained in the formal nature of a church service (Gollin, 1967).

Another form of community is expressed in many services of mainstream Christian churches today, where it has become customary for there to be a moment when the 'peace is passed' at the Eucharist. This is a traditional liturgical act which can be conducted in a strictly formal way. In some churches, however, especially those influenced by the Charismatic Movement of a more enthusiastic and emotionally explicit style of religion, this period introduces a much less formal moment when people wander around the church hugging or otherwise greeting each other. This could be interpreted as a form of *communitas* which sometimes demonstrates a spontaneous character and at others a level of intensity that merely hints at the possibility of spontaneity.

IDENTITY AND AUTHENTICITY

The relationship between a stated theological ideal and an actual personal experience of the truth enshrined in it is complex within Christianity. In many Protestant traditions a person comes to a full sense of identity after religious conversion or, as in the case with some renewal movements associated with charismatic groups, when they have a new kind of experience enabling them to speak in tongues or heal other people. It is not easy to determine if and when people will undergo such transformations so that formal rites of passage do not usually exist in these groups, but the experience itself can be a kind of rite of passage. For it is when people first speak in tongues or receive a vision in a communal context that they are, as it were, accorded recognition as being part of the acceptable inner circle of the faithful.

In terms of Christian thinking, the relationship between a formal ritual status and the inner life of a person is of vital importance. Individuals are called to live their lives in a heart-felt and sincere way and not simply to obey official rules attached to a social status. In the world of everyday life husbands and wives must love each other and not simply follow rules for married people, just as leaders in the Church must have an inner sense of identity with their calling rather than simply follow rules attached to their social status.

EMBODIMENT REPLACING ROLE

This is one reason why it is important to think of self-identity as something a person grows into. Individuals come to a deep awareness of their place in the world through their life experience, through what can be called a sense of embodiment. Our bodies and our life experiences are not simply intellectual or rational things, they are also deeply emotional, and this is why the idea of embodiment is important: it is as thinking and feeling bodies that we live, change and enter fully into ourselves as we express ourselves to others (Levin, 1985). It is as embodied individuals that we undergo rites of passage. If we speak about people only in terms of the roles they have in life or, for example, of the parts they play in social dramas, then we get the idea that humans are actors who wear their costume and cosmetics only on the outsides of their lives. The idea of roles played in life is useful but it has its limits. Excessive stress on roles and role-models easily leads to a superficial understanding of people and needs to be kept firmly in place through the perspective of embodiment. In rites of passage many of the symbols used touch the experience of people in an emotional way and can enter quite deeply into what we might call their mood memory.

So it is that identity involves depth of emotion in embodiment as well as including roles that are learned in more formal ways. The links between status and growing awareness of identity may be quite complex. We have already discussed the fact that in churches where baptism often takes place while people are still babies Christian status comes long before any personal sense of identity as a follower of Christ. In that case, a sense of identity grows with time as a person enters into the status that has already been given in baptism. In a similar way people are formally given the status of husband and wife on the day of their marriage but it may take time for them to grow into their own sense of identity as married partners. Conversely, they may already have lived together in practical terms as husband and wife some time before they undertake the ritual of marriage.

Conquering life

The theoretical ideas lying behind this chapter began with van Gennep's rites of passage and continued with Turner's development of the phase of liminality. We now conclude with the still more recent perspective of the anthropologist Maurice Bloch and his idea of rebounding conquest (1992). Bloch criticized van Gennep's view that rites of passage simply changed people's social status because he sees many forms of initiation rites as important existential moments which change an individual's personal awareness and self-understanding. Bloch focuses on the major issue that while the ordinary facts of life involve the process of birth, growth and death there is another view of life which begins with the language of death and goes on to talk about a new kind of birth. In many forms of ritual people are said to die in some ritual or moral sense as a prelude to a new-birth of a religious or cultural form. For Bloch this symbolizes a kind of transcendence of one level of existence and its replacement by a higher order of awareness.

This idea can be applied to Christian theology in numerous ways. For example, this idea of rebounding conquest helps interpret the events, already mentioned above, surrounding the coming of the Holy Spirit described in the Acts of the Apostles when, finally, the old human nature is transformed by the new power of God and the new Christian community sets out on a path of evangelistic conquest (D. J. Davies, 1995). Running alongside this conquest is a serious consideration of how to live the new life and to harness the new-found energy to a routine pattern of social existence, and this we discuss in the following chapter on the moral life.

Further reading

Augustine (1945) *City of God*. London: Dent.

Campbell, V. C. (1987) *A Dictionary of Pastoral Care*. London: SPCK.

Davies, D. J. (1990) *Cremation Today and Tomorrow*. Nottingham: GROW-Alcuin Books.

Davies, J. G. (1986) *A New Dictionary of Liturgy and Worship*. London: SCM Press.

Stevenson, K. W. (1982) *Nuptial Blessings: A Study of Christian Marriage Rites*. London: Alcuin Club.

8. Making moral decisions

Making moral decisions involves living in accord with the principles of a religion, and this lies at the heart of religious faith where issues of good and evil come into sharp focus. To understand the moral law of a religion we need to grasp the principles motivating religions and to see not only how they give shape and pattern to people's lives, but also how they motivate believers in living the good life. How, then, should Christians make moral decisions, what are the motives that control their way of life?

Like Jesus, many early Christians were Jews. One consequence of this was that Christianity inherited the Jewish belief that morality starts with God and reflects the very nature of God. God was believed to be specially concerned with both holiness and justice in individual and social life. Israel, and especially its prophets, realized early on that God was as much concerned with honesty in ordinary affairs as with the dutiful performance of religious ceremonies (Isa 1:12–17; Mic 6:6–8). The early Christian communities in some of their writings also stressed the importance of an inward love for the laws governing human life.

The word 'communities' (in the plural) is important, because it is a reminder that there was no one, single, 'Christianity' from the earliest moments, but rather a quest for the meaning and significance of Jesus, which took many different forms. It included disputes and conflicts. It is true that in general Jesus was recognized as Lord, as the one who had lived and died and risen from the dead in order to reconcile us to God and to each other. But when Jesus was also recognized as Christ (as the Messiah for whom the Jews had been waiting), what would the consequences of that recognition be for moral life and behaviour? Did the detail of the Law remain in place, as a control over life? Or had the detail of the Law been subordinated to a new command of love? Is a good life to be achieved by works (feeding the hungry, visiting the sick, clothing the naked), or is it to be accepted as a work of God's grace and of the working of the Holy Spirit within individuals? The New Testament does not display one answer to these questions, but rather a struggle to see and understand more clearly what answers are in accord with 'the mind of Christ'.

The last phrase is not entirely vague. From the outset, followers of Jesus clearly felt that they were to make moral decisions in accordance with the teaching Jesus gave and the life which he led. This dual emphasis on teaching and example was to remain importantin later Christian history. In the Sermon on the Mount (Matt 5 – 7) we have several examples of Jesus challenging people on the way they should live. For example, Jesus tells his listeners that they have all heard the traditional Jewish law that they must love their neighbour as themselves, but now he tells them that, in addition to loving their neighbours, they must also love their enemies (Matt 5:43–46). The reason for loving enemies comes from God's own moral nature, which all can see in the fact that God gives the benefit of sun and rain to all alike, irrespective of their attitude towards God. In other words, God is generous and not discriminatory.

Jesus finishes this part of his argument with the very simple point that even non-religious people are kind to those from whom they expect some benefit in return. Everybody knows that such 'give and take' is basic to life: I shall treat you well so that you will treat me well. This is part of being worldly-wise, but, in the teaching of Jesus, it is not true wisdom according to the values of the Kingdom of God. God's values are characterized by generosity, where people get more than they give, and certainly more than they deserve. All this is very pointedly taught towards the end of Matthew's gospel in the story of a man hiring workers for his vineyard (20:1–16). Men are hired at different times of the day, but, when pay-time comes, they all receive the same amount of money. Those who have worked all day long are disappointed at being paid the same as those who had done only one hour's work, even though they are given what they had originally agreed upon. We are not told the reaction of those who received a whole day's pay for just one hour's work, but we are told that the employer is a very generous person. In other words, the basis on which this employer operates is not the normal scheme of things.

Those hearing Jesus' teaching would have to get used to operating in a similar way if they too wanted to be disciples. Their moral decisions also would have to be based on the values of generosity and love. Just as important is the fact that without this knowledge they will misunderstand the way God treats them and the way they treat God. These simple points lay the foundation for understanding how Christians should set about making moral decisions and living morally themselves in their personal, social and private lives. Matters of morality on a national or state-wide level raise different (or at least additional) issues, as in the case of war, which need separate consideration.

'Give and take' in daily life

Rules governing ordinary social life are often linked to the rules of religion. Sometimes they parallel each other but they may also be contradictory. We show later in this chapter how anthropologists understand reciprocity and obligation, and how it affects moral life and being. In the case of Christianity, the moral meaning of relationships is focused on an entirely new answer to the question 'And who is my neighbour?' The question was asked by a lawyer who had already asked Jesus what he should do to inherit eternal life. Jesus told him in reply that he already had the answer in his own religious tradition: the absolute love of God, and the love of his neighbour as himself. 'But he, seeking to justify himself, said, "And who is my neighbour?" '

The parable of the Good Samaritan extends the boundary of obligation to everyone and reduces the expectation of reciprocity to zero. This constitutes the identity of a Christian believer in a correspondingly new relation to God, with the content of obligation (in terms of ritual observance) reduced to zero (or at least 'near-zero') as a priority in human life, and with the expectation of reciprocity increased to the maximum, because it is recognized that everything is received as gift, including life itself. ('You see how he clothes the flowers of the field ... ? Shall he not much more clothe you, O you of little faith?'). Thus the moral life and being of a Christian become a radical attack on idolatry, far more profound than breaking carved images of God. The point here is that if human beings do tend to invest the other sources of their identity with great significance, even to the extent of seeing those sources as sacred, then idolatry may be only a step away.

IDENTITY, WORSHIP AND IDOLATRY

In Christian thinking, idolatry occurs when God as the ultimate reality is replaced by some lesser concern. It is perfectly possible for individuals to gain their sense of identity from their family, spouse or children, from their career, profession, or hobby. A total focus on money, sex, or some other aspect of life may also serve the same end, giving an individual a sense of meaning and purpose in life. But in Christian thinking such things are secondary to God. So if individuals draw their identity solely from such partial things they are caught up in idolatry. The temptation to become selfishly focused on these items may lead to ethical choices which are the opposite of God's open generosity. In this sense, it is easy to see the miser as one who idolizes money and is certainly not generous.

This situation is also the opposite of true worship in one important sense. Idolatry reinforces the individual's own sense of self. Worship, by contrast, stresses the centrality of God, and directs the worshipper away from self towards the divine. Such a movement from self towards God is one form of transcendence. It is basic to worship and closely related to ethics or the way people ought to live the good life.

This raises the question of reciprocity once more. In idolatry individuals give because they expect to receive benefit in return. They may offer to the gods to receive back as much. The form of prayer that goes with such idolatry takes the line: 'If you, O God, save me from this trouble, I will give money to the Church.' In contrast, in worship the believer offers thanks or praise to God simply because of the nature of God. In ethical decisions the believer acts in accordance with the nature of other people, who are made in the image of God. There is no expectation of benefit or return. This brings us to the important issue of self-sacrifice and self-offering.

The goal of Christian living is self-sacrifice. The believer lives for others and for God because Christ lived in that way, and because Christ lived and died for the sake of all people. The sacrifice of Christ draws out a response of self-sacrifice in the believer (Rom 12:1). The Letter to the Galatians (2:20) expresses it in this way: 'I have been crucified with Christ; it is no longer I who live but Christ who lives in me: and the life I now live in the flesh I live by faith in the Son of God, who loved me and gave himself for me.'

Moral decision-making

What has been said so far is important as the foundation for morality. Christian morality, focused in the love of God, revealed in Jesus Christ, is grasped in such a way that a response is expressed in social justice. In other words, moral decisions are Christ-focused and socially enacted; they are also closely related to the idea of salvation.

Salvation is the identity of the Christian granted by God. This is a very important idea since it sets the boundaries for the way people think about themselves, and that perspective itself influences the way people think about others and act towards others. Salvation involves the believer in a new set of 'obligations' to God and to others. This is a very delicate area of debate and needs careful spelling out. One interesting way to do this is by relating the social ideas of gift and reciprocity to the theological ideas of grace and merit.

The Hebrew Bible set the social basis for salvation within the framework of God's covenant with Israel. God had promised a chosen people that he would cause them to flourish and to have a land for their own possession. In return, they were to live justly according to divine laws. The one problem with this view was that individuals might ignore their personal responsibility by putting the emphasis upon the group to which they belonged. As a counter-measure against this evasion of personal responsibility there is a trend of thought in the Hebrew Scriptures which underlines the fact that all individuals are responsible for their own personal sins. Both Jeremiah and Ezekiel quote the same proverb ('The fathers have eaten sour grapes, and the children's teeth have been set on edge') in order to stress the point that a child should not suffer for the sins its parent committed, but rather that individuals should take responsibility for their own sin (Ezek 18:1; see also 2 Kings 14:6). The law of God was applicable both to the nation and to individuals within it.

Among the followers of Jesus and in the early Christian community there was much debate about whether this Jewish law of God also applied to Christian Jews. And what of Christians who were not Jews at all? In other words, did God's covenant with Israel embrace Christianity?

One reason why these were real and pressing problems was because early Christianity quickly came to establish itself as separate from Jewish identity and community life. Some of the early

Christians were probably not Jews themselves, some of them were freed slaves or people who did not belong to fixed communities. The Christian churches of the first and second centuries came to provide an alternative community for many who lacked a community of their own. What would be the rules controlling these new congregation-communities, both within their own life and as far as the wider world was concerned? This became an even more pressing question because of the early Christian belief in the value of individuals in their own right, irrespective of their national, religious, or even their gender differences. In the teaching of Jesus, each individual has to decide on how to live after hearing the message of the Kingdom of God. Part of the process of making moral decisions lies in knowing what you have to decide for yourself, and that each believer is a responsible agent. Tradition was insufficient. One answer to these questions on how the new Christian community of otherwise unrelated yet 'saved' individuals should be governed emerges in the letters and theology of Paul. Central to his argument is the issue of grace and merit, which was to prove increasingly important throughout the future history of the emergent Christian Church.

Grace, merit and salvation

God is the central starting point in Paul's thought. God is the first to act both in creation and in salvation. It was God's decision to save humanity from its evil state. God did this through Jesus of Nazareth who was himself God's appointed Messiah and was also in some distinctive way God's 'son'. Not only did Jesus live a perfect life, but his death was a sacrifice which paralleled the sacrifices of the Jewish Temple and also went far beyond them. This intense, spontaneous activity of God was grounded in divine mercy and love towards the human race. Humanity, by contrast, is depicted as being quite unable to rouse itself to any activity at all. All are, in Paul's terms, quite dead. Salvation originates in God and comes to men and women to enliven them, enabling them to respond to God's love.

Grace is the divine attitude of generous love revealed to needy human beings through Jesus. In his Letter to the Romans, Paul describes men and women as not only helpless and ungodly, but as enemies of God (5:6, 10). In a vivid expression, Paul speaks of God's love being poured into human hearts; as dying from thirst, they are revived, saved by a love which forgives their sins and creates them anew to love God and to serve others. Paul goes to great pains at this point to argue that human effort plays no part in God's process of salvation. Nobody can boast that their own religious life or endeavours have won them God's favour; it was God who came and lavished riches upon them. Once individuals appreciate just what it is that God has done, they become touched by this expression of divine generosity and thus find it possible to become generous themselves.

We might even interpret 'faith' as this new sense of being generous. Faith is not the outcome of human endeavour: it is newly created in individuals as grace makes an impact upon their lives. There is a sense, then, in which grace and faith are true partners: grace expresses God's generous love, and faith expresses humanity's open acceptance of it. But this is where the problems start.

Because human beings are so used to living by reciprocity, they think that religion works on the same basis. In everyday life there is cause and effect in matched payments of give and take. Work produces wages and nobody ever gets anything for nothing. On that approach to life you would expect God to favour humanity because of some human endeavour or action. Paul's firm conviction is that nobody anywhere has any reason to think like that as far as the Christian message is concerned.

GRACE AND MORALITY

Through Christ a new morality has been created. It resembles the Old Testament scheme of God's prime action towards a chosen people, but this new scheme is grounded in God's self-sacrifice in Christ and has resulted in a people of faith. The ethic or rule by which this people must live is the new commandment of love, which is not based on a balanced reciprocity. This rather technical term, 'balanced reciprocity', means that people expect to be repaid for what they do. 'A fair day's work for a fair day's pay' is one example of balanced reciprocity, and it underlies most social life. Christ's ethic argued against such a careful give and take. He argued that if someone takes your coat you should give him your cloak as well (Matt 5:40). This outlook is grounded in generosity, and modelled on God's generosity to humanity.

In a very basic sense the teaching of Jesus seems to start on the normal assumption of reciprocity, that you should do to others what you expect them to do to you. This has a basic logic to it which all can understand (Matt 7:12), and it is sometimes even called the Golden Rule. But then Jesus passes on to an ethic of love which involves loving your enemy, an idea contrary to normal reciprocal rules. In human life enemies exist to do evil and harm; they are to be resisted and opposed, not only by individuals but by society at large. Christ's teaching throws a question mark over such normal views. Grace and faith together describe this new style of living. Ethical decisions should be taken on the basis of this ethic of love, according to the Sermon on the Mount; by so doing believers will truly reflect the generosity or 'perfectness' of God (Matt 5:48). The problem comes when people confuse ordinary reciprocity with the model of divine generosity. This is one of the best ways of understanding what is often called the 'faith–works' issue in Christian thought.

As this occurs in the letters of Paul (particularly in Galatians, 1 Corinthians, 2 Corinthians, Romans, to give them in the probable order in which they were written), it is the tension between, on the one side, the radical incapacity of humans to earn their own salvation, above all through an attempted obedience to the commands of law, and on the other side, the language of command which Paul uses, when instructing Christians how to live. Christian life is summarized in the love of God and the love of one's neighbour, but what does that general principle mean in detail and in practice? J. W. Drane summarized the issue in the title of his study of it, *Paul, Libertine or Legalist?*: 'The least we can do', he argued, 'is to observe that whereas in Galatians Paul was able to reject legalism in all its forms, in 1 Corinthians he reintroduces the form of legal language, which in turn leads him into a position in 1 Corinthians not so very much different from the legalism he had so much deprecated in Galatians' (1975: 65).

But in the context of gift-giving and reciprocity, the apparent conflict dissolves. If we have received all things as a gift, including the Holy Spirit – the capacity to 'walk in newness of life' – then the language of a human life will become one of love, joy, peace, etc. Some behaviours so contradict the utterance of the Spirit that they can be condemned; others so exemplify it that they can be commanded. But they are not commanded as bribes (gifts from ourselves to God of a coercive kind) to ensure our own salvation.

211

Justification is not a statement that God has decided to overlook our sins because now we are doing a little better, but rather it is a statement that he has cancelled altogether the condemnation that we all undoubtedly deserve.

But although we can see now how the apparent tension between grace and works in relation to salvation might be resolved, the fact remains that the whole of Christian history has been an exploration of emphasis between these two, as they affect the practice and worth of morality.

The ideas of human endeavour, merit and reciprocity, can all be seen within Christian doctrine in the debate about salvation conducted by Augustine and Pelagius in the early fifth century. Augustine was a philosopher who converted to Christianity, and became Bishop of Hippo in North Africa. Pelagius was a lay monk who went from the British Isles to Rome and then on to Africa.

AUGUSTINE AND PELAGIUS

Augustine thought that individuals were saved from the conse- quences of sin because God willed that they should hear the message of divine mercy and respond to it. He developed the idea of predestination, which is already found in the Bible, and said that God chose some people to believe in divine grace whilst others were not so chosen. Here the great stress is on God's wise decision and on the fact that salvation is a gift given to men and women. It is by God's mercy that they are able to understand their plight and sinfulness, and by God's mercy that they come to decide to live as Christians. The idea of prevenient grace has been used to describe God's grace 'preventing' or, in a modern equivalent of that term, 'going before' an individual on the road to faith. This made great sense to Augustine, as it did later to Martin Luther, against the background of human moral weakness and God's plan of predestination. What is important, as far as our earlier discussion of reciprocity is concerned, is that grace stands out as a gift in this scheme of salvation. Because all of God's actions are free and not conditioned by human activity, so too with grace; grace is free and unmerited, and shows God's goodness and love.

This pattern of faith which stresses God's initiative above anything that a person does is typical of those who have been described as 'twice-born' individuals. This descriptive term, already discussed in the context of worship in Chapter 6, was elaborated by the psychologist and philosopher William James when speaking of people who saw the world as evil, and who felt themselves inwardly disturbed by guilt and other negative forces. This outlook he called the religion of the 'sick-soul'. But these individuals often experienced a conversion and a sense of freedom from guilt through a kind of new birth. Paul, Augustine, and Luther all seem to have had such an experience.

Another and different sort of life is led by the 'once-born' type of religious believer. William James spoke of these people as having a religion of 'healthy-mindedness'. They did not experience a critical moment or period of conversion but tended to grow into their religious faith over a lifetime. They tended to stress the goodness of both God and human beings and did not emphasize evil and guilt. The once- and the twice-born styles of Christian religion can, in a very broad way, be related to the form of theology in more Catholic and more Protestant traditions. Catholic doctrine does speak of being born again but means by that the ritual process of baptism through which a child is said to be born again as the Holy Spirit works through the ritual of the Church. As far as the psychological and experiential life of individuals is concerned, there is no expectation that a moment of conversion will occur. Within the more Protestant tradition the idea of a personal act of commitment to God is more directly related to a conversion involving an experience of change.

The Catholic, once-born, style of life lived through the sacraments of the Church corresponds with a disciplined form of existence. In fact this idea of discipline can be stressed to a marked degree. This was one of the features emphasized by Pelagius, Augustine's opponent, as discussed in Chapter 3. In some respects Pelagius resembles a 'once-born' Christian. Being a monk he knew the significance of a disciplined life as a means of improving himself. Humanity, he believed, possessed the capability to do good because God had made that possible, but it depended upon individuals whether they willed to do good or not. If the belief was too widely accepted that individuals could do nothing to help themselves as far as salvation was concerned, then they would cease to strive to be better and would then simply become worse.

Augustine could not agree with this. God alone, he believed, was the source of salvation. Men and women could do nothing to help themselves. People could not choose and carry out morally good things simply because they were not morally good themselves. The doctrine of the Fall of mankind was influential in Augustine's thinking, arguing that, although humanity was created morally good, all people have disobeyed God and have been tainted with evil ever since. The generations after Adam and Eve have inherited and been influenced by evil in ways described in Chapters 3 and 5.

We are now in a position to see why this debate between Augustine and Pelagius on salvation is important for the total theme of making moral decisions. The question hangs on the nature of human beings and the capabilities they possess. Are they capable of making moral decisions on their own, unaided by divine help? Is human nature so corrupted by sin that nothing good can come of it? Or are human beings intrinsically good and able, at least partially and perhaps fully, to do good deeds?

Moral theology

Generally speaking most Christian traditions accepted that men and women are at least inclined to evil. The majority of modern theologians, who would not accept literally the idea of a historical Adam and Eve and their original disobedience, still recognize the radical human inability to do good and avoid evil at all times. But it makes relatively little difference whether we speak of the Fall as a historical event or as a metaphor of the fallenness of humanity as a present experience: the significance lies in the fact that men and women know themselves to be other than they ought to be. As in most religions of the world Christianity stresses this flawed aspect of life. Men and women have a sense of what it means to be good, they know that there are religious laws and general principles of goodness, and they know that they fail to keep them.

For Augustine God is always good in electing people to be amongst those who believe. These, in turn, when they come to believe and to experience the merciful love of God acknowledge that God is the source of their own good will. They speak of themselves as having received grace from God, and express a passive sense of having been helpless until the divine mercy worked within them. Other terms were used to describe different aspects of grace, and all show how vital the idea was to Catholic and Protestant traditions alike. Protestant theology, for example, stressed irresistible grace which meant that even God's chosen ones might fall by the wayside if God did not ensure that grace worked for them irresistibly until they attained heaven itself. 'Actual grace' was a Catholic term for God's special help in assisting an individual achieve some great endeavour but which would not stay with that person permanently.

So when it comes to making moral decisions many Christians are aware that deciding what is good is one thing, but actually doing it is another. To love God with all one's heart, mind, and strength, and to love one's neighbour as one's self are two great commandments which many people support but few are able to practise. The reason for this inability is the incapacitating power of sin. It is for this reason that assistance is needed from God. Just as Augustine argued that God gives grace to enable people to believe, so grace is needed to enable them to live as believers.

In the centuries following after Augustine, and especially with Thomas Aquinas in the thirteenth century, moral theology emerged as a special form of theology to help believers live in a Christian way. Rules were constructed using the Bible, the teaching of the Fathers of the Church, and employing human reason to interpret these sources. They were especially important for helping large numbers of converts to Christianity, and for guiding priests when they gave direction to people after confession of sin.

Penance, grace, and indulgences

The growth of the Church, with priests as leaders and an increasing lay membership, involved increased concern over discipline. By about the third century church members who behaved immorally were placed under penance and not allowed to attend the Eucharist for a specified period. But if particularly worthy people, such as those awaiting martyrdom, prayed for them, then they could be let off some of their penance time and be readmitted to full fellowship. When the idea of purgatory developed, this idea of release from penance was transferred from this world into the next. Purgatory was where the souls of the dead were purged of remaining sin and guilt prior to finally gaining the ultimate vision of God.

Just as martyrs might pray for fellow Christians and their

readmittance to fellowship so the prayers of worthy believers would avail for the dead and speed their journey to heaven. It was here that the idea of merit became important. Within the total membership of the Church were some particularly meritorious people, not only Christ and the Blessed Virgin Mary his mother, but martyrs and other saints. Together their good works constituted a kind of treasure chest of merit which could benefit less saintly Church members. By the twelfth century it was possible to be granted a portion of this merit in what was called an indulgence.

Church leaders granted these indulgences to believers for some endeavour such as engaging in the Crusades against the enemies of Christianity, performing some penance, making a pilgrimage, and so on. This was a system of reciprocity in which the freedom from a period in purgatory was given for some work done on earth. It depended on the idea of a treasury of merit within the Communion of Saints of the Church, and on church leaders, especially the Pope and some others, administering the system.

MARTIN LUTHER

Indulgence was a system far removed from the New Testament and was open to abuse. This was something that made a strong impact upon Martin Luther (1483–1546), a German scholar and monk whose own search for a personal sense of satisfying religion had involved him in a conversion experience and a deep conviction that the grace of God was fundamental to salvation. He emphasized the doctrine of justification by faith which was derived from Paul's Letter to the Romans and gained great support from Augustine. This argued that faith alone was the human side of that relationship with God which is one of grace. For Luther, it was Jesus Christ who fully expressed God's grace to men and women. In his own study of chapter 12 of Paul's Letter to the Romans, Luther expanded this point, arguing that Jesus is the foundation of Christian ethics, and that foundation is God's free gift to humanity (Pauck, 1961).

For Luther, moral decisions emerged from the experience of God's grace which made the Christian into a free individual. The salvation that came by grace and was received in faith gave to each individual a sense of freedom, a freedom from having to satisfy religious legal requirements, a freedom which could be used as a basis to serve other people. Having a knowledge of their own salvation Christians need no longer strive to please God, since that was an impossibility for weak and fallen humanity. Having been forgiven by God they were now at liberty to serve God and their neighbour. Merit and gift were two important ideas for Luther, but as this quotation from his commentary on Romans shows, they were entirely focused on Christ:

> For if through the offence of one many died, much more the grace of God, and the gift, by the grace of one man, Jesus Christ, has abounded to many (Rom 5.15). The apostle connects grace and the gift of grace as if they differed from one another, but he does this in order to show clearly the nature of him who was to come, as he said, namely, that as we are justified by God and receive his grace, we do not receive this grace by any merit of our own, but it is a gift the Father gave to Christ in order that he should give it to men.

Luther adds a further note that this grace of God is not like a gift one friend gives to another but is much broader, since it is the enemy of God – fallen humanity – that receives the gift of grace through Jesus Christ.

What is now obvious is that human endeavour is out of the question as far as salvation is concerned, and moral decisions cannot be taken in order to impress God or to achieve some merit which will contribute towards salvation. Moral decisions to serve and love one's neighbour must now, inevitably, spring up from the living faith which God's grace has created within the person of faith. Morality is a consequence of faith and an outcome of salvation, it is not a means of meriting salvation.

For Luther, as for many subsequent Christian thinkers, there is a powerful sense of freedom underlying this commitment to morality, even though he argues that the Christian is a divided person, being both justified and yet also a sinner. Luther's theological emphasis sketches a picture of Christian individuals who are responsible before God for their lives. This focus on faith, on the individual, and in particular on the sense of freedom that comes with salvation, was to be even more important in Kierkegaard, a Protestant thinker of a later generation for whom the making of moral decisions constitutes the central process of becoming truly Christian.

Søren Kierkegaard: deciding to be yourself

Søren Kierkegaard (1813–55) was a Dane. His own life experiences led him to be extremely critical both of the official Church and of contemporary philosophical trends. For him, truth concerned the inward and personal dimensions of existence rather than proofs about the objective world. Subjectivity, knowledge of self, rather than objectivity and knowledge of the world, lay at the heart of his outlook. This is the reason why many see Kierkegaard as the father of existentialism, a philosophical outlook focusing on the existence and experience of individuals. It has taken definite non-religious and anti-religious directions in the work of people such as Heidegger, Camus and Sartre, and more Christian directions with Karl Jaspers and especially Gabriel Marcel. Kierkegaard wanted individuals to be true to themselves, to discover their own identity through their own bitter experience of life. The greatest moral decision that can be made is the decision to face oneself and not to turn away into trivial pursuits.

This is an extremely important point as far as moral decisions in Christianity are concerned. We normally talk about morality in terms of making judgements affecting our behaviour towards others. We accept rules for life and act upon them. Kierkegaard asked something more of his hearers than that. He asked people to realize that the greatest of all moral decisions they would ever have to take was to decide to become themselves. Rather in the way that Jesus told his disciples that they had to take the great log out of their own eye before they could possibly see clearly to take a speck of dust out of somebody else's eye, so Kierkegaard calls individuals to see that they must actively decide to become themselves before they can act truly and with integrity towards God and towards others.

But this is no easy task. For as individuals begin to see themselves as they are, they encounter sin. It is not easy for one person to describe sin to another person, each individual must know his or her own sin. Sin involves a kind of dread or anxiety which comes over individuals as they learn about their own freedom and the many possibilities open to them. Freedom is part of the dread anxiety of being human, freedom is related to sin. Sometimes Kierkegaard speaks of a kind of 'dizziness' surrounding our sense of freedom, and it is this dizziness which gives us a sense of dread. But such an awareness is absolutely vital before individuals can begin to become themselves.

The dread must be accepted as an act of faith, but it can only be accepted through the paradoxical belief that God became an individual in Jesus Christ. To think that God became a particular individual on this earth is something that reason rejects, argued Kierkegaard, because it is so hard to understand. Objectively it cannot be proved, but Kierkegaard had abandoned such objective proof. It is subjectively and inwardly that individuals come to faith and believe that God became man in Jesus. It is as people begin to experience these things and to act decisively on them that they come to be themselves and come to be Christian. Prayer was important as an opportunity to be what each one is before God. The acting and posturing of social life must give way to becoming a real self before God.

Existence and ethical vitality

One idea, drawn from the field of social anthropology, is of considerable use in understanding moral decision-making in relation to social life and to the religious idea of salvation. In an important essay entitled 'The ideology of merit', S. J. Tambiah described the way in which in some Buddhist traditions boys become monks for limited periods of time. They observe the necessary Buddhist rules of life by sacrificing their own wishes and desires. It is believed that they earn or make merit through this sacrificial form of religious duty and use it to offset demerit in the lives of their family. Tambiah expresses the issue in these terms:

> Youths become temporary monks to make merit for the elders and community members. In effect ... the older generation persuades its youth temporarily to renounce its vitality and sexual potency and undergo an ascetic regimen. In a sense it is the sacrifice of this human energy that produces ethical vitality which can counter *karma* and suffering. (1968: 105)

One way of understanding how this process of merit-making works is to remember that humans are both social and self-conscious. As social beings we live in organized groups with rules to control our communal existence. The ideas of goodness and badness behind these rules are related, as we have seen, to the group's survival and welfare. As social beings we also invest our rules with emotionally charged value. This emotional power binds people to central cultural values which seem so real and true that they are placed beyond contradiction.

As self-conscious beings we reflect upon these rules of life and realize their importance for our survival. Here the word 'moral' comes very close to meaning the same as 'social', so that when we say something is morally good we regard it as good for society too, just as something that is morally bad is thought to work against the welfare of society.

In the above quotation Tambiah lays great emphasis on the control of human energy in keeping particular rules. In this case it is sexual energy that is especially important, as the youths are expected to live like ascetic monks. This shows us that merit is related to effort, it is not simply an abstract idea but is quite definitely linked to individuals. It is keeping rules through personal effort that earns merit; self-sacrifice is part of this endeavour. The vigour and energy of life which could go into selfishness and rule-breaking is controlled, and in this sense sacrificed, to prove that rules are good and that the moral way of life is the right way.

ETHICAL VITALITY AND JESUS

All this means that in terms of the ethical vitality and merit-making Christianity makes a radical change of emphasis: even when the effort of individual believers is discounted as a way to salvation, as it clearly was in the Reformation and teaching of Martin Luther, the earning of merit is still personal. But, instead of each individual being involved in gaining merit, it is the one person Jesus Christ who is believed to be the source of all merit. Thus, instead of thinking of a part of a youth's life being given up to live according to religious precepts, Christian theology sees the whole life of Jesus as being lived fully in accordance with the will of God. When in the prime of life, Jesus gave himself to death in actual self-sacrifice. This pattern of life and death produces the fullest possible degree of ethical vitality, so much so that Jesus is said to die for the sin of the whole world. The merit generated by his perfect life which is finally yielded up in death is enough to count against all the lack of merit of the rest of humanity (D. J. Davies, 1995). In the teaching of Paul there is another application of ethical vitality directed to those who have already become Christians through the merits of Jesus Christ and not through their own efforts. Paul addresses believers in this way: 'I appeal to you therefore, brethren, by the mercies of God, to present your bodies as a living sacrifice, holy and acceptable to God, which is your spiritual worship' (Rom 12:1). Because Christ's merit has already won salvation for believers they can now devote their own ethical vitality to living out their Christian lives especially in service to their neighbour. But such freedom is very hard to live with, its acceptance is not easy. In moral terms, as we have just seen, it may well be easier to have strict rules to keep than to be a free agent who has to decide how to live for the sake of others. Something of the same problem, arising from the pull between freedom and the need for certainty, emerges in the idea of the Protestant ethic.

The Protestant ethic, the morality of work

The Protestant ethic is another idea derived from the social sciences, in this case from the German sociologist Max Weber (1976). First appearing in *The Protestant Ethic and the Spirit of Capitalism* in 1904–05, this argument involves a fundamental attitude to the morality of work in the sense of labour. It deals with the relationship between wealth creation and salvation.

Weber believed that the Puritan religious outlook, which followed on from the Protestant Reformation in Europe in the sixteenth century, linked the realms of salvation and work in a very distinctive way. The Protestant Christian believed that salvation came from God to the extent that God selected or predestined people to be saved. This was all God's doing. There was, as we have already seen, no merit in human action by means of which men and women might save themselves. But people want a degree of certainty in their lives, and are not content with the idea that *perhaps* they are in the group that God has chosen to save rather than in the group God has chosen to damn. So a practical answer emerged as a way of coping with this dilemma: the Protestant ethic.

Christians set themselves the task of doing their work in careful and efficient ways resulting in success and profit. They interpreted success as a divine blessing and assumed that God would only bless those specially chosen for salvation. So wealth was an indirect proof of salvation. The moral decision to live carefully before God, and not to waste the riches that were earned but to spend them in capitalist investment or charitable work, produced a whole cultural outlook.

Although the Protestant ethic is not normally associated with the idea of ethical vitality, the two are very closely related. They are especially closed linked through the idea of asceticism. Max Weber saw Protestants who were dedicated to work as practising a sort of asceticism, which he called a worldly asceticism. Though they have not gone into a monastery and away from the world to control their life, they are still engaged in ascetic activities. Their life is highly organized, ordered, and controlled. They do not waste their wealth indulging their appetites; and just as much as monks this commitment is for life. The similarity with monks, whether they are Christian or Buddhist monks, is obvious, in that life's energy is devoted to living according to strict moral principles related to salvation even if not causing salvation.

Here then, in Protestant ethical vitality, we have one important sort of moral decision. It is the decision to live a controlled and organized life to prove one's membership in God's company of elect people. The desire is still for a sense of certainty and approval rather than an open attitude of trust in God. Some, like the Protestant theologian Dietrich Bonhoeffer, whom we consider below, find such an outlook on life and faith inadequate for genuine Christian morality. Given this long history in Christianity of debates about freedom and obedience, grace and works, the questions arise whether Christian moral decision-making is a matter of obedience to the law or authority of God, or whether it is a response to the grace of God which looks at every situation and tries to decide what the Holy Spirit urges as the best expression of love in that circumstance.

Absolute and relative morals

Those questions have to be asked in the context of more general questions: What is the basis for making a moral decision? Are there absolute moral values true for all times and places? Why can I not do as I like?

So far in this chapter, we have looked at the creative tension in

Christianity as it has tried to answer these questions – the tension between grace and merit, faith and works, generosity and obedience. There has been general agreement that moral values have an absolute character and can legitimately make a demand on all people, at all times and in all places. The idea that moral laws have been revealed by God is common to Judaism, Christianity, and Islam. God is believed to be a moral being who has communicated the moral law to humanity, whose duty it is to accept and practise the good way of life. The question is, how to do so?

The Old Testament contains instruction, Law, or Torah, which Jews believe to have been given by God as the basis for the divine covenant relationship with ancient Israel. In the New Testament this Law is interpreted in a Christian way, especially by Paul. He thought that the Law showed people their own inability to keep it and therefore served as a means to bring them to trust in Jesus, the only perfect Jew, whose fulfilling of the Law became the basis for salvation. The demands of the Law were absolute and needed absolute observation which all failed except Jesus.

A firm and fixed Law of this sort can become a two-edged sword. On the one hand, everyone can be sure of how to live and need be in no doubt about what to do, but on the other hand, when failure occurs, because the Law is not kept, then some penalty is encountered. The penalty can vary from a personal sense of guilt to the belief in damnation. This is an important point because moral codes usually involve penalties for those breaking them. This raises the important distinction between moral codes as a rule for life as opposed to moral codes as a guide in life.

The New Testament has no doubt that God revealed his will, in the form of specific commandments, to the people of Israel. The Ten Commandments (Deut 5:7–21) might be summarized in the two great commandments, but they still represent an expression of absolute moral values. The covenant community is defined as those who live by those standards, by keeping the Law. Yet in general the New Testament writers no longer believe that the definition of a good or a right decision can be found simply by checking its conformity with the Law of the *old* covenant. The *new* covenant, or testament, is characterized by an application of rules and laws in the overriding direction of love. Put in a very extreme way, it was this perception which produced what is known as 'situation ethics' (Fletcher, 1966).

Situation ethics argues that love is the principle underlying Christian religion. If individuals genuinely have love at heart, and are open to learn from the traditional wisdom of the Church, then they can trust themselves to act morally in any particular situation. Certain fixed laws may be inappropriate in one specific context. It may, for example, be wrong to lie but it would be right to lie to a murderer, who was seeking his victim's whereabouts. Here the emphasis upon the individual takes over from rules laid down by an entire society. Situation ethics is one reflection of the modern trend to emphasize the significance of the individual who must act on the basis of commitment to a moral principle applied in the light of the needs of others and the circumstances of the day.

In the Christian tradition, authority (coming from the will of God mediated through the Church) and individual responsibility to make moral decisions in relation to particular situations, are held together in the understanding of conscience.

Conscience

Traditionally speaking, conscience refers to the human ability to judge the difference between good and evil behaviour. It is often taken to be a given part of human nature. In the New Testament Paul speaks of the human conscience several times in his Letter to the Romans. The conscience of Gentiles accuses or excuses them depending on how they behave (Rom 2:15). But this is not the whole story as far as Paul is concerned. Speaking for himself he says that he knows the difference between good and evil, but his problem is that he cannot bring himself to do what is good. In other words he has an active conscience but his will to do the good thing is powerless (Rom 7:15–24). For Paul as for many thinkers in later centuries the human conscience has to cope with imperfect human nature. Some think that the conscience itself has been spoiled through sin while others see the conscience as having to deal with an imperfect human nature surrounding it.

Nevertheless, the word 'conscience' stands for each individual as absolutely and solely responsible before God for the formation of her or his decision, thought or action. This is what is known as 'foundational conscience'. No authority, neither pope nor parent, can invade that conscience to control or coerce it. Each person stands before God. But each person is immersed in the issues and decisions of daily life. The individual exercise of judgement in detail is known as 'situational conscience'. Since no one can know all the relevant facts or consequences of a situational decision, it is here that the authority of Scripture and of tradition becomes important, *informing* conscience. Even so, it cannot take over the foundational conscience, which is the individual decision before God and in the light of eternity.

The primacy of conscience over authority indicates why Dietrich Bonhoeffer saw the human conscience as a means through which individuals come to a unity within themselves. It is a form of self-protection and self-control as individuals live in society, helping them to find integrity in their lives. Bonhoeffer argued that conscience 'is directed not towards a particular kind of doing but towards a particular mode of being. It protests against a doing which imperils the unity of this being with itself' (1955: 211).

But, says Bonhoeffer, the Christian conscience is more than this. If we talk only in terms of self-identity and protection we are in a realm of selfishness and self-rule. When an individual has Christian faith, such self-rule is no longer the goal. Jesus Christ replaces self-rule. The individual conscience can be full of ungodly self-justification, but for the Christian Jesus Christ sets the conscience free from having to justify itself. In a most dramatic proclamation Bonhoeffer writes in a simple single sentence: 'Jesus Christ has become my conscience' (1955: 213).

Moral decisions can now be made in a different way and without fear of self. In a way that is not initially easy to understand, Bonhoeffer argues that the conscience which is set free by Jesus Christ will not be timidly afraid of what it does. It will even be free to 'enter into the guilt of another man for the other man's sake, and indeed precisely in doing this it will show itself in its purity'. The making of moral decisions is not something individuals do just for themselves. Following the example of Jesus Christ they must live for others and this will involve them in taking decisions that are risky and problematic. Such risk involves freedom and dangerous possibilities. It is the fact that Jesus Christ stands as the final judge of those who seek the good of others and who risk acting in freedom to achieve this, which gives the courage to live. They hope for mercy from God rather than the praise of their own self-satisfied conscience.

Societies and social morality

Much of what we have looked at so far has focused on the individual. But individuals cannot live as Robinson Crusoes, each one an island, separate from everyone else. We live necessarily in societies and social groups (like families or schools), and morality concerns them as much as it concerns individuals. In groups or organizations, rules governing conduct are more likely to obtain, because there is no single person weighing up each situation: evaluation is diffused through an organization, even though the decisions may be taken and expressed by authority figures. Individuals may agree or disagree (and that is a classic instance of conscience), but the rules and norms of the group or a society will continue.

But given that rules are likely to be prominent in groups or organizations or societies, and that these ultimately rest on a sufficient consensus among those who make up the membership, what happens when the rules of one group or society conflict with those of another? Cultural and moral relativity is a fact, at least in the sense that different societies endorse different items as good or evil (though they are, nevertheless, exemplifying the human universal of making judgements and distinctions of that kind). The Christian belief that the capacity to recognize goodness (however much we may fail to act upon it) is a human universal does not mean that the diversity of different life-styles has to be obliterated. There will be considerable agreement on some items, but equally important diversity in moral codes, which may nevertheless be regarded as good.

But what happens when there is a conflict between two systems, or societies? It is easy to talk theoretically about differences in moral codes. When morals clash in real situations, however, calm discussion gives way to action as in the case of war. If one nation sees another being treated badly by a third party, what should it do? Did Hitler, for example, have the right to kill Jews because he wanted to eliminate them from his 'perfect' society? Should one country not respect the rights of rulers in another society to do what they want?

In the history of Christendom the idea of the Just War has explored some of these issues. Augustine (354–430) developed the idea of a Just War on the basis that war was commanded by God to restore the world to peace and not waged for personal benefit. This idea is reflected in Article 37 of the Thirty-nine Articles of Belief in the Church of England where it says 'it is lawful for Christian men, at the commandment of the Magistrate, to wear weapons, and serve in the wars'.

But in order to argue like this two distinctions have to be made: on the one hand, the distinction between the morality applicable to individuals and the morality applicable to nations; and on the other hand the distinction between love and justice.

From what was said earlier it is obvious that the teaching of Jesus applies directly to individual morality. Here one should love not only one's friend but also one's enemy. Waging war is obviously not a way to love, so war would have to be excluded from a morally acceptable way of life. But, as some subsequent Christian theologians have argued at length, the issue of justice takes the personal ethic of love into another level of discussion. The theologian Reinhold Niebuhr, who was born in 1894, was very much concerned with the way in which an ethical system for society could be related to an ethical system of the individual Christian. This he saw as relating the themes of love and justice within a world where sin was a fundamental problem affecting human behaviour. In his *Interpretation of Christian Ethics* (1935) he explored the idea of personal and social evil and at one point came very close to a deep insight of a German contemporary, Dietrich Bonhoeffer.

Niebuhr argued that 'There is no deeper pathos in the spiritual life of man than the cruelty of righteous people' (1956: 203). Here he tried to get at the fact that very religious people can be merciless and, through a false sense of their own goodness, adopt critical and unloving judgements. Love and justice do not coincide in a satisfactory way. Bonhoeffer pressed the case of evil even more firmly in the book *Ethics* which was published in an incomplete form after his death and concerned Christian morality focused on the most difficult themes of morality, of war, justice, love, selfishness and self-sacrifice.

Today there are once more villains and saints, and they are not hidden from public view ... They emerge from primeval depths and by their appearance they tear open the infernal or the divine abyss from which they come and enable us to see for a moment into mysteries of which we had never dreamed. What is worse than doing evil is being evil. It is

227

worse for a liar to tell the truth than for a lover of truth to lie ... One sin is not like another. They do not all have the same weight. (1955: 3)

This quotation powerfully illustrates the critical nature of his situation. From this modern theologian, we come to the heart of the matter – the title of a novel by Graham Greene which reminds us that fiction, as well as philosophy or biblical exegesis, may also manifest truth about the problems of making moral decisions. Fiction acutely makes the point that it is in the struggle of making moral decisions (or in *not* making them) that human character is formed – not just 'human beings' but humanity in being. It is character which is the consequence of morality, either as a work of beauty, or as one of hideous deformity.

My moral choices

It is, then, our character which is reflected in the moral decisions we make and is, to a degree, created by those decisions. As we saw so clearly in Kierkegaard, we have to decide to become ourselves. If we decide to steal or break the law we might well find ourselves convicted of a crime and becoming a criminal. If we decide to ride roughshod over people as part of our career development we may well find ourselves becoming callous and alienated from those who otherwise might be friends.

This is vitally important in the process of becoming a mature individual. As children we find many decisions taken on our behalf, we are taught how to behave. Becoming adult involves deciding how to behave. We have to take responsibility for our own actions and for the consequences of our actions.

There may, of course, be serious obstacles to our apparent freedom of choice. Indeed, this issue of freedom is a constant element in the Christian tradition of morality. In most Christian traditions the idea of sin is seen to weaken such freedom. We saw a classic expression of this in Paul, who knew what was good but felt unable to carry it out. The human state of sinful deprivation is often believed to require the grace of God to overcome it, both in the saving work of Jesus, and also in the power provided by the Holy Spirit within individual lives. A similar idea of disability is also encountered in secular social opinion, as in the view that an impoverished childhood environment leads people into crime and delinquency. In a very similar way, some psychological theories about infancy and childhood explain problems later experienced by adults. While there may be some truth in these theories, it is important to distinguish between ideas of determination and ideas of human possibility. Religious ideas of predestination and secular ideas of conditioning can both work against individuals taking responsibility for themselves despite the problems they have experienced.

Respect is an integral part of moral development: respect for self and respect for others. If we look at others as deprived then they might begin looking at themselves in a similar way. As long as there is a real opportunity for people to take responsibility for themselves they should at least be respected as having the option to decide for themselves. In terms of Christian morality, both sorts of respect are grounded in our attitude of respect for God. The command to love our neighbour as ourselves is grounded in the command to love God with all our heart: it is important to notice that God, neighbour, and self are all included in this outlook. Respect expresses the worth of a person. A sense of our own worth derives in Christianity from the belief that God both made us and loves us. We are worthy because God says so through the acts of creation and redemption. This divine statement must take precedence even over any sense of personal unworthiness.

Sources of morality

'In the beginning is the decision.' This, for a Christian, might be said to be the first word on morality. All have to decide on the source and authority of morality for themselves. As they become alert to moral issues they must consider the laws of their society which, as citizens, they are obliged to obey. Why obey them? Should people make moral decisions at the personal level which match those of their society? This is not a simple question as far as Christian morality is concerned. The law of the land may regard as legal things which some Christians take to be sinful. The long-standing issue of abortion is one such question. Some aspects of financial dealing and tax paying might be others, as are forms of homosexual behaviour.

Traditional sources of morality for Christians have been the Bible, Church tradition, and the inward guidance of the Holy Spirit. Any or all of these can be emphasized in relation to our natural reasoning about life and the world. If making moral decisions is so important that we are formed through those decisions then we could identify morality as part of the total creative process. In terms of Christian theology our morality should be grounded in love and not in fear. So fear as a source or justification for morality might have to be ruled out of court. The idea of hell as a punishment for the wicked is no basis for Christian morality. Not to sin because of the fear of consequences will not help a person become mature. Love as a respect for the worth of others is a far better motive for making moral decisions.

Other motives for morality include a sense of responsibility for the world of which we are all a part. The closing decades of the twentieth century have witnessed a tremendous growth in awareness of the danger to ecology from modern industry. This responsibility can be interpreted in Christian terms as part of our stewardship of nature, or it can have a secular origin in a human concern for our planet as the place of our survival and life.

Ecological morality highlights the major moral issue of whether my personal behaviour should be influenced by the good of others. My own freedom to use chemicals that are useful for my life but which endanger the lives of future generations is called into question. I am not the only person who matters. Here the profoundly religious theme of the self-centred life meets head on the necessity of shared living. We have to make moral decisions precisely because we live with others. To say that only the individual counts and that my decisions must be based on what, for example, gives me pleasure is to deny the Christian morality of mutual concern. The genius of Christian theology lies in the belief that morality helps us become more than we would be alone. Making moral decisions is part of the creative work of making persons.

Further reading

Augustine (1950) *The City of God*. London: J. M. Dent.
Bonhoeffer, D. (1959) *Letters and Papers from Prison*. London: Fontana.
Gill, R. (1985) *A Textbook of Christian Ethics*. Edinburgh: T. & T. Clark.
Hume, D. (1969) *A Treatise of Human Nature*, ed. E. C. Mossner. Harmondsworth: Penguin.
Poggi, G. (1983) *Calvinism and the Capitalist Spirit*. London: Macmillan.

9. Attitudes to nature

In Christian thought it is as moral and social creatures that we frame our attitudes to nature. At first glance these attitudes appear relatively simple, so simple that advertisers within a Christian cultural heritage use images of crystal clear mountain streams, of natural mineral water, of healthy young people running free through woodlands, or living in a flower-decked cottage in the countryside, to conjure up our sense of what is natural. And what is natural is believed to be good. But habits regarded by some people as perfectly natural are strongly opposed by others. There is, for example, some stiff opposition in Britain to the hunting of animals whether by people or dogs, as though this was an obviously bad practice despite the fact that hunting has been part of human behaviour for a very long time. Similarly, some people think it socially proper, physically healthy, and morally good, to be naked at what are called naturist clubs, while others think such behaviour morally questionable and even humanly degrading.

These simple examples show how the word 'nature' comes with many built-in values and social conventions. Each society has its own relative emphasis to place upon natural things so that what is true in one country may well be false in another. The British image of rural idylls with its desire to have an historic country cottage is not, for example, entirely shared by the French, many of whom would prefer to live in modern houses in towns.

In this chapter we attempt to show how Christian ideas drawn from the Bible and its interpretation, as well as from church traditions, enter into our view of 'nature'. As we do this we will become aware of the interplay between various cultural views, some Christian and some non-Christian, which almost naturally seem to guide our outlook. As far as human beings are concerned there seems to be no such thing as 'nature' existing as an untouched world of its own. Whether we see certain natural phenomena as pure and innocent or red in tooth and claw depends upon the values and beliefs which human society brings to bear upon them. An understanding of nature requires an analysis of how cultures classify aspects of the world, and in terms of Christian religion it begins in the belief that God created all that is.

Creation

For Christian theology attitudes to nature have been formed through the doctrine of creation, a doctrine grounded in the belief that the world is really there, surrounding us and forming our environment. Though this might seem a strange way to start discussing Christian attitudes to nature it is nevertheless important because the reality of the world lies at the heart of all Christian theology.

Central to the belief in the reality of the world is the conviction that when we open our eyes and look around us we are not deluded by what we see. The world of nature is no figment of our imagination, nor is it a trick played upon us by some supernatural being. The hard and fast reality of the universe and of our earth as part of it is guaranteed by the fact that God is responsible for it. Here, in God's responsibility, we have the first theological principle of creation. In traditional theological language this prime responsibility of God is expressed through the slightly misleading Latin phrase *creatio ex nihilo*. This phrase, 'creation out of nothing', means that it is God who establishes and creates all things, it speaks of the primacy of God. It is precisely because God wills that the universe should exist and calls it into existence that we may speak of a further principle of creation, namely the dependable nature of the world. It was this dependability of nature that allowed later generations of scientists to study it in systematic ways on the belief that the world would not change its nature between one day and another.

Initially and in a fundamentally important way Christianity drew heavily from the Hebrew Scriptures when developing a doctrine of creation and in coming to understand the wisdom of God in creation. In the book of Genesis there are two accounts of creation. The first account (1:1 – 2:4) presents us with an orderly view of creation stemming from the Priestly tradition of Israel. At the outset God creates humanity as male and female. Following the pattern of a week, a day-by-day series of creative acts makes everything according to its kind. A similar Priestly motivation of order occurs in parts of the books of Leviticus (chs 1ff.), and Deuteronomy (chs 5ff.), where a close parallel is drawn between the perfection of the natural world and the perfection of the social life to which God's people are called.

The second account of creation in Genesis (2:4ff.) according to the Yahwistic tradition of Israel starts from a different perspective and begins with the creation of the male. Only after a clear discussion of the loneliness of the man is woman produced from the man's rib.

The Priestly strand of the Old Testament accentuates both the careful orderliness of the world and the boundaries that surround Israel. Here it is difficult to separate the geographical territory of Israel from the social world of God's people, and to this we return shortly in exploring the symbolism of food taboos in Israel. Before that it is worth stressing how relatively infrequently the idea of creation occurs throughout the rest of the Old Testament.

In the Wisdom literature of Psalms (74:12–17 and 89:5–12), in Proverbs (8:22–31), in Job (chs 38 and 39), and among the prophets (Isa 42:5; 66:1–2; Jer 10:12–13), there are some passages expressing God's power and responsibility as creator but by far the greater number of references to God's creative power in the world preface a statement about God's right to be obeyed by Israel. An interesting feature of these accounts involves the place of humanity. Hebrew and Christian outlooks on creation always involve and implicate men and women within the total scheme. Because Old Testament writings were intended as expressions of social ideals and practical rules for a whole nation or people they embrace aspects of life which are absent in the New Testament which is itself aimed at a more restricted community of believers already existing within wider social frameworks.

Relationship and responsibility

So it is that the Genesis portrayals of God's work describe the universe as a setting for human life. The universe is no neutral place. It is a place for men and women. But it is a place full of relationships

233

and responsibilities. In fact these two words, relationship and responsibility, offer a direct way of grasping a Christian interpretation of the Hebrew idea of creation.

The very idea of relationships, whether between things, people, or between people and God, provides the framework of creation in the first Genesis story. Everything is created according to its own kind and is related to all other kinds of things in an orderly way. In fact orderly relationships constitute God's perfect world and in some senses reflect God's perfection. In the second creation story (Gen 2:4ff.) one heavily stressed relationship is that between human life and the very dust of the earth. People are left in no doubt that they came from and will return to the very earth itself, an idea which radically influences attitudes to the world and to nature. In powerful imagery human beings are said to come from the dust of the earth in exactly the same way as do the animals. Because of this earthy origin humanity and animals are portrayed as having a relationship with each other even though it is an unsatisfactory relationship as far as the human male is concerned. It is this very inadequacy that leads God to create woman out of man and at the same time to establish a new quality of relationship on the earth, that between man and woman.

So the doctrine of creation embraces not only the very ground itself along with plants, animals, and humans, but it also involves human relationships. In other words social life is part and parcel of creation itself. So it is that no hard and fast line should ever be drawn between natural things and social things. For Christian theology distinctions between nature and culture are inappropriate, a point to which we shall return later when considering theologies focusing on ecological and social issues.

The close relationship between nature and society is an important fact when we turn to the second key word in the Christian doctrine of creation, namely, responsibility. Responsibility involves moral issues and in the Old Testament it is closely linked to commandments. God commands Adam and Eve not to eat of the tree of the knowledge of good and evil (Gen 2:17). They quite simply disobey this command and do not carry out their responsibilities towards God and his Law. This act of disobedience, this irresponsibility, leads to a change in relationships. This whole situation is often referred to as the Fall and depicts the moral weakness and flawed nature of men and women. In further strong imagery the woman is condemned to suffer pain in childbirth so that one of the most natural of acts is now to become a problem (Gen 3:16). In a very similar way men are to find their natural work of farming hard and strenuous.

So it is that the creation embraces a strong moral component. In the Hebrew Scriptures all life possesses a moral dimension. Issues of good and evil surround all life, and are directly linked to the law and commandments of God. Here there is no possibility of looking in an abstract way at the world, nature is not there simply to be appreciated, it is an arena of moral life speaking of God and involving God. Men and women cannot regard themselves simply as artists enjoying the world in a dispassionate sense because the world is a vehicle for divine ends and is not an end in itself. Human beings are living members of a complex world existing within all sorts of relationships with it and possessing all sorts of responsibilities towards it.

World and society

We have already said that the social world is part and parcel of creation itself. One of the clearest insights into this Hebrew view of the world comes through the idea of a promised land and a chosen people. Running throughout much of the Old Testament is this deeply held belief that God had promised an actual territory to his own chosen people, and within it very particular areas for each of the major tribal clans (Num 34). It was from this perspective of a divine society in a divine territory that the rest of the world made sense. And the rest of the world was not to be seen simply in geographical terms but also in terms of social life. One of the most important distinctions drawn in the Old Testament is between God's chosen people and those other nations who did not belong to that covenant community. These outsiders, or Gentiles as non-Jews later came to be know, inhabited their own distinct territories so that from the perspective of the Old Testament, as in most parts of the world today, geography and politics were practically the same thing.

As Christianity emerged from Jewish stock it too, in the course of time, came to draw a distinction between members of the Christian community, and outsiders not of the faith. Christianity also came to establish itself as a territorial religion, and it has not been unknown for some Christian groups to use the idea of a promised land as a way of thinking about God's will for them. A major way of looking at the world from one Christian perspective is found in the title Holy Roman Empire which Charlemagne gave to his Western empire on his coronation in 800 CE and which lasted a thousand years until Napoleon brought it to a close in the early nineteenth century. Even in modern times we have become used to thinking of some societies as being Christian, Hindu, Muslim, Buddhist, Sikh, secular, or atheist. In other words countries are still often categorized by virtue of their dominant religious or ideological outlook.

Humans and animals in nature

We have already shown that the Jewish tradition argued that both humankind and animals originated from the dust of the ground and because of that shared a certain kinship. As a kind of analogy we might say that this joint origin in the Book of Genesis resembles the theory of evolution when it argues that humans and animals all come from pre-existing animal stock.

In the Old Testament animals are distinguished from one another in several ways. In the first Genesis creation myth sea creatures are distinguished from the birds both of which were said to be created on the fifth day. Beasts, cattle, creeping things, and mankind, were all created on the sixth day as distinct groups. Humanity is given a distinct command to be fruitful and fill the earth, to subdue it and to have dominion over these various animal groups. It is a dominion that follows from the fact, clearly linked in the text, that male and female were created in the image of God (Gen 1:27, 28).

In the various laws associated with the running of God's ideal society those animals that may be regarded as domesticated have certain rights associated with them. An individual should, for example, assist an ox or an ass that has fallen. Even a bird's nest with eggs, young, and mother should be treated with due care; the eggs may be taken but the mother must be allowed to remain free (Deut 22:4, 6).

Unclean animals and food

In the books of Leviticus (11:2–23) and Deuteronomy (14:3–20) fixed rules are given as to which animals may or may not be eaten by Jews.

236

These rules are interesting showing as they do just how closely attitudes to nature are linked to religious ideas. Although these rules have been interpreted by biblical scholars in different ways one of the most suggestive explanations of why they exist came from the British social anthropologist Mary Douglas (1966).

She argued that the picture of the world drawn out in the Levitical and Deuteronomic codes of life is one of order and tight control. There was a place for everything and when everything was in its place the overall harmonious picture of society reflected and symbolized the unity of God. Social order expressed divine order. Orderliness had a strong moral dimension, order was good, chaos was bad. This was all the more important given the fact that Israel was much concerned with its identity as God's people. Marriage, for example, should be with members and not with outsiders. All of which led to a preoccupation with boundaries of behaviour.

And this is where the rules for eating come in as a sort of perpetual reminder and symbol of the good order, because those creatures deemed unclean for eating had something about them which indicated disorder or chaos. The pig, for example, is classified as unclean because it has a cloven hoof but does not chew the cud (Deut 14:8). The logic of this prohibition is that animals which have cloven hoofs and also chew the cud are like the normal grazing animals familiar to the tribes of Israel, such animals express the good order of society. But the pig possesses only half the qualification for inclusion in that normal category: it has a cloven hoof but does not chew the cud. In that sense the pig is an anomaly, it shares the features of two different categories of creature and because it straddles the boundary line it is a bad example of perfection. In a similar way anything that comes from river or sea and has fins and scales as do ordinary fish is clean. But anything that comes from the water and lacks such fishy signs is deemed unclean.

This sort of interpretation can be extended to explain why the Jews were commanded not to weave two types of cloth together, nor plough using a donkey and an ox (Deut 22:10–11). In all aspects of life everything should be 'according to its kind' as the first creation myth expresses the orderliness of creation, for that order helps distinguish God's people from other nations, and also expresses the divine orderliness of God. Here there can be no attitude towards nature that is not at the same time an attitude towards society and, indirectly, towards God.

This point becomes extremely clear in the symbolism of Peter's dream in the Acts of the Apostles (Acts 10:9ff.) where there is presentation of the Old Testament food law which is immediately transcended. Peter has a vision of food which is unclean. When told to eat it he recoils saying that he has never eaten anything that is unclean. The answer that comes to him is very powerful, saying that what God has cleansed none should call unclean. The clear implication is that former rules of a closed society and a closed religion are now overcome as the Christian religion opens the way for all to come and worship God. Immediately afterwards Peter is summoned to preach to the Gentiles.

In its subsequent history Christianity has been remarkably open on the matter of food. We might even say that because Christianity emerged from Judaism and possesses a very clear abandonment of the Old Testament food regulations it was easy for it not to fall into extensive new food rules. One consequence of this is that Christianity has had relatively few food problems as a missionary movement entering new cultures.

Scripture, worship, and nature

The belief that God's creation of nature is a cause of worship and praise is already found in the Jewish Scriptures and furnished Christianity with a fundamentally important view of the universe. A few of the Psalms dwell quite specifically on the wonders of God's work in nature. Psalm 104 expresses the idea of God's wise creativity at some length. It is a creativity which stimulates the human response of worship. God it is who stretches out the heavens, establishes the earth, causes grass to grow, gives the sea its depth and fills it with creatures. God it is who gives life to all things and who ultimately takes away their breath of life causing them to return to the dust of the earth. As men and women ponder these facts they praise and bless God. The world of nature is a world in which the Christian, like the Jew, takes delight precisely because it is an expression of God's will and power. The Psalms are one particular source of such worship: 'The heavens declare the glory of God', begins Psalm 19, before it goes on to say how both day and night and the sun express and obey the divine command. But it is true to say that throughout the Psalms, as also in the book of Job (chs 38 – 41), practically any mention of natural phenomena is associated with their divine originator. Very little biblical material dwells on nature as such. Nature exists not in its own right but as a created entity. Humanity may appreciate it and use it but never focus solely on it.

Another aspect of creation reinforces this point, a perspective in which the world stands as a witness to God over against humanity. In early Christianity Paul speaks of this invisible power and God as being revealed in and through the visible aspects of the world. He even argues that humanity is without an excuse for not believing in God precisely because the visible world should leave them in no doubt about God's existence (Rom 1:19–20). Subsequent Christians such as Augustine could speak of the world as a kind of great book written by God but with real objects in the place of words.

It is here that human beings can easily look at nature, or read it, in a wrong way and instead of praising God because of it, see it as an end in itself and become idolaters. The worship of nature is fundamentally wrong for Christians because created things are put in the place properly belonging to the creator. Paul in the same early section of his Letter to the Romans speaks in just this way about people worshipping and serving the creature rather than the creator (1:19–25). So it is that, biblically speaking, there is no such thing as an attitude to nature devoid of a parallel attitude to God its creator.

While the natural world may cause men and women to reflect on God and to turn their minds in a divine direction, as in Psalm 19 where the heavens are said to declare the glory of God, Christian theology has always maintained a sharp distinction between God and the created order. Some mystical trends occasionally employ the idea of pantheism to suggest that God is one with the universe, as the philosopher Spinoza (1632–77) had argued. Orthodox theology has denied this on the basis that God was transcendent over creation. Perhaps one of the reasons why humankind often talks about itself as distinct from nature is because Christian men and women see themselves related to the world in a similarly separate way. Even here theological ideas help influence attitudes to natural realities.

Flawed but renewable

Although the Bible emphasizes the reality of the world it also argues that this very real world is not what it should be. The first Genesis story of creation depicts God looking upon the creation and pronouncing it to be very good (Gen 1:31). But, as we shall see in more detail later, with the sinful disobedience of humanity, the world is cursed. This theme recurs in the Old Testament prophets who see God blessing the world when the chosen people are obedient and blighting it when they are disobedient. This theme is developed in some of the Jewish prophets with the divine promise to make new heavens and a new earth in which perfection will exist. This sense of perfection involves the obedience of God's people and also a world of justice and orderly life with all chaos removed, a place where 'the wolf and the lamb shall feed together, the lion shall eat straw like the ox' (Isa 65:25).

Christians adopted much of this Jewish approach to the physical world both in seeing the present order as imperfect and in believing that God would transform it in the last days. One strand of New Testament teaching speaks of Christians as 'waiting for new heavens and a new earth in which righteousness dwells' (2 Pet 3:13). Biblical teaching about such a final period, or eschatology as it has been called over the last century and a half, binds the destiny of believers close to the destiny of the world. Paul's important contribution in his Letter to the Romans speaks of the creation as being caught up in a process of decay. He speaks as though the creation is caught in the painful pangs of birth. Believer and world together are prisoners and groan as they seek release. But the hope is sure and the 'glorious liberty of the children of God' will come to believer and to the world (Rom 8:21). But perhaps the best known description of this Christian longing comes in the book of Revelation. There the visionary sees a new heaven and a new earth following on from the old heaven and earth which had passed away. Central to the vision is a new Jerusalem which comes down to the new earth and is the centre of divine blessing for mankind. As we show at several points in this chapter New Jerusalem is both a city and a garden, it combines within itself images of the old Jerusalem and of the Garden of Eden. A river of life flows through its central street, which is bordered by the tree of life (Rev 22:2).

This clear vision of a renewed world has seldom played a central part in mainstream Christian thinking but some sectarian movements have focused on it in a very powerful way. In the mid and late nineteenth century the Mormons in Utah saw their own geographical area as a special place to which God had led them. By their hard work and careful social organization arid land was becoming very fruitful. In biblical terms, following Isaiah (35:1), they saw the desert blossoming as a rose and becoming a new kind of promised land. Once more the idea of a promised land went hand in hand with their belief in themselves as a chosen people.

In the twentieth century the Jehovah's Witnesses stressed the wrongness of the present system of things in the world, and testified to their belief that it would take a major act of God to restore the world to the divine plan. In many ways the Mormon and Jehovah's Witnesses examples illustrate the 'this-worldly' orientation of biblical religion which many central Christian views had forgotten in their growing tendency to see salvation in terms of the destiny of the human soul in heaven after this earthly life is ended.

Nature and heaven

There have been tendencies in Christianity to draw a line between sacred and secular aspects of life and to view nature in a negative light. The contrast between spirit and flesh was used by Paul in his Letter to the Romans (8:5) and appears in a similar way in the First Letter of John where Christians are exhorted not to love the world or the things in the world (1 John 2:15). In an interesting way we find that in the case of asceticism the first two Christian centuries show little concern with it, instead there is a basic acceptance of the world. It is only in the third century that asceticism begins to make its presence felt, and by the time of Ambrose of Milan in the fourth century asceticism assumes a major significance so much so that virginity is deemed superior to the married state of life. Marriage becomes one formal expression of worldly life as opposed to spiritual existence, a distinction not found in the Bible itself.

The more directly biblical distinction between flesh and spirit is reflected, for example, in the fifth century when Augustine followed a similar path in *The City of God* where his two cities depicted two loves, of God and of self. Such a spirit–flesh distinction, even though it does not refer directly to aspects of nature, is a view that encourages asceticism and sees the spiritual life in a rather narrow way. Some traditions where monks and nuns have remained unmarried and live quite apart from the ordinary world illustrate this distinction between spirit and flesh which comes to match a

241

distinction between heaven and earth. For such people the truly religious life is lived on the border between earth and heaven, and this is why regular worship in churches was so important.

Another tradition within Christianity has taken quite a different approach affirming a 'this-worldly' rather than an 'other-worldly' perspective. There have been religious orders which have stressed this perspective, as in the modern case of Mother Teresa and her nuns. In the twentieth century this strongly affirmative outlook has been emphasized both by Liberation Theologians in their stress on social justice and by theologians with ecological concerns to care for world resources. Before considering this very recent Ecological Theology in the next part of this chapter we will explore one major theological concern which prepared the ground for these recent developments.

Incarnational theology and nature

Christianity has, formally, spent more time discussing human nature than it has the nature of animals, plants, or the cosmos. There are some exceptions to this and, for example, the historian Keith Thomas has shown how popular religion in Britain often regarded animals as capable of having some sort of religion. Indeed in the period after the Reformation it was argued by some that animals could gain immortality (1984: 137ff.). Even so in modern theology attitudes to nature have often ignored animals and plants and focused on human nature and on the precise identity of Jesus of Nazareth. In one very real sense then Christian attitudes to nature focus on attitudes towards Jesus. This is very clear in the history of doctrine which, over the first five hundred years of Christian history, was preoccupied with the relationship between human nature and divine nature within the one person of Jesus.

Christian orthodoxy came to be formulated through great Councils of church leaders as at Nicaea (325 CE) and Chalcedon (451 CE). Central to their conclusions was the belief that Jesus was fully human and also fully divine, a single person possessing two natures. This was believed to be important for Christian theology to ensure the salvation of men and women: because their humanity had been fully assumed by Jesus it had also be redeemed through him. As we have repeatedly stressed in this book, there was a deep awareness of this need for human nature to be fully entered into and taken on by Jesus before human beings could be saved from sin. This was the generally accepted position of orthodoxy. Implicit in this belief was that God loved human beings enough to become one of them in Jesus of Nazareth. Human nature had now become associated with divine nature in the person of one individual. This meant that human beings could reflect on their own identity through the belief that God had not only created humanity but had also entered into humanity. This divine approval or validation of human nature, in the very process of salvation, gave to men and women the opportunity of looking positively on their own life and its significance.

Because God had assumed humanity in one concrete individual it was now not only perfectly proper, but also necessary, for all Christians to look on other people in a profounder way (2 Cor 5:15–19). So it is that attitudes to human nature are forged not only through the doctrine of creation, but also through the doctrine of redemption.

This process of God entering into humanity in the individual man Jesus of Nazareth is spoken of in theology as the doctrine of the Incarnation. It is a doctrine closely associated in Christian belief with what is often called sacramental theology emphasizing how ordinary aspects of life can be endowed with religious significance. This refers not only to official church sacraments using wine, bread, or water as in the Eucharist or baptism, but to many other aspects of life and in one sense embraces the very matter of the universe itself. In this incarnational–sacramental theology God employs natural phenomena as vehicles for religious truth. For Christians committed to this view of the universe attitudes to nature are grounded in a world of divine value and significance.

Evolution

Religious values have not, however, been the sole influence on people's interpretation of the world, and religious ideas themselves changed shape because of the impact of other philosophical and scientific ideas. Because the Christian religion has been closely bound up with the total cultural life of Europe for at least the last 1500 years it is quite understandable that major shifts in general thought are reflected in religious thinking, just as theological thought makes

243

its own impact upon wider social currents. In looking at some of these changes and influences as they affect attitudes to nature we shall take history a little out of step by looking first at some nineteenth- and twentieth-century issues before returning to the sixteenth century. We do this because one of the most important changes in human self-understanding belongs to Darwin's work in the mid-nineteenth century, as discussed in Chapter 3 above. Darwin's biological studies reinforced the more speculative philosophical and sociological work of scholars like Herbert Spencer (1820–1902) and caused much debate in the last third of the nineteenth century (Andreski, 1972).

The basic problem was that traditional Christian thought, like thought in general, believed that God had created human beings fully formed and identifiably human shortly after the creation of the world of nature. Darwin's biological theory of evolution combined with the findings of geologists to argue that the world was very much older than traditional theology had assumed, and that human beings had emerged from pre-human forms of animal life. More than this, his idea of the survival of the fittest implied that divine will and providence was not the cause behind the emergence of men and women. Natural biological processes were the fundamental processes of life.

Some nineteenth-century Christians regarded this theory of evolution as quite antagonistic to Christianity as witnessed in a debate at Oxford in 1860 when the bishop of that diocese, Samuel Wilberforce, tried to ridicule the idea of evolution but was himself politely humbled by the scientist T. H. Huxley. A few nineteenth-century Christians such as F. B. Jevons (1858–1936) of Durham warmly accepted evolutionary theories and saw them as complementing the doctrine of creation. It was in this later nineteenth-century period that Christian approaches to nature were challenged and stimulated into new thinking about God and the world.

These questions are still important because some Christians think there is a sharp distinction between the doctrine of creation and the theory of evolution. At its simplest this argument sets the intentional creative act of God in opposition to the accidental or random event of the origin of the universe with the subsequent evolution of life. Intention versus accident is a key distinction here and no compromise is believed to be possible between the two world-views.

EVOLUTION AS CREATION

Another view, adopted by some Christians and raised earlier in Chapter 3, accepts the general process of evolution but assumes that the universe itself, however it came into existence, was intended by God. The origin of the cosmos and the evolution of life on earth are both seen as part of God's overall creative scheme. Here evolution is creation. Ultimately this view does not accept that the existence of life is accidental and random. The Catholic priest and scientist Pierre Teilhard de Chardin (1881–1955) developed his own modern religious philosophy of creation grounded in an evolutionary perspective. Central to it was the belief that Christ was the centre of love for our cosmos which is a dynamic system of interrelationships, even matter is endued with a degree of dynamic awareness. Christ is the focus and goal for human existence, making sense of the past as well as providing hope for the future. Much of Teilhard's language and terminology was unacceptable to the church authorities of his day who prevented him publishing his work and sent him to work in China for long periods; it is also unacceptable to most scientists. Even so Teilhard de Chardin shows the importance of evolution and of Christ for a modern Christian perception of the world. He shows how important it is to consider theological issues in the light of scientific knowledge and to strive seriously to integrate them. Some problems are inevitably caused by such thinkers because older forms of argument and older patterns of theology cannot quite cope with new insights. One important example of this concerns sin.

Nature, sin, and evolution

As we saw earlier in Chapters 3 and 5, one major stream of traditional Christian theology speaks of sin in relation to the Fall of mankind. God's perfect creation comes to be spoiled through the disobedience of humanity as in chapter 3 of the book of Genesis where the very ground is cursed to produce weeds because of Adam's wickedness. One consequence of this approach is that the world of nature is viewed as a sorry scene. The golden age is in the past and only in some future age will it be restored in heaven, or in some dramatic act of the last days. There is little place in this tradition for a view of evolutionary development of the world and its moral nature.

245

This scheme of a Fall in the past and some future divine restoration belongs to a world-view which tends to take some aspects of Genesis and of the book of Revelation as literally true. It reminds us that the question of creation and evolution often involves a very particular kind of biblical interpretation, one that stresses the literal truth of biblical passages.

Views which give an important place to evolutionary ideas will almost certainly not follow that kind of literal path focusing on a very few passages of Scripture. Instead they will draw from numerous aspects of the Bible and other Christian traditions of doctrine interpreted in non-literal ways.

This is true for what has been called Process Theology. Following the philosophy of A. N. Whitehead (1861–1947) Process Theologians have interpreted the world as a developing and dynamic reality intimately related to God and progressing in such a way that God's love increasingly comes to the fore (Pittinger, 1967). The stress on love is related to a strong emphasis upon human personality and its development, not only within the individual but throughout history and human culture. Events in the here and now are also given pride of place in order to emphasize the ongoing process of evolution. It is the task of men and women to engage themselves with this ongoing work of creation to ensure that love increasingly influences human life. In this scheme of things sin and evil can be understood as hindrances and backward movements in the process of world creation. In Process thought both the idea of love and that of evil demonstrate the intimate association of human beings with the material world (Ogden, 1967). Process Theology makes an important contribution to a Christian understanding of nature by arguing that human life is part and parcel of the universe itself, sharing in the shaping of the world for the future. Natural and moral values are closely combined, just as God is intimately involved in the evolving world of nature and humanity; here there is no place for a sharp distinction between the world and the Church. In historical terms this link between theology and science has not always been so obvious and easy as was particularly true in the sixteenth century.

The universe, God, and orthodoxy

The sixteenth century was a period of astonishing change as far as

Western Christendom was concerned; part of this change deeply affected attitudes to nature. The religious reformation of Martin Luther (1483–1546) was matched by the scientific revolution inaugurated by Nicolas Copernicus (1473–1543) and discussed in Chapter 3. For us, today, the idea that the earth moves round the sun is accepted as an ordinary fact of life. But this simple change of outlook was to be radically important in giving humanity a different sense of its own importance. Instead of being the central inhabitants of the universe human beings could now see themselves as resident upon a subsidiary and peripheral planet. Subsequent astronomers and physicists reinforced this new perception of the universe. Sometimes, as with John Kepler (1571–1630) who formulated some basic laws explaining the movement of the planets, these new interpretations were linked with theological ideas. Kepler, for example, thought that the orderliness of nature expressed something of the nature of God. He saw analogies between the sun as God the Father, the fixed stars and God the Son, and the realm of the planets and God the Spirit and the other planets. The orderliness of the universe was something that appealed strongly to another profoundly religious scientist, Isaac Newton (1642–1727). His discovery of the law of gravity is well known, but it is also worth remembering his religious convictions which were not always orthodox. Not only did he find the doctrine of the Holy Trinity rather contrary to reason but he was much given to speculation on millenarian ideas about the end of the world.

The emergence of scientific ideas influencing our view of the world has, occasionally, led to major opposition from church authorities. We have already seen this with Darwin's evolutionary theories in the nineteenth century. But there was a far starker conflict in the early seventeenth century when the astronomer Galileo (1564–1642), who incidentally discovered four satellites of Jupiter with his new invention of the astronomical telescope, forcefully argued the Copernican theory of the sun's centrality to our universe. The Catholic Church took exception to his utterances and formally condemned the Copernican theory in 1616; the Church still affirmed and supported the traditional Ptolemaic view of the universe, where everything revolved around the earth. Galileo was summoned to Rome, was subject to the Inquisition and forced to recant under threat of torture. His support of the Copernican theory was regarded as a form of heresy. After nearly a decade he was permitted to return to Florence where he died. After his recantation he is reckoned to have added words to the effect that 'it does move all the same'. This episode in the history of science is at the same time a moment in the history of theology, showing how attitudes to nature are intrinsically linked with theological beliefs about creation. It also opens the meaning of the word 'nature' showing that it embraces our total understanding of the universe and not simply on what we think about animal rights or ecology.

Many aspects of thought in the seventeenth and especially in the eighteenth century emphasized human reason in arriving at a sense of what the world was about. One strand of thought discussed the place of mankind within the broad flow of nature, or the great chain of being, and argued that there was a kind of principle of continuity with all parts of the world filled with appropriate creatures. This philosophical outlook prepared the way for the nineteenth century's more scientific discovery of the theory of evolution. But perhaps the Scottish philosopher David Hume (1711–76) can be taken as a more typical exponent of the eighteenth-century age of reason in which the world of nature was very largely given a secondary place because of the preoccupation with human thought and human knowledge. As a response to the alienation of mankind from nature inherent within the age of reason we find at the close of the eighteenth century the rise of Romanticism, a general outlook which brought the world of nature back into the forefront of experience and thought. It is not surprising that the Romantics like Wordsworth (1770–1850) used poetry to express the power and significance of nature in sharp contrast to the logical, philosophical, treatises of the rationalists.

One important aspect of Romantic thought is the belief that nature impresses upon human beings a sense of the significance and unity of things, a kind of sense of presence. Nature is perceived as dynamic and is not simply there as an object to be observed. Some of Wordsworth's thoughts expressed in his 'Lines Composed a few Miles Above Tintern Abbey' touch on this outlook:

And I have felt
A presence that disturbs me with the joy
Of elevated thoughts: a sense sublime
Of something far more deeply interfused,
Whose dwelling is the light of setting suns,
And the round ocean and the living air ...

248

This outlook is not far removed from mystical religious individuals who prefer to speak of encountering God through nature rather than of having some sort of objective view of nature. The material world becomes the arena within which a knowledge of God is born and expands, so much so that the believer may feel quite at one with all that is. At such a moment the world of nature is the means by which the believer reckons to gain an intuitive knowledge of reality. Before the Romantics the seventeenth-century English mystic Thomas Traherne (1637–74) could say 'You never Enjoy the World aright till the Sea itself floweth in your Veins, till you are Clothed with the Heavens, and Crowned with the Stars ... till you delight in God for being Good to all' (*Centuries* 1.29).

A secular dynamic world

Within broad Christian culture it is important to consider the ideas of those who do not start from theological or even from any official Christian standpoint because of the mutual influences which always seem to be at work in society. J. E. Lovelock (1979), for example, published a book that has become influential in discussions of ecology and human responsibility for the world. He called his book *Gaia* after the Greek goddess of the earth, a suggestion made to him by his novelist neighbour William Golding. *Gaia* is subtitled 'A new look at life on earth', and is really a hypothesis about the world we inhabit. The hypothesis is that the actual chemical and physical nature of the earth's surface, its atmosphere and oceans, has been brought about by the presence of life itself. More than that, it is a self-regulating system with a capacity to keep the world as a healthy system capable of sustaining life, in this sense it is an intelligent system. It also embraces humanity.

In Lovelock's outlook many people have an implicit under-standing of the fact that life is one immense system of interlinked parts; this reflects a kind of long standing folk-wisdom or paganism which the churches do not like to admit still exists. Even so Lovelock suggests that the churches, along with humanist movements, have come to see the power of environmental campaigns and have revised their own theology to catch up with the mood of the age. He particularly criticizes the continuing Christian concern to stress mankind's stewardship of the world, because he sees in this a continued desire to keep mankind centre-stage. With this in mind it is interesting that one popular book on Christian faith in relation to nature was entitled *To Care for the Earth* (1986), a title reflecting the Christian sense of responsibility for the world alongside the centrality of men and women within it. Its author, Seán McDonagh, was well aware of the Gaia hypothesis and argued for the emergence of a Christian spirituality developed from a modern understanding of the earth. But still the commitment to the Christian idea of human importance comes to the fore as is, perhaps, inevitable in the light of the doctrine of creation. For Lovelock, by subtle contrast, men and women along with all other animals, plants, and chemical systems, exist together in a mutual overall system of things which is Gaia. There is no precedence accorded to mankind, even though it might be that human intellect and technology will, in the future, be able to help the total system of nature to protect itself.

In terms of Christian theology it is practically impossible not to see humanity as central to the world of nature. This is because of the fundamental distinction between the Christian belief that God willed and intended a world of which mankind should be a part, and that kind of scientific interpretation which sees the emergence of the cosmos, of the earth, and ultimately of life, as accidental. We have already mentioned this distinction between intention and accident but its importance demands a re-emphasis since it is this sharp difference between an intended and an accidental universe which stands at the centre of the religion and science debate over the universe. Some Christians wish to stress this divide and to sharpen the distinction between the creative will of God and the accidental events of matter. There are some, especially in the United States of America, who actively oppose the theory of evolution precisely because they see it as godless. They press other Christians not to accept evolutionary theories because to do so is to deny belief in the divine will to create the world. For these individuals a Christian view of nature, often based on a literal understanding of the book of Genesis, necessitates a clear belief that God willed the world into existence in an intentional way. They do not wish their children to be taught evolutionary theory in school because they see that as a form of secular indoctrination and contrary to Christianity.

Other Christians, probably the majority, accept the theory of evolution but bring to it a theological assumption. They, too, start with the belief that God is fundamentally responsible for the universe, the earth, and for mankind, but they accept evolutionary processes in a qualified form by arguing that these are the means by which God creates things. We have already seen this in the work of Teilhard de Chardin. A more recent English scientist and theologian, A. R. Peacocke (1971), has also argued on the assumption that evolutionary processes are fundamental to the way God continually creates the universe.

As mentioned in Chapter 3, several contemporary scientists and theologians have raised the issue of the anthropic principle, the idea that human self-consciousness is not an accident of the evolutionary process but the consequence of the very way life-systems are organized in the universe. Another related issue is the fact that the world is so intelligible in terms of physics and mathematics. In fact the mathematicians and physicists often seem to speak of the universe as a far more intelligible place than do philosophers and scholars of literature.

What these various arguments from science and religion show is that Christian attitudes to nature are not simply concerned with such things as the beauty of flowers but with the meaning of the universe itself. Christian theology deals with this immense question of the meaning of the universe in philosophical ways, as we have already showed, but for many believers the theme is also pursued through the medium of worship in what we might call a celebration of nature.

Celebrating nature

Because many Christians understand and express their faith more through worship than through formal theology it is wise not to ignore attitudes to nature developed through worship. So although we have already mentioned some psalms in relation to the doctrine of creation we now go on to look at other canticles and hymns which have given expression to Christian perspectives.

One of the longest standing hymns of praise to God which celebrates nature and calls upon natural phenomena to worship God is the *Benedicite*. This Latin title ('Bless ye') begins a hymn of praise put into the mouths of the three men in a fiery furnace in the Jewish Song of The Three, placed in the Apocrypha. It has been used in Christian ritual from very early days and was widespread in Europe by the fifth century. In the Church of England, for example, it stands as a canticle in the service of Morning Prayer in the Book of Common Prayer. It embraces many aspects of nature:

O all ye works of the Lord, bless ye the Lord:
Praise him, and magnify him for ever.
O ye sun and moon ... stars of heaven ... showers and dew ...
winds ... winter and summer ... frost and cold ...
O all ye green things upon the earth ...
Whales ... fowls of the air ... beasts and cattle ...
Praise him and magnify him for ever.

A very similar message runs through the hymn 'All creatures of our God and King', which is based on St Francis of Assisi's 'Canticle of the Sun' from the early thirteenth century. Francis is renowned as a Christian whose simple life involved a closeness to animals and nature, and some Christians have recently heralded him as a prophet of ecological theology. It is always unwise to force or project the issues and problems of one generation back onto another, and this is probably also true of Francis, whose sense of unity with natural things was not prompted by worries over survival (Sorrell, 1988), but by a sense of common purpose and fulfilment in the service of God. This is clearly expressed in 'All creatures of our God and King' where sun and moon, wind, and flowing water, along with mother earth and her flowers, are all called to praise and worship God.

HARVEST THANKSGIVING

A few more recent hymns of the eighteenth and nineteenth century have focused on 'the little flowers and birds' but usually in hymns for children such as 'All things bright and beautiful, All creatures great and small' of 1848, but more frequently attention is fixed on the harvest and the relation of the natural elements to harvest. 'We plough the fields and scatter The good seed on the land' is a favourite hymn of many churches, written in the late eighteenth century, and always used at Harvest Festival or Harvest Thanksgiving Services in Britain. It expresses the rural nature of much European and North American Protestant religion, and summarizes human response to God for the produce of nature: 'All good gifts around us Are sent from heaven above, Then thank the Lord, O thank the Lord, For all his love'. Even so this hymn, like the similar 'Come ye thankful people come', is an agricultural hymn. Both focus on cultivated fields rather than on wild animals and plants. God's providence is connected with the supply of food, and in this sense the attitude to nature is an extension of human need. It is interesting that Harvest Thanksgiving services are relatively modern as church-based events in Great Britain. Although secular celebration of harvest had long occurred in Britain as in most agricultural societies it only became specifically linked with the church in the nineteenth century.

In 1843 the Vicar of Morwenstow in Cornwall developed and extended a custom relating to Lammas Day in late summer when the bread for Holy Communion was baked from new corn that had just been harvested. This church-focused custom became increasingly popular with the decoration of churches with corn, fruit, vegetables, and flowers. By 1862 the Church of England produced a form of service for the occasion. As time went on, and especially in industrial towns and cities, other aspects of human endeavour such as coal or manufactured products were often added to the harvest goods as an expression of human work and of thanks to God.

Whether dealing with harvest or nature in general these hymns are few in number. Most traditional hymn books have more hymns on heaven and the afterlife than they do on earth and the environment of nature. This is fully in accord with the fact that Christianity's overarching concern has, traditionally, been more with the salvation of individuals couched in terms of church membership and the world of heaven rather than the protection of earth's ecology.

Animal rights

Among the few theologians whose attitude to nature struck a distinctively different note is Albert Schweitzer. He was one of the most remarkable scholars of the twentieth century, having made important contributions to philosophical, biblical, and musical scholarship. After all that he learned medicine and became a medical missionary in Africa. In his volumes on the philosophy of civilization Schweitzer developed the idea of what he called reverence for life. This concern, which embraced the belief that even insects should be respected and not killed, is strange as far as Christianity is concerned, being a more distinctive feature of Buddhism. Even so this man, who was awarded a Nobel Peace Prize, did emphasize and seek to practise reverence for nature, a strange phrase given the fact that Christians normally use reverence only in respect of God. For Schweitzer it was something of a passion and stemmed from a personal conviction that had dawned upon him in a radically profound way, it was more of an ethical motive for life than any sort of celebration of nature.

In many respects it is this ethical aspect of attitudes to nature that has come to predominate widely in Western countries in this last third of the twentieth century. The very idea of animal rights stands in the tradition of ethical concerns over which religious values have had such an influence. But the major concern for animal rights has tended not to originate specifically within theology but from wider public opinion and pressure groups such as the World Wide Fund for Nature and Greenpeace. The protection of endangered species has been a major concern on the ethical basis that it is wrong for humanity to destroy another species. Concern for pandas, dolphins, and whales has been accentuated through extensive media coverage and has led to many people gaining a knowledge of the way of life of these animals far beyond former levels of popular awareness.

One attitude to nature that has also developed more recently within traditionally Christian Western societies is vegetarianism. Vegetarianism enshrines for many the belief that it is wrong to be cruel to animals by farming them intensively and then slaughtering them just for food. There is no strictly theological or biblical basis for vegetarianism or for this attitude in Christianity, but it can be viewed as an extension of the ideal of love. The growth of animal rights follows on from an immense increase of awareness of human rights throughout the twentieth century and shows how attitudes to nature are intimately bound up with attitudes to human nature and ultimately to theological beliefs about the human condition.

Attitudes towards nature have, inevitably, included attitudes towards human nature and the place of men and women within the world and cosmos. One of the most dramatically important areas of theological analysis in this field, in recent decades, has been that of sexuality and gender, most especially focused upon women. The final chapter of this book explores this topic and, also, shows how the social contexts of earlier generations influenced their interpretation of the Bible.

Further reading

Hendry, G. S. (1980) *Theology of Nature*. Philadelphia: Westminster Press.
McDonagh, S. (1986) *To Care for the Earth*. London: Geoffrey Chapman.
Sorrell, R. D. (1988) *St Francis of Assisi*. New York: Oxford University Press.

10. Attitudes to women

Clare Drury

As we saw in Chapter 4, the primary source of authority for Christians has always been the Bible and, while it is on biblical texts that Christian attitudes to women are based, this does not mean that there is any straightforward biblical teaching about women which everyone accepts. For the Bible is made up of many different books written and altered over many centuries and not designed to be bound together as one volume. Furthermore, the interpretation of the Bible changes as society changes, so that what seems to fit the scientific and cultural ideas of one century may look quite different in the next.

For some Christians, however, even now, the Bible is felt to have an authority which transcends time and place, so that words written centuries ago in an entirely different culture can be read and believed without reference to the social, cultural or religious conditions in which they were written. But modern scholarship has brought an awareness of the importance of a society's historical and cultural background when interpreting its documents, so that Christian scholars read Paul's teaching on marriage in 1 Corinthians 7, for example, with the knowledge that he expected the world to end in a very short time. When Paul discourages his readers from marrying, it is because 'the appointed time has grown very short', and they should be concentrating on their new faith and not on the worldly cares of the newly married. Jesus, too, had called people to prepare for the coming Kingdom of God, proclaiming its imminence and its radical demands. In the centuries following, some Christians have taken these demands seriously even without the urgent eschatological motivation of the earliest teachers, while others have tried to accommodate the teaching to existing social conditions. In the present century, feminists have been able to point out how radical some of the New Testament teaching about women really was when understood against its contemporary background. They claim that this radicalism was lost during centuries of patriarchal domination of the Church.

Attitudes to the position of women in Christianity, therefore, depend first on which biblical texts one chooses, then on how one reads the Bible and how much weight is given to the contexts in which it was written. The women's movement has begun to interpret the Bible in its own, feminist, way, recognizing the almost total male dominance of both writers and interpreters of the Old and New Testaments, drawing out teaching more positive towards women which has often been overlooked before. Following the extreme change in attitudes towards sexuality and gender issues in modern Western society, Christian women have begun to assert their right to equality inside the Church as well as in secular life. Recently, as women have gained unprecedented freedom in the West, the Churches have begun to mirror these changes. But in societies which have given women a more restricted role and function, the Church has continued to reflect this state of affairs. Some modern scholars have recognized that many of the most influential ideas about women in the Church have come from celibate male writers whose fears about their own sexuality were projected on to women (Warner, 1976; Bynum, 1987; Southern, 1970). They chose to emphasize teaching that was negative towards women so that women could be kept at a safe distance and in a secondary position within the Church.

A less radical, but still inegalitarian, view of women, found today among some conservative Protestant groups, is that they have a role different from, but complementary or subordinate to, men. Some Churches, such as the Quakers, the Methodists, the Baptists and some provinces of the Anglican Communion, treat women as men's equals at all levels and some appoint them as ministers, priests or even bishops, while others, such as the Roman Catholics, still demand celibacy of their all-male priesthood. Some allow women control over their bodies in, for instance, contraception and even abortion, while others regard both as sinful. Since the Bible is the primary authority for these contradictory positions, it is necessary first to look at what it has to say about gender, sexuality and

257

marriage and then at how the Church has interpreted these texts. Much of the seminal work of interpretation was done in the first four centuries of Christianity and those interpretations have formed the basis of most Christian attitudes towards women until the twentieth century.

Women as part of the created order

Christians adopted the Jewish Scriptures as their own because they believed that Jesus was the Christ, or Messiah, to whom the Scriptures referred. They soon began to write their own books some of which, in time, also achieved the status and authority of Scripture. The two groups of writings together came to be called the Old and New Testaments. Both are thought by Christians to record the activities of the same God who is responsible for creating the world and sustaining it, and for providing salvation for his people. So Christians, like Jews, believed that the world had been created by God, that God was beneficent, that he approved his creation and wished it well, 'And God saw everything that he had made, and behold, it was very good' (Gen 1:31). However, the world was obviously not a perfect place where God's work was undeniably present; suffering and pain could not be explained as the creation of a good God. Genesis 3 placed the responsibility for the sufferings of the human race on the shoulders of Adam and Eve for their act of disobedience to God. Christians accepted the stories of creation they found in the Jewish Scriptures and adapted them only to the extent of introducing the pre-existent Christ into the scheme of creation, so that the redeemer of the world was also seen to take part in its creation (John 1:1–18; Col 1:12–20; Heb 1:1 – 2:13). They felt that through the death and resurrection of Christ, God had provided a way of reversing the sin of Adam and Eve. 'For as in Adam all die, so also in Christ shall all be made alive' (1 Cor 15:22; cf. Rom 5:12ff.). Because Christians believed that Jesus was the Jewish Messiah and that Jewish history had been building up to and working towards the coming of the Messiah, they felt entirely justified in interpreting the Jewish Scriptures in ways which suited their own purposes, but which were foreign both to the probable original intentions of the writers and to their Jewish interpreters.

The story of the Creation and Fall in Genesis 1 – 3 was perhaps the most influential Old Testament text affecting woman's place in society, her relationship with her husband and with God. The first thing that must be said is that Genesis 1 – 3 clearly incorporates two distinct accounts of the creation myth; Genesis 1:1 – 2:3 dates from about 400 BCE and is more sophisticated than the Genesis 2:4 – 3:24 account, which includes the story of the Fall and which may have been written about five hundred years earlier. From the woman's point of view the separation of the two stories is vital. In the later account, God creates the world in six days ending with the creation of human beings. In this account man and woman are created at the same time, they are the high point of creation and are given dominion over all the other creatures, 'So God created man in his own image, in the image of God he created him; male and female he created them' (Gen 1:27). There is no distinction in status, there is no subjugation of one sex to the other implied. Both are created in the image of God, and the significance of the gender difference is made clear immediately with the injunction 'Be fruitful and multiply'. Male and female are differentiated primarily for procreation – the commandment to procreate was understood in a positive way by the Jews as long as sexual intercourse took place within marriage. The image of God is not tied to the male, the whole human race is in the image of God. There was a tendency among Christians to conflate the two accounts so that the one in Genesis 1:1 – 2:3 is seen to describe the perfect state of human beings in Paradise before the Fall, the state which, through Christ, it was possible to regain. This may be the basis of a passage in Galatians where Paul seems to be describing Christianity as a faith in which distinctions of race, social status and gender do not apply. 'There is neither Jew nor Greek, there is neither slave nor free, there is neither male nor female; for you are all one in Christ Jesus' (Gal 3:28). This text has been important for Christian women from the earliest Quakers to modern feminist Christians such as Elizabeth Schüssler Fiorenza (1983, ch. 6). The equality of the status of the sexes before God is therefore recognized among redeemed – that is Christian – men and women, at any rate by Paul. But as far as most Christian women are concerned, the equality of status has had little effect in their everyday lives until this century, especially since elsewhere in Paul's letters and in those written by his followers, this egalitarian ideal seems to be contradicted (e.g. 1 Cor 11:7–9; 14:34–36; 1 Tim 2:9–15).

The older account of the Creation (Gen 2:4 – 3:24) is more

primitive in style. God uses the dust of the ground to create Adam, the first man, and breathes into his nostrils the breath of life, 'and man became a living being'. God went on to create a garden for man to live in with trees bearing fruit for him to eat. He only commanded Adam not to eat fruit from the tree of the knowledge of good and evil. God then created all the birds and animals with the aim of finding a helper fit for man, but he could not. So God sent Adam into a deep sleep and created the woman, out of Adam's rib. She is created to provide a companion suitable for him, and their original belonging together as one creature is the explanation for 'the two becoming one flesh' in marriage (Gen 2:24; cf. Mark 10:8). It is she who persuades Adam to disobey God's commandment not to eat of the tree of the knowledge of good and evil.

Christian writers from Paul onwards used this story in two ways. First, it showed that women are subordinate to men because they are created after men and from men and for men. It is the origin of the idea, which many feminist Christians find abhorrent, that human-kind is to be understood in terms of the male. There is a natural hierarchy; to be male is the norm, the female half of the human race is other and subordinate. Paul uses the story to justify his system of authority, explaining it as a kind of divine order given in nature: 'For man was not made from woman, but woman from man. Neither was man created for woman, but woman for man' (1 Cor 11:8–9).

The second way in which Christian writers came to use this version of the creation myth was to emphasize the fundamental wickedness of women. They are responsible for leading men astray; if the woman had not tempted the man, he would not have sinned. 'For Adam was formed first then Eve; and Adam was not deceived, but the woman was deceived and became a transgressor' (1 Tim 2:13–14). The punishment meted out to Adam and Eve after their disobedience is in line with this sort of interpretation. Adam will find it difficult to provide a livelihood because the earth has been cursed and growing food will be arduous and painful. But the woman's punishment is more integral to her very existence and her purpose in life. She will have pain in child-bearing and yet she will desire her husband and he will have authority over her (Gen 3:16–19). This emphasis on Eve's primary guilt is exacerbated by the idea which became prevalent among many Christians that the knowledge which Adam and Eve gained from eating the fruit of the tree of knowledge was carnal knowledge. In other words, Eve was responsible for introducing Adam to sexuality. Women are temptresses in what came to be seen in the Church as the greatest of all temptations, sex. According to the gospels of Matthew and Mark, Jesus joined the two stories together to support his radical opposition to divorce.

> But from the beginning of creation, 'God made them male and female.' 'For this reason a man shall leave his father and mother and be joined to his wife, and the two shall become one flesh.' So they are no longer two but one. What therefore God has joined together, let no one put asunder. (Mark 10:6–9; cf. Matt 19:5–6)

The two accounts have been conflated in Christian tradition ever since. So, it has been necessary to reconcile the idea that women, like men, were made in the image of God, with the idea that men were made in the image of God and women, created later, were secondary and inferior.

This latter view became prevalent in the Church partly because it meshed so well with most secular views in the world of late antiquity in which Christianity grew up. Aristotle (fourth century BCE) had introduced the idea that the male seed provides the 'form' of the human body. The woman's part is passively to receive the formative power of the male seed and so conceive a child. If all goes well, the baby will be male, but if some accident occurs the male form is subverted and produces an inferior or malformed, that is female, baby (Aristotle, *Generation of Animals*, 2.3). He believed that there was a natural hierarchy with free men, who were naturally more rational than women, ruling over wives, slaves and children (e.g. *Politics*, 12.1). Men were seen as fiery, hot and active; women as cold, clammy, wet and passive. Aristotle's writings continued to be very influential in the Church for many centuries, partly because they seemed to reflect the actual state of affairs. It was not until 1827, for instance, when K. E. von Baer discovered the ovum, that it was recognized that women have an equal share in the reproductive process. In the early centuries of this era, every girl baby was deemed a failure, less than the ideal, useful only for her ability to bear children, 'Yet woman will be saved through bearing children, if she continues in faith and love and holiness, with modesty' (1 Tim 2:15).

Although the Church chose to emphasize the sin of Eve by concentrating on the older creation story, yet Genesis 1:27 could not be entirely ignored: 'In the image of God he created him; male and female he created them.' Augustine, Bishop of Hippo in North Africa, was possibly the most influential Christian writer of all outside the New Testament. He combined the texts of Genesis 1:27 with 1 Corinthians 11:7–16 to argue that woman was not made in the image of God in the same sense that man was.

> But we must see how the words spoken by the Apostle, that not the woman but the man is the image of God are not contrary to that which is written in Genesis ... For he says that human nature itself, which is complete in both sexes, has been made to the image of God. For after he had said that God made man to the image of God, he went on to say: 'he made them male and female'. In what sense then are we to understand the Apostle, that the man is the image of God, and consequently is forbidden to cover his head, but the woman is not, and on this account is commanded to do so? The solution lies ... in that the woman together with her husband is the image of God, so that the whole substance is one image. But when she is assigned as a help-meet, a function that pertains to her alone, then she is not the image of God; but as far as the man is concerned, he is by himself alone the image of God, just as fully and completely as when he and the woman are joined together in one. (Augustine, *de Trinitate*, 12, 7, 10).

He believed that the serpent had approached Eve first, because she represented 'the frailer part of human society', the more gullible partner. Later theologians such as Thomas Aquinas (d. 1274) revived Aristotle's definition of a woman as a malformed male, but claimed that the innate inferiority had been exacerbated by sin. He followed closely Aristotle's view of the relations of men and women. Woman was only created for her role in procreation; children were encouraged to follow their fathers rather than their mothers: 'The father is more to be loved than the mother because he is the active generative element, whereas the mother is the passive' (*Summa Theologiae* II/II, q. 26, a. 10). Women were more sexually incontinent than men (ibid., q. 156, a. 1). Aquinas believed that for companionship at any rate, another male was superior because of his greater rationality and self-control.

These are only two examples of male writers in late antiquity and the Middle Ages, but they are typical of the prevalent attitude among educated men of the whole period. Their ideas are responses to their own life situations and their social contexts where women were perceived as a threat to men's ability to avoid sin. But the very persistence of such statements from many different writers reveals that in reality women's lives did not always conform to this pattern. There were noble and notable exceptions to the rule; for example, two powerful and erudite abbesses in the twelfth century – Hildegard of Bingen and Heloïse, whose tutor, Abelard, had become her lover, thus giving substance to some of the male fears about women – were admired and praised by even the most misogynist celibates. Many other aristocratic women were educated to an advanced level, often as well as their brothers, to enable them to take on responsibilities when their husbands were away from home (Labalme, 1980). Some were taught the arts of medicine and herbs so that they could heal the sick and wounded. But this was a two-edged sword; learned women and particularly those skilled in medicine were in danger of being feared as much as revered. A combination of men's fear of women's sexuality and of their skill and erudition could lead to accusations of witchcraft which in turn resulted in inquisitions and terrible persecutions (Cohn, 1976).

It was, however, usually perfectly acceptable for a woman to be well-educated, fluent in languages, well-read in the Scriptures and the Christian Fathers, as long as she did not try to teach men or produce theology of her own, for they claimed that Paul had taught the same. 'Let a woman learn in silence with all submissiveness. I permit no woman to teach or to have authority over men; she is to keep silent' (1 Tim 2:11–12). Mysticism was sometimes an exception to this rule, and mysticism was an area of Christianity particularly attractive to women in the Middle Ages for the revelations given to mystics came directly from God or from Christ, they by-passed the authority of the leaders and teachers of the Church. One such woman was Julian of Norwich, a fourteenth-century anchoress or recluse whose *Revelations of Divine Love* were written down by a scribe. She, like others before her, understood Christ's role partly in terms of motherhood.

> Thus in Jesus, our true Mother, has our life been grounded, through his own uncreated foresight, and the Father's almighty power, and the exalted and sovereign goodness of the Holy Spirit. In taking our nature he restored us to life; in his blessed death upon the cross he bore us to eternal life; and now, since then, and until the Day of Judgement, he feeds and helps us on – just as one would expect the supreme and royal nature of motherhood to act, and the natural needs of childhood to require. (*Revelations*, 63)

Her understanding of the motherhood of God is revealed in Christ, both as nurturing carer, and as creator and saviour of the whole person, body and soul. As well as these lofty and inspiring exceptions, there are indications that the realities of everyday life for ordinary women in the Middle Ages did not always conform to the theories of celibate male writers. The Wife of Bath's Prologue in Chaucer's *Canterbury Tales*, published in the fourteenth century, deals at length with contemporary attitudes towards sexuality and the scriptural texts on which they were based. Here she summarizes the misogyny of the priests:

> For take my word for it, there is no libel
> On women that the clergy will not paint,
> Except when writing of a woman-saint ...
> By God, if women had but written stories
> Like those the clergy keep in oratories,
> More had been written of man's wickedness
> Than all the sons of Adam could redress. (trans. Neville Coghill)

Margery Kempe, a fifteenth-century married woman from Norfolk, who had borne fourteen children, decided to take a vow of chastity and to travel on pilgrimages throughout Europe and as far as the Holy Land. She was guided in her actions by revelations of Christ, who encouraged her at one point to bargain with her husband that if she ate with him on Friday instead of fasting, he would make no sexual demands on her. Her outlandish behaviour and outspoken teaching led to accusations of heresy and of disobeying Paul's injunction that women should not preach. She defended herself bravely before the Archbishop of York and the Mayor of Leicester, arguing her case as an equal.

The attitude of Protestant theologians in the sixteenth century was a little more positive towards women than that of the celibate priests of the Catholic Church, for although they also emphasized the sin of Eve and her innate inferiority to Adam, they thought that she also was created in the image of God and was destined to 'inherit the glory of the future life' (Luther, *Lectures on Genesis*, 1.27).

> For the punishment that she is now subjected to the man was imposed on her after sin and because of sin, just as the other hardships and dangers were: travail, pain and countless other vexations. Therefore Eve was not like the woman of today: her state was far better and more

264

excellent, and she was in no respect inferior to Adam, whether you count the qualities of the body or those of the mind. (2.18)

This means that Eve's sorrows, which she would not have if she had not fallen into sin, are to be great, numerous and also of various kinds. The threat is directed particularly at birth and conception ... Now there is also added to those sorrows of gestation and birth that Eve has been placed under the power of her husband, she who previously was very free and, as the sharer of all the gifts of God, was in no respect inferior to her husband. This punishment too springs from original sin; and the woman bears it just as unwillingly as she bears those pains and the inconveniences which have been placed upon her flesh. The rule remains with the husband, and the wife is compelled to obey him by God's command. He rules the home and the state, wages war, defends his own possessions, tills the soil, builds, plants, etc. The woman, on the other hand, is like a nail driven into the wall. She sits at home ... the wife should stay at home and look after the affairs of the household as one who has been deprived of the ability of administering those affairs that are outside and concern the state ... In this way Eve is punished. (3.16)

Martin Luther, himself a married man who had started his career as a celibate, could value women in a positive way even if still very much from a male point of view; 'wives are adorned with the blessing and glory of motherhood, namely that we are all conceived, born and nurtured by them' (*Lectures on Genesis* 3.16). He claims that it is the fault of 'ungodly celibacy that aspersions are cast against the female sex' (2.18), yet he accepts that God has assigned to them the care of children and kitchen: to *Kinder, Küche, Kirche* under the authority of their husbands.

In the religious turmoil of mid-seventeenth-century England, a group of Dissenters, led by George Fox, held radical views about the equality of women and men which proved in the long term to be very influential. The sect which became known as the Quakers flourished in England in spite of persecution, and soon spread to America. Fox and an early convert, Margaret Fell, who later became his wife, believed that women and men were both created in the image of God; inequality was a result of the sin of Adam and Eve, and that equality had been restored by Christ for those who followed him. So that in a Quaker marriage husband and wife are theoretically equal. The woman does not promise to obey her husband, both husband and wife promise to obey God. The Quakers have no priests, no set forms of worship or sacraments. At meetings the Spirit descends on men and women alike, there is no need for priestly authority, the emphasis is on the individual's sense of the divine and responsibility for others. The Quakers set up their own educational system, since, as Dissenters, the universities were closed to them, and boys and girls were educated in schools together as early as the eighteenth century. Women quickly developed a sense of responsibility against this background; in 1666 separate women's meetings were established to supervise marriages, women's and children's affairs and the welfare of the poor.

The Shakers, a sect which originated in an eighteenth-century Quaker revival, flourished in North America. They went further in egalitarian behaviour than the Quakers. The Shakers live a celibate life (though marriage is not absolutely forbidden), but one in which brothers and sisters are equal; separated from the world, they live in 'family' communities. There is no natural hierarchy of gender, so there is no difference in status between men and women in their communities.

Such groups represent a trend which ran against the tide of mainstream Christian thought until the nineteenth and twentieth centuries, when the increase in biological knowledge and a belief in some sort of evolutionary process rather than divine creation in seven days made the churches rethink their most fundamental beliefs. As discussed in Chapter 4, a different attitude to biblical texts, for example, reading Genesis 1 – 3 as mythological rather than as historical truth, has allowed more Christians to accept the principle of sexual equality and to remove guilt from women just for being women. This is still not universally true, however, and the Church's negative attitude to sexuality and to women as the dangerous 'other' who might lead men astray, still persists in many places.

The ideal of celibacy

In the world of the Roman Empire in which Christianity took shape, the need to produce children to replace the lives of those lost in war or from disease was very great. People were expected to get married young – many girls would marry at fourteen – and to produce several children. Life expectancy was short, few people reached the age of fifty, so marriage and procreation were strongly encouraged. Christianity was remarkable for its idealization of celibacy and virginity: 'Their contempt for death is patent to us every day, and likewise their restraint from intercourse. For they include not only men but also women who refrain from intercourse all through their lives' (attributed to Galen).

Although virginity was not unknown in pagan religions, it was often not undertaken for life; it was frequently not chosen by the individual herself, but by her father or other authorities, and the need for virgins or celibates was usually related to the need for purity at the altar. So although Christianity's sexual restraint was unusual, the traditionally accepted view that the Church provided a haven of respectability in a pagan world of debauched sexuality is far from the truth. Apart from a recognition that adolescent boys would experience strong sexual urges, Graeco-Roman society expected its citizens to be reasonably chaste and monogamous after marriage. This was partly for biological reasons: 'Frequent sexual activity was frowned upon. It decreased the fertility of the male seed and hence the father's chance of children' (Brown, 1988: 369ff.). Sexual intercourse, if conducted with proper decorum, would have a positive effect on the character of the child. But the values of the State were to be reflected in the life of the family and household; loyalty and self-control were highly valued in the Roman Empire of the first few centuries CE.

The Christian ideal of celibacy which flourished against this background had different roots as well. For women especially, virginity was seen as a way of becoming closer to the lost ideal of being in the image of God, closer to what Eve was before she sinned and was cursed. It also has roots in the Jewish idea of single-minded devotion to God, the idea that the whole person owes him allegiance. Whereas in the Graeco-Roman world the soul was thought to rule the rebellious body – the body could be held in check by the restraint of the soul – for the Jew, both body and soul were part of God's creation, and both would be liable to judgement.

The Essenes, a Jewish sect contemporary with Jesus, shunned pleasure and disdained marriage (Josephus, *War*, ii:119f.). The Qumran sect – possibly to be identified with the Essenes – also encouraged celibacy, openness and wholehearted obedience to God: 'That they should seek God with a whole heart and soul ... and no longer follow a sinful heart' (*Community Rule* 1). These Palestinian

Jewish ideas about wholeness and single-heartedness helped form the Christian attitudes towards sexuality, even when the religion had left Palestine and was predominantly a religion of the Graeco-Roman cities.

Celibacy as an ideal is found in the New Testament both in the teaching of Jesus and in that of Paul. According to Matthew 19:10–12, Jesus encouraged celibacy in his followers: 'Not all can receive this precept, but only those to whom it is given. For there are eunuchs who have been so from birth, and there are eunuchs who have been made eunuchs by men, and there are eunuchs, who have made themselves eunuchs for the sake of the Kingdom of Heaven.' In third-century Alexandria, Origen took the saying quite literally and castrated himself for the sake of the Kingdom of Heaven. But much of the Church's teaching on celibacy, as on marriage and divorce, derives from Paul's First Letter to the Corinthians:

> I wish that all were as I myself am [i.e., able to exercise sexual self-control]. But each has his own special gift from God, one of one kind and one of another. To the unmarried and the widows I say that it is well for them to remain single as I do. But if they cannot exercise self-control, they should marry. For it is better to marry than to be aflame with passion. (7:7–9)

Paul seems to be advocating celibacy as the best way, and allowing marriage as a concession to those whose sexual feelings are so strong that otherwise they would commit the sin of fornication. For Paul, brought up as a strict Jew, sexual intercourse was intended for the purpose of procreation and should therefore only take place between married couples.

This passage, along with Matthew 19:10–12, has been used by the Church over the centuries to argue for the ideal of celibacy. Until recently the teaching was taken out of its context and accepted as authoritative just as it stood, without reference to its time or place of composition and ignoring the clear evidence elsewhere in the letter and in the gospels that the earliest apostles were married (1 Cor 9:5; Mark 1:30 and parallels). In the West, in 1139, it became illegal for priests to marry, or for married men to become priests. The legitimacy of married priests had been a subject for discussion in the Church since the fourth century, and it was one important element in the split between Eastern and Western Churches. For the Eastern

Churches continued to allow their priests to marry, though their bishops had to be celibate. The effect of this on women has again been to see them as second-class citizens; not only could women not be priests, but in the Roman Catholic Church at any rate, they were not even allowed to marry priests.

However, looking at the historical and sociological background of 1 Corinthians will produce a different picture of what Paul was trying to say. Since Paul expected the world to end very soon, his somewhat negative attitude to marriage arises as much from a recognition that a married man is bound up in worldly cares because of his wife, as from a disdain for sexual passion: 'Yet those who marry will have worldly troubles, and I would spare you that. I mean, brethren, the appointed time has grown very short' (1 Cor 7:28–29). In fact, Paul's attitude to sexual intercourse within marriage is surprisingly egalitarian:

The husband should give his wife her conjugal rights, and likewise the wife to her husband. For the wife does not rule over her own body, but the husband does; likewise the husband does not rule over his own body, but the wife does. (7:3–4)

He even goes on to teach against complete celibacy within marriage:

Do not therefore refuse one another except perhaps by agreement for a season, that you may devote yourselves to prayer; but then come together again, lest Satan tempt you through lack of self-control. (7:5)

The eschatological dimension forms the background to all Paul's teaching. If one really sees no future ahead in worldly terms, then undertaking marriage, which is a commitment to a particular worldly future, becomes nonsensical. So marriage is permitted as a concession to prevent fornication because the other more positive reasons for getting married, such as having children, are no longer relevant.

Sociological studies of first-century Corinth also provide a picture which is different from the traditional one (Meeks, 1983: 76, 77, 106). There seems to have been an enthusiastic, spirit-filled group in Corinth who were taking ideas about sexual equality too literally and their behaviour was threatening the stability of the Corinthian church, which depended for its continuing success on its acceptance by the well-to-do heads of households. So Paul's teaching on marriage and divorce is a holding action, designed to permit such families to continue to live normally in their pagan societies while accepting his teaching in their Christian lives. Paul was not afraid to compromise for the sake of the spread of the Church. He was 'all things to all men'.

Paul's teaching on divorce arises out of the same social and eschatological background. There is no time to waste on the business of getting divorced; attention should rather be focused on the individual's faith and the coming transformation of the world: 'Are you bound to a wife? Do not seek to be free. Are you free from a wife? Do not seek marriage' (1 Cor 7:27). Paul argues that no one should try to change the state in which they were called to be a Christian – they should not seek freedom from slavery or a change in marital status; such changes involve time and attention which would be diverted from the important matter in hand.

In the centuries which followed, when eschatological fervour had died down, the ideals of celibacy and virginity gained popularity as ways of demonstrating one's wholehearted acceptance of the Gospel message. For women especially, retaining one's virginity was a sign of freedom and equality in Christ. At a time when women were regarded as inferior to men in every way, and were under the authority of a man, whether father or husband, a refusal to become married was tantamount to rebellion. It was a denial of the principles on which the Graeco-Roman world was founded. Women had to choose between obedience to their earthly father and obedience to God. One of the earliest accounts of a case like this is the fictional account of Thecla, found in the second-century *Acts of Paul and Thecla*. Thecla was engaged to a man named Thamyris, but was converted to Christianity on the eve of her marriage by Paul's preaching. She took a vow of celibacy and refused to marry Thamyris. Her family and fiancé were so incensed that Thecla was persecuted and condemned to death. Saved by a miracle, she accompanied Paul to Antioch. Condemned to fight with wild beasts in the arena, she baptized herself and the beasts did her no harm. Many people, particularly women, were converted by stories of her activities and her preaching. Like Paul she travelled the Mediterranean proclaiming the Christian message, and converting many to the faith. Thecla's story is the first of many accounts of women all over the Christian world, many of whom came to be revered as saints, who refused marriage on the grounds of wholehearted devotion to the Gospel message. But, at the same time, they were exercising their independence and freedom to be individuals in their own right, quite separate from fathers and husbands.

There were other models of celibacy growing up alongside these rather spectacular ones. Women of well-to-do families would renounce marriage because they felt that virginity left them closer to the ideals of the Kingdom as proclaimed by Christ (Matt 19:12; Luke 20:35) and by Paul (1 Cor 7:6). Others, like the wealthy Melania, in the fourth century, submitted to her family's demands that she marry, and to her husband's demand that she produce two children, but she then became celibate and with her husband, Pinian, renounced the world and lived a life of penitent obedience to Christ. Jerome, an older contemporary of Augustine, and an ascetic of great erudition, set himself up as a spiritual mentor to a group of rich, aristocratic women, first in Rome, then outside Bethlehem. Jerome claimed that virginity and chastity were infinitely superior to marriage and would bring with them rewards of eternal life better than those awaiting married people. He warned his female followers repeatedly against the dangers of mixing in worldly company:

> Do not court the company of married ladies ... women of the world, you know, plume themselves because their husbands are on the bench or in other high positions ... Learn in this respect a holy pride; Know that you are better than they. (Jerome, *Epistle to Eustochium*, 22.16)

This teaching had tragic consequences for the family of one of Jerome's most faithful supporters in Rome, the wealthy widow, Paula. The superiority of asceticism and chastity was impressed so strongly on two of her daughters, Blaesilla and Eustochium, that when Blaesilla's husband died, she acceded to Jerome's suggestion that she should adopt a radically austere regime which, within three months, led to her death. Jerome was fiercely criticized and blamed by many of his contemporaries for her death. In fact, his negative attitude towards sexuality was by no means universally popular. Jovinian, a celibate Christian monk, criticized the growing popularity of Jerome's views, arguing that God himself had commanded Adam and Eve to procreate, 'Be fruitful and multiply and fill the earth', and that this command, first found in Genesis 1:28, was repeated by Jesus himself. Concentrating on deutero-

Pauline texts, he was also able to draw out teaching positive to marriage from the epistles. 'I desire, therefore, that younger widows marry and bear children', and 'marriage is honourable to all, and the marriage bed undefiled' (1 Tim 5:14 and Heb 13:4, quoted in *Jerome Against Jovinian*, 1.5). However, the opposition was too great, and the idealization of virginity and celibacy as the most desirable way of following Christ continued to grow in strength. This controversy illustrates the difficulty of basing the Church's teaching on scriptural proof. The texts are chosen selectively, and there are always other texts which can be used to disprove the case.

Not long after Jerome's departure from Rome, Paula and Eustochium also travelled to Bethlehem and set up a community of celibate women there near Jerome's small monastic community, supporting both him and themselves with their great wealth. These women found the advantages of their celibate state lay not only in the renunciation of the social and marital obligations of high-born Roman women, but also that they were able to read, study and absorb the Scriptures in their original tongues and the Christian writers who had interpreted them under the guidance of learned men such as Jerome. Although it was the norm for aristocratic women to be highly educated, for they often had to take responsibility for their husbands' estates and businesses when they were away from home, Christian women who adopted the celibate life had greater freedom in the disposal of their money and their time than their married sisters. The women who followed Jerome into a life of intellectual asceticism were not encouraged to write themselves, but their minds and intellects were as highly trained and learned as many of their male contemporaries (Brown, 1988: 369ff.).

Throughout the Middle Ages, the tendency continued, among aristocratic women at any rate, to renounce the life of marriage and follow the more meritorious route of celibacy. Virginity was recognized as a powerful and compelling religious ideal. The woman who was intact and whole, who had devoted herself mind and body to Christ, was felt to have extraordinary power and was open to the inspiration of the Spirit in a unique way. During the twelfth century the number of women choosing to follow the only religious role available to them grew rapidly, but the rules defining how they could renounce the world were still firmly in the grasp of men. When, in the thirteenth century, St Clare tried to follow Francis of Assisi as a mendicant, she was refused and forced to retire to a convent, to keep some of her wealth and her servants. Such a dangerous and wandering life was not suitable for a woman. Within convents, in the tenth to the twelfth centuries, women had even had some authority to exercise clerical roles such as hearing confessions from the nuns under them, preaching and sometimes even celebrating Mass. But in the later Middle Ages this was stopped; the powerful abbesses of the earlier period are no longer found.

At the same time women were finding new ways of living their religious lives. The established orders demanded such high dowries from women wanting to enter their convents that only the very rich could afford it. Among the new bourgeoisie and the lesser nobility of the towns in northern Europe, many women chose to become beguines. Beguines were women who set themselves apart from the world and devoted their lives in celibacy to prayer, manual work and charity. They took no vows, had no rules or hierarchy, but lived in loosely organized groups or at home. In southern Europe, the movement of tertiaries developed at the same time; these were women who were affiliated with mendicant orders but who devoted themselves to prayer, asceticism and charitable works. The rapid rise in the number of women religious in this period has been explained by social historians as resulting from their desire to avoid the dangers of childbirth and the possible brutalities of marriage, or on the difficulty and expense of finding a husband and a dowry. But the religious life of renunciation and the women's wish to express their faith through their whole lives must still have been the main impetus.

So there was a variety of ways for women to express their religious ideals in the Middle Ages, generally involving the vow of chastity. The decision to give one's whole life to God was the most powerful decision a girl or a woman could make. It expressed total devotion to God but at the same time enabled her to exercise control over the only area of her life where she had control – her body. She also gained, thereby, a measure of autonomy not otherwise to be found in the world of men. It is no accident that this autonomy through renunciation fitted so neatly with the idea prevalent at the time that women were dangerous tempters of men.

The Virgin Mary

The theory of learned, celibate men, based on their readings of

273

Scripture, that women were second-class human beings and a threat to men, was supported by the growth of the popularity of the cult of the Virgin Mary. Reverence for the Virgin bridged the gap between popular feelings and intellectual theories. The New Testament basis for the growth of the cult is extremely sparse. Paul, the first New Testament writer, mentions Jesus' birth only once, in Galatians 4:4: 'But when the time had fully come, God sent forth his Son, born of a woman, born under the Law.' This amounts only to a claim that Jesus was a Jewish male baby; it says nothing about who his mother and father were. Similarly, in Mark's gospel, which is commonly thought to be the earliest of the four gospels, apart from a reference to Mary, his mother and his brothers and sisters, to point out how incredible is the authority with which Jesus teaches (Mark 6:1–6), Jesus' mother appears only once, again in the company of his brothers, and is treated by Jesus with some disrespect:

> And his mother and his brothers came; and standing outside they sent to him and called him. And a crowd was sitting about him; and they said to him, 'Your mother and your brothers are outside, asking for you. And he replied, 'Who are my mother and my brothers?' And looking around on those who sat about him, he said, 'Here are my mother and my brothers! Whoever does the will of God is my brother, and sister, and mother.' (Mark 3:31–35)

Certainly Mark does not seem to be aware that Mary was a virgin, and she is not shown the deference which was later to become her due. John's gospel also gives Jesus' mother no name, and although she appears at his first miraculous sign (John 2:1–11) and at the crucifixion (John 19:25–27), she is never said to be a virgin and there is little in these stories to give rise to her adoration.

It is on the birth narratives in Matthew and Luke that the cult of the Virgin Mary is based. Whether or not Jesus' mother conceived him as a virgin, gave birth to him as a virgin or continued to be a virgin for the rest of her life, as the Roman Catholic Church claims, is not at issue here and has been very fully discussed elsewhere (Warner, 1976). What is significant is that both Matthew and Luke believed that Jesus' birth had been special, possibly unique, and that in some sense it originated with God. The title 'Son of God', understood elsewhere in the New Testament in a metaphorical way as referring to God's special messianic envoy, was apparently understood by Matthew and Luke in a physical sense. At a time when the biological understanding of how conception took place was dominated by Aristotle's active and passive, giving and receiving imagery, the possibility of a girl conceiving by the Holy Spirit was universally believable and not unparalleled in pagan mythology.

The story of the conception and birth of Jesus is told in quite different ways by Matthew and Luke. Matthew portrays Mary as a passive character. The story is told from the point of view of Joseph, the putative father, who is instructed by an angel not to divorce his betrothed, as she has not been unfaithful, 'for that which is conceived in her is of the Holy Spirit' (Matt 1:20). In typical Matthean fashion, the conception is said to have come about to fulfil the Scriptures. The rest of Matthew's story – the visit of the Magi, the massacre of the children, the flight into Egypt (none of which appear in Luke's account) – also fulfils scriptural prophecy or has scriptural resonances. Like Matthew, Luke names Mary and Joseph, and, like Matthew, places the birth in Bethlehem, but, whereas in Matthew's account Mary and Joseph seem to live in Bethlehem, according to Luke, they come from Nazareth in Galilee and travel to Bethlehem because of a census. It is shepherds, not the more glamorous Magi, who visit Jesus, but most important of all, it is Mary to whom the announcement of the birth is made by the angel Gabriel, and Mary who responds first with incomprehension and then with faithful acceptance: 'Behold, I am the handmaid of the Lord; let it be to me according to your word' (Luke 1:38). Each evangelist told the story of Jesus' birth in a way which suited his own purpose in writing and the needs of the people for whom he was writing.

However, as with the creation narratives in Genesis, the two gospel stories were soon conflated by the Church in worship and doctrine so that a much more elaborate picture of Mary developed, fleshed out by material in other writings such as the *Protevangelium of James* (M. R. James, 1924) where her 'immaculate conception' is described. Not only did she conceive her son without a human father, she herself was conceived without sexual intercourse when her parents embraced after a period of separation and penitential prayer. Her young life was dedicated to God from the start (*Protevangelium of James* 7:1 – 8:1). The idea gained popularity because only if Mary herself was free from sin could her body provide a womb fit for the Son of God. So either she must have been preserved from actual sin, or, by conception without sexual intercourse, she was preserved from original sin which has tainted the rest of the human race from Adam onwards. Some medieval theologians found it impossible to accept the idea that Mary, uniquely among human beings, was free from the contagion of sin and therefore not in need of the redemption brought by Christ. They got round this by believing that the redemptive gifts had been awarded to her in advance by God so that she was fit to bear his Son. In 1854 Pope Pius IX declared the immaculate conception of Mary to be a dogma of the Roman Catholic Church. The Church had also decided officially, though the idea had been current since the second century, at the First Lateran Council in 649 CE that Mary was a virgin not only before Jesus' birth, but during it and ever afterwards as well (Warner, 1976: 22ff.). The brothers of Jesus mentioned in the New Testament were considered to be either sons of Joseph by a previous marriage, or merely cousins.

In parallel with the separation of Mary from ordinary human sexual experience, she began to assume her own soteriological significance. The second-century writers Justin and Irenaeus portrayed her as the new Eve, who by her obedient acceptance of the angel's message showed herself to be the disobedient Eve's opposite. Just as Jesus had undone the sin of Adam (Rom 5:12–21; 1 Cor 15:20–22, 45–50), so Mary had reversed the condemnation of Eve. Just as a man and a woman had been involved in introducing sin into the world, so Mary with Jesus came to play a part in the redemption of the world.

Alongside this anti-sexual imagery, there grew up the veneration of Mary's motherhood. This is the image so familiar in Christian art from earliest times throughout the Middle Ages, of a mother holding an infant in her arms, in various poses, with expressions from that of the happy mother proudly presenting her infant son, to the mother whose look shows that she knows what fate awaits him. These artistic representations of Mary as mother are reflections of the popular interest in her motherhood. In 451 CE at the Council of Chalcedon, the title 'Mother of God' was accepted by the Church after decades of bitter dispute. But the result of the decision was to open the way for her veneration almost as a goddess. For Christianity, like Judaism and later Islam, is notable for having only one God and he is decidedly male. Although there are occasional references to God in a female role in the Old Testament (e.g. Isa 49:1, 15; 66:13), and Jesus refers to himself as being like a mother hen protecting her chicks (Matt 23:37), and uses the image of a woman searching for lost coins to represent God seeking sinners (Luke 15:8–10), nevertheless the overriding biblical picture of God is of a male deity with stereotypical male characteristics – he is strong, warlike, vengeful, a judge; the husband of unfaithful Israel, or the father of his people. For Christians the masculinity is emphasized by teaching about God's fatherhood. Jesus, the Son of God, became human so that human beings can become sons of God (e.g. Rom 8:3 and 14). The paradigmatic prayer taught to his disciples by Jesus begins 'Our Father ...'. God is male and so is his Son. The third member of the Christian Trinity, the Holy Spirit, is of indeterminate gender – the Greek word for spirit is *pneuma*, a neuter word, and the Latin, *spiritus*, is masculine. But female the Holy Spirit is certainly not. So the gradual rise of the cult of Mary, first as virgin, then also as mother, and later still as Queen of Heaven, filled a need in Christianity, especially among the less well-educated.

Because there was no mention of her death in the gospels, popular stories grew up about the end of her life. Some believed that she had not actually died, but this view was never officially sanctioned because it would deny her full humanity. So, in the Eastern Church the tradition of the Dormition grew up. Mary's body is laid to rest and Jesus receives her soul into heaven. In the West, she is taken to heaven body and soul. Although this element of the story did not become dogma as the Assumption until the papal decree of 1950, it had been the basis for believing in Mary as Queen of Heaven since the early Middle Ages. During the Middle Ages, she was worshipped as the Queen of Heaven and became an object of prayer and devotion. She was seen as a mediator, someone who, because of her femininity and motherhood, could sympathize with and plead the case of Christian sinners. As the *mater dolorosa*, the bereaved mother, sharing the universal human experience of grief and loss, she became the great focus as comforter and consoler.

In the courtly life and literature of the twelfth and thirteenth centuries, the idealization of the Virgin, which was reaching its zenith in the Church, was reflected in the idealization of the chaste and untouchable female figure familiar to us from the Arthurian legends and other traditions of courtly love (Warner, 1976, ch. 9). It was during the same period that the Church began the long process of sacralizing marriage, introducing rules of degrees of blood relationship, the enforcement of monogamy and indissolubility, and most important of all for women, consent. Although in theory the woman's situation had improved, she could be revered as a chaste and obedient wife, or the object of devotion of a faithful knight, yet she was still her husband's inferior and subject to his control. Idealized in a role designed by men, she had little freedom and certainly no sense of equality. In northern Europe in Protestant Churches, this idealization diminished as reverence for the Virgin gradually disappeared, but the role assigned to women by Luther continued to be generally accepted for centuries.

The other woman and other women

The cult of the Virgin Mary and the corresponding idealization of chastity caught the imagination of people and scholars alike, presenting fascinating intellectual problems as well as spiritual and emotional solace. But the ideal she presents of perfect mother as well as spotless virgin has always had its negative aspects for women as well. It is an impossible ideal for a human mother to live up to. Feminists argue that that is partly why celibate male priests have encouraged it for so long: women can never attain the ideal of redeemed womanhood as presented by the virgin mother and feel confident in their femininity. The ideal is unattainable. The best a woman can do is remain celibate and deny herself her biological destiny as a mother.

There are plenty of other women in the New Testament and in the tradition of the Church who provide different sorts of role models from the virgin mother, but whose part in the origins of Christianity has usually been played down. In the gospels, many women appear as part of Jesus's following whose lives are by no means blameless but who are praised by Jesus for their faith and insight. The most well-known story is that of the 'woman of the city who was a sinner' who anointed Jesus for burial before his death. This story is told in all four gospels (Matt 26:6–13; Mark 14:3–9; Luke 7:36–50; John 12:1–8).

And while he was in Bethany in the house of Simon the leper, as he sat at table, a woman came with an alabaster jar of ointment of pure nard, very costly, and she broke the jar and poured it over his head. But there were some who said to themselves indignantly, 'Why was the ointment thus wasted? For this ointment might have been sold for more than three hundred denarii, and given to the poor.' And they reproached her. But Jesus said, 'Let her alone; why do you trouble her? She has done a beautiful thing to me. For you always have the poor with you and whenever you will, you can do good to them; but you will not always have me. She has done what she could; she has anointed my body beforehand for burying. And truly, I say to you, wherever the gospel is preached in the whole world, what she has done will be told in memory of her.' (Mark 14:3–9)

All except Luke place the story at the beginning of the Passion narrative so that the anointing is seen to have direct relevance to Jesus' death. Luke is the only evangelist actually to state that the woman was a sinner, but the story in all the gospels is an illustration of one of the main complaints by the authorities against Jesus and his followers, that he mixed with and sat at table with tax-collectors, sinners and prostitutes (Mark 2:16). For a first-century Jew this was extremely radical behaviour. Tax-collectors and criminals were social outcasts, and women, let alone prostitutes, would not be acceptable table companions. The details of the story are different in each gospel; Luke, for example, places it in the house of Simon the Pharisee to highlight more clearly the contrast between the sinner whose act of goodness is praised and the official 'good' man, the Pharisee. But the point is made in all of them, that forgiveness or approval by Jesus is given to a woman of dubious character. She 'belongs' in a way that some of his friends and close followers do not: 'Truly, I say to you, the tax-collectors and harlots will go into the kingdom of God before you' (Matt 21:31). This woman came to be identified with Mary Magdalene by the Church, though there is no link in the gospels between the woman who washed Jesus' feet with her tears and the woman who in all the gospel accounts was one of the first witnesses to the resurrection.

In John's gospel there is another story where a 'sinful' woman is contrasted with 'good' scribes and Pharisees. The woman had been caught in adultery, which was a capital offence for a woman; the authorities brought her to Jesus to test his attitude. He responded by saying 'Let him who is without sin among you be the first to throw a stone at her'. Obviously she survived, and was sent on her way by Jesus with the words 'Neither do I condemn you; go, and do not sin again' (John 8:1–11). Although the authenticity of this passage is very doubtful, it reflects an image of Jesus as the protector of the female 'sinner'. He gets into conversation with a Samaritan woman in John 4, a woman who had had five 'husbands', and reveals his messiahship to her. He heals a woman who was ritually unclean because of her constant haemorrhage (Mark 5:24–34), and a Gentile woman's daughter (Mark 7:24–30). All these women would have been outcasts in contemporary Jewish society, but the evangelists seem to be making a point of their inclusion among those who are to enter the Kingdom of God. Other well-known women from Old Testament stories whose sexual life was the cause of disapproval are mentioned in Matthew's genealogy of Christ. Along with the famous patriarchs and kings, Tamar, who slept with Judah, her father-in-law, Rahab the harlot and Ruth, who slept with Boaz before she married him, are also part of his ancestry. Perhaps Matthew wanted to provide the unmarried mother, Mary, with some suitable prototypes, who were Jewish heroines in spite of their tarnished reputations. Rahab is also mentioned in the Letter to the Hebrews as one of the people who showed great faith during Israel's past (Heb 11:31), and in James 2:25 she is praised as an example of faith demonstrated by works. The 'good harlot' became a stereotype in Christianity as an alternative to that of the virgin.

In 1666, while in prison for her Quaker beliefs, Margaret Fell wrote *Women's Speaking Justified by Scripture*, a pamphlet which defended women's right to speak in public religious contexts. Basing her arguments on examples from Scripture, she demonstrated that women were capable of receiving divine inspiration and that they had been of central importance throughout biblical history. She pays special attention to the women in the gospels:

> Thus we see that Jesus owned the love and grace that appeared in women, and did not despise it, and by what is recorded in the Scriptures, he received as much love, kindness, compassion and tender dealing towards him from women, as he did from any others, both in his life time, and also after they had exercised their cruelty upon him, for Mary Magdalene, and Mary the mother of Joses, beheld where he was laid ... Mark this, ye despisers of the weakness of women, and look upon yourselves to be so wise: but Christ Jesus does not so, for he makes use of the weak: for when he met the women after he was risen, he said to them, 'All hail', and they came and held him by the feet, and worshipped him, and then said Jesus unto them, 'Be not afraid, go tell my brethren that they go into Galilee and there they shall see me.' ... What had

become of the redemption of the whole body of mankind, if they had not believed the message that the Lord Jesus sent by these women ...

It is not surprising that the authorities found this kind of argument hard to take. Both Margaret Fell and George Fox, who supported her arguments to the full, found themselves repeatedly persecuted and imprisoned for publishing such statements.

Although in the narrative parts of the New Testament – the gospels and Acts – women do seem to have played an important part in earliest Christianity in all sorts of roles, it is from the teaching within the letters, especially those that come from second- or third-generation Christians, such as Ephesians, and the pastoral letters to Timothy and Titus, and the letters of Peter, that much of the material comes which has kept women in a secondary role in Christianity, subordinate and obedient to men: 'Wives be subject to your husbands as to the Lord. For the husband is the head of the wife as Christ is the head of the church' (Eph 5:22–23; cf. also Col 3:18); 'And so train the young women to love their husbands and children, to be sensible, chaste, domestic, kind and submissive to their husbands, that the word of God may not be discredited' (Titus 2:4–5). They had to be quiet and submissive in public, and were denied the authority to teach or preach to men: '... the women should keep silence in the churches. For they are not permitted to speak, but should be subordinate even as the law says' (1 Cor 14:34; cf. also 1 Tim 2:11–12). The difference can be explained by a recognition that the gospel accounts reflect the radical nature of the renewal movement of first-generation Palestinian Christianity, while the deutero-Pauline letters reflect the later, more settled, urban situation of the Church in Hellenistic society.

Women as priests and ministers

It is to this primitive, radical form of Christianity that Christian women have always turned when seeking to be treated as men's equals in the Church. The mention of women playing significant roles in the Church in the lists of greetings in the letters, in Acts and in apocryphal works like the *Acts of Paul and Thecla*, led Margaret Fell in the seventeenth century, as it does women today, to argue for equal status within the Church. Paul names several women in Romans 16 who are active in the Church, for instance, Phoebe the

281

deacon (Rom 16:1) and Prisca, a fellow worker with Paul (Rom 16:3), who also appears in Acts 18 as Priscilla. The arguments have prevailed in some Churches; the Lutherans, the Methodists, the United Reformed Church all have women clergy. Among the Churches of the Anglican Communion, opinion is still divided, but most now have women priests, and in the United States and New Zealand there are women bishops as well as priests and deacons. The Roman Catholic and Eastern Orthodox Churches, however, still find authority in their traditional teaching about women and resist the idea. There is little that is new in any of the arguments; they have all been rehearsed before, but changes that have taken place in society in the West during the twentieth century have made it much easier for women's voices to be heard. Women are seen publicly in roles of importance and authority in secular life, so that some of the old arguments based on women's innate inferiority to men have disappeared in the Church as well.

But the influence has not been only in one direction; it was the firmly held belief among Quakers that women and men were equal in the sight of God which enabled Quaker women to fight for the emancipation of slaves in the nineteenth century and the liberation of women in the nineteenth and twentieth centuries. It was not just their beliefs which enabled them to contribute so much to changes in attitude, but also the fact that from the beginning they were used to running their own meetings, and to concerning themselves with the poor and under-privileged, and so they had the resources to organize and equip themselves to help (Bacon, 1980).

The movement towards equality for women within the Church has picked up speed enormously in the twentieth century, and their status as men's equals is now accepted by many Christians. The question remains: how far-reaching will be the effect of having women as priests, ministers and bishops on the religious language and doctrines of the Church, dominated by men for so many centuries? (see Loades, 1990).

Further reading

Brown, P. (1988) *The Body and Society: Men, Women and Sexual Renunciation in Early Christianity.* New York: Columbia University Press.

Chaucer, Geoffrey (1951) *The Canterbury Tales*, trans. Neville Coghill. Harmondsworth: Penguin Classics.

Loades, A. (ed.) (1990) *Feminist Theology: A Reader*. London: SPCK.

Pagels, E. (1988) *Adam, Eve and the Serpent*. London: Weidenfeld and Nicolson.

Sanders, E. P. (1990) *Paul*. Oxford: Oxford University Press.

Schüssler Fiorenza, E. (1983) *In Memory of Her*. London: SCM Press.

Trevett, C. (ed.) (1989) *Women's Speaking Justified: And Other Seventeenth Century Quaker Writings about Women*. London: Quaker Home Service.

Warner, M. (1976) *Alone of All Her Sex: The Myth and Cult of the Virgin Mary*. London: Weidenfeld and Nicolson.

Ziesler, J. (1983) *Pauline Christianity*. Oxford: Oxford University Press.

Bibliography

Andreski, S. (1972) *Herbert Spencer: Structure, Function and Evolution.* London: Nelson.

Anselm, *Cur Deus Homo?* (Numerous editions)

Arrington, L. J. and D. Bitton (1980) *The Mormon Experience.* New York: Vintage Books.

Augustine (1950) *The City of God.* London: J. M. Dent.

Aulén, G. (1970) *Christus Victor.* London: SPCK. (First published 1931)

Bacon, M. H. (1980) *Valient Friend: The Life of Lucretia Mott.* New York: Walker & Co.

Badcock, C. R. (1980) *The Psychoanalysis of Culture.* Oxford: Blackwell.

Barr, J. (1973) *The Bible in the Modern World.* London: SCM Press.

Barr, J. (1981) *Fundamentalism.* London: SCM Press.

Beckwith, J. (1970) *Early Christian and Byzantine Art.* Harmondsworth: Penguin.

Berger, P. (1969) *The Social Reality of Religion.* Harmondsworth: Penguin.

Berger, P. (1971) *A Rumour of Angels.* Harmondsworth: Penguin.

Berger, P. L. and T. Luckmann (1967) *The Social Construction of Reality.* Harmondsworth: Penguin.

Bethell, D. (1972) 'The making of a twelfth century collection' in G. J. Cumming and D. Baker (eds), *Popular Belief and Practice.* Cambridge: Cambridge University Press.

Bloch, M. (1992) *Prey into Hunter: The Politics of Religious Experience.* Cambridge: Cambridge University Press.

Bloom, A. (1971) *God and Man.* London: Darton, Longman and Todd.

Bonhoeffer, D. (1955) *Ethics.* London: SCM Press.

Bowker, J. (1973) *The Sense of God.* Oxford: Oxford University Press.

Bowker, J. (1978) *The Religious Imagination and the Sense of God.* Oxford: Oxford University Press.

Brown, P. (1988) *The Body and Society: Men, Women and Sexual Renunciation in Early Christianity.* New York: Columbia University Press. (1989 edn London: Faber and Faber)

Bultmann, R. (1960) *Jesus Christ and Mythology*. London: SCM Press.
Bultmann, R. and K. Jaspers (1958) *Myth and Christianity*. New York: Noonday Press.
Bynum, C. W. (1987) *Holy Feast and Holy Fast*. Berkeley: University of California Press.
Casey, M. (1991) *From Jewish Prophet to Gentile God*. Cambridge: James Clarke.
Christie, Y. *et al.* (eds) (1982) *Art in the Christian World: A Handbook of Style and Forms*. London: Faber and Faber.
Cohn, N. (1976) *Europe's Inner Demons*. London: Paladin.
Colvin, H. (1991) *Architecture and the After-Life*. London: Yale University Press.
Cox, H. (1965) *The Secular City*. Harmondsworth: Pelican.
Cullmann, O. (1962) *Christ and Time*. London: SCM Press.
Cumpsty, J. S. (1991) *Religion As Belonging: A General Theory of Religion*. London: University Press of America.
Dandelion. P. (1996) *A Sociological Analysis of the Theology of Quakers*. New York: Mellen Press.
Davies, D. J. (1984) *Meaning and Salvation in Religious Studies*. Leiden: E. J. Brill.
Davies, D. J. (1991) *F. B. Jevons: An Evolutionary Realist*. New York: Mellen Press.
Davies, D. J. (1995) 'Rebounding vitality: resurrection and Spirit in Luke–Acts' in M. D. Carroll, D. Clines and P. Davies (eds), *The Bible in Human Society*. Sheffield: Sheffield Academic Press, pp. 205–23.
Davies, J. G. (ed.) (1986) *A New Dictionary of Liturgy and Worship*. London: SCM Press.
Dix, G. (1945) *The Shape of the Liturgy*. London: Dacre Press.
Douglas, M. (1966) *Purity and Danger*. London: Routledge and Kegan Paul.
Drane, J. W. (1975) *Paul, Libertine or Legalist?* London: SPCK.
Durkheim, E. (1976) *The Elementary Forms of the Religious Life*. London: Allen and Unwin. (First published 1915)
Eliade, M. (1960) *Myths, Dreams and Mysteries*. London: Fontana.
Eliade, M. (1979) *A History of Religious Ideas*. London: Collins.
Evans, I. (1969) *The Welsh Revival of 1904*. Port Talbot: Evangelical Movement of Wales.
Feuerbach, L. (1957) *The Essence of Christianity*. London: Harper and Row. (First published 1841)
Fletcher, J. (1966) *Situation Ethics*. London: SCM Press.
Freud, S. (1960) *Totem and Taboo*. London: Routledge & Kegan Paul.
Freud, S. (1973) *The Future of an Illusion*. London: Hogarth Press.
Fukuyama, F. (1992) *The End of History and the Last Man*. London: Penguin.

Geldof, B. (1986) *Is That It?* London: Sidgwick & Jackson.

Glenny, M. (1990) *The Rebirth of History: Eastern Europe in the Age of Democracy.* London: Penguin.

Gollin, G. L. (1967) *Moravians in Two Worlds.* New York: Columbia University Press.

Goody, J. (1986) *The Logic of Writing and the Organization of Society.* Cambridge: Cambridge University Press.

Gutiérrez, G. (1974) *A Theology of Liberation.* London: SCM Press.

Hartshorne, C. S. (1967) *A Natural Theology for Our Time.* Peru, IL: Open Court.

Harvey, D. (1989) *The Condition of Postmodernity.* Oxford: Blackwell.

Hendry, G. S. (1980) *Theology and Nature.* Philadelphia: Westminster Press.

Hick, J. (ed.) (1977) *The Myth of God Incarnate.* London: SCM Press.

Hume, D. (1969) *A Treatise of Human Nature*, ed. E. C. Mossner. Harmondsworth: Penguin.

James, M. R. (1924) *The Apocryphal New Testament.* Oxford: Oxford University Press.

James, W. (1902) *The Varieties of Religious Experience.* London: Longman.

Jevons, F. B. (1896) *Introduction to the History of Religion.* London: Methuen.

Jevons, F. B. (1906) *Religion in Evolution.* London: Methuen.

Labalme, P. (1980) *Beyond Their Sex.* New York: New York University Press.

Leach, E. (1969) *Genesis As Myth and Other Essays.* London: Cape.

Leeuw, G. van der (1967) *Religion in Essence and Manifestation.* Gloucester, MA: Peter Smith. (First published 1933)

LeFevre, P. D. (1956) *The Prayers of Kierkegaard.* Chicago: Chicago University Press.

Levin, D. M. (1985) *The Body's Recollection of Being.* London: Routledge & Kegan Paul.

Lévi-Strauss, C. (1964) *Structural Anthropology*, vol. 1. London: Allen Lane.

Lewis, I. M. (1986) *Religion in Context.* Cambridge: Cambridge University Press.

Ling, Trevor (1968) *A History of Religion East and West.* London: Macmillan.

Loades, A. (ed.) (1990) *Feminist Theology: A Reader.* London: SPCK.

Lovelock, J. E. (1979) *Gaia: A New Look at Life on Earth.* Oxford: Oxford University Press.

McDonagh, S. (1986) *To Care for the Earth.* London: Geoffrey Chapman.

Martin, D. and P. Mullen, (eds) (1984) *Strange Gifts.* Oxford: Basil Blackwell.

Meeks, W. (1983) *The First Urban Christians*. New Haven: Yale University Press.

Mol, H. (1976) *Identity and the Sacred*. Oxford: Basil Blackwell.

Murray, M. C. (1981) *Rebirth and Afterlife*. Oxford: British Archaeological Reports.

Niebuhr, R. (1956) *An Interpretation of Christian Ethics*. New York: Meridian Books. (First published 1935)

Ogden, S. M. (1967) *The Reality of God and Other Essays*. London: SCM Press.

Ogden, S. M. (1979) *Faith and Freedom*. Nashville: Abingdon.

Otto, R. (1924) *The Idea of the Holy*. Oxford: Oxford University Press.

Pauck, W. (ed.) (1961) *Luther: Lectures on Romans*. Philadelphia: The Westminster Press.

Peacocke, A. R. (1971) *Science and the Christian Experiment*. Oxford: Oxford University Press.

Pittinger, N. (1967) *God in Process*. London: SCM Press.

Poggi, G. (1983) *Calvinism and the Capitalist Spirit*. London: Macmillan.

Rieff, P. (1966) *The Triumph of the Therapeutic*. Harmondsworth: Penguin.

Rogerson, J. (1974) *Myth in Old Testament Interpretation*. Berlin: Walter de Gruyter.

Russell, J. B. (1977) *The Devil*. New York: New American Library.

Schüssler Fiorenza, E. (1983) *In Memory of Her*. London: SCM Press.

Schweitzer, A. (1914) *The Mystery of the Kingdom of God*. London: A. & C. Black.

Schweitzer, A. (1931) *The Mysticism of Paul the Apostle*. London: A. & C. Black.

Skultans, V. (1974) *Intimacy and Distance*. London: Routledge.

Smart, Ninian (1996) *Dimensions of the Sacred*. London: HarperCollins.

Smith, Wilfred Cantwell (1962) *The Meaning and End of Religion*. New York: Macmillan.

Smith, Wilfred Cantwell (1976) 'Objectivity and the humane sciences' in W. G. Oxtoby (ed.), *Religious Diversity*. New York: Harper and Row.

Sorrell, R. D. (1988) *St Francis of Assisi*. New York: Oxford University Press.

Southern, R. W. (1970) *Western Society and the Church in the Middle Ages*. Harmondsworth: Penguin.

Spencer, P. (ed) (1985) *Society and the Dance*. Cambridge: Cambridge University Press.

Stroup, G. W. (1981) *The Promise of Narrative Theology*. London: SCM Press.

Swanson, G. (1960) *The Birth of the Gods*. Ann Arbor: University of Michigan.

Tambiah, S. J. (1968) 'The ideology of merit and the social correlates of Buddhism in a Thai village' in E. R. Leach (ed.), *Dialectic in Practical Religion*. Cambridge: Cambridge University Press.

Teilhard de Chardin, P. (1965) *Hymn of the Universe*. London: Collins.

Thomas, K. (1984) *Man and the Natural World*. London: Penguin.

Thornton, L. S. (1928) *The Incarnate Lord*. London: Longman.

Thornton, L. S. (1950) *Revelation and the Modern World*. Westminster: Dacre Press.

Tillich, P. (1953) *Systematic Theology*. London: Nisbet.

Towler, R. (1984) *The Need for Certainty*. London: Routledge.

Turnbull, C. M. (1984) *The Human Cycle*. London: Jonathan Cape.

Turner, B. S. (ed.) (1990) *Theories of Modernity and Postmodernity*. London: Sage.

Turner, V. (1969) *The Ritual Process*. London: Routledge & Kegan Paul.

Turner, V. (1982) *From Ritual to Theatre*. New York: PAJ Publications.

Warner, M. (1976) *Alone of All Her Sex: The Myth and Cult of the Virgin Mary*. London: Weidenfeld and Nicolson.

Weber, M. (1965) *The Sociology of Religion*. London: Methuen. (First published 1922)

Weber, M. (1976) *The Protestant Ethic and the Spirit of Capitalism*. London: Allen and Unwin.

Whitehead, A. (1926) *Religion in the Making*. Cambridge: Cambridge University Press.

Wilson, B. R. (1970) *Religious Sects*. New York: World University Press.

Yannaras, C. (1991) *Elements of Faith: An Introduction to Orthodox Theology*. Edinburgh: T. & T. Clark.

Index